KU-098-093

A *dictionary of*

EPONYMS

Third edition

Cyril Leslie Beeching

HOUSE OF COMMONS
LIBRARY

DISPOSED OF
BY AUTHORITY

THE LIBRARY ASSOCIATION
LONDON

© Cyril Leslie Beeching 1979, 1983, 1989

Published by
Library Association Publishing Ltd
7 Ridgmount Street
London WC1E 7AE

All rights reserved. No part of this publication may be photocopied, recorded or otherwise reproduced, stored in a retrieval system or transmitted in any form or by any electronic or mechanical means without the prior permission of the copyright owner and publisher.

First published 1979 by Clive Bingley Ltd
Second revised edition 1983
This third revised edition 1989

British Library Cataloguing in Publication Data

Beeching, Cyril Leslie
    Dictionary of eponyms. — 3rd ed.
    1. English language. Eponyms — Dictionaries
    I. Title   II. Library Association
    423'.1

    ISBN 0-85365-559-6

HOUSE OF COMMONS
       LIBRARY
CATALOGUED

Typeset in 10/11pt Palacio by Library Association Publishing Ltd
Printed in Great Britain by
Dotesios Printers Ltd, Trowbridge, Wiltshire

Contents

Introduction to the First Edition

The English language contains a large number of eponymic words – words derived from the names of people. Yet this is a rare distinction for a living person and is a lasting memorial to the dead only if there is sufficient awareness of the connection between the word and the name.

To give advice on how to get your name in the dictionary, or how to become eponymous, would be difficult. An easy answer might be to suggest, 'Become a famous scientist'. Most of the eminent men of science (Ohm, Ampère, Galvani, Watt, Newton, Rutherford, et al.) have given their names to something or other. One could point to the Danish physicist Hans Christian Oersted, who is remembered (by scientists, at least) as the man who gave his name to the unit of magnetic field strength; while his brother, Anders Oersted, is quite forgotten today though he was once Prime Minister of Denmark. However, the names of some prime ministers have passed into the language, but more often than not for reasons unconnected with statesmanship – for example, Anthony Eden and the *Anthony Eden* hat.

Certain professions and callings do seem less productive of eponyms than others. The names of painters are rarely to be found in the dictionary, and musicians fare little better. There are some surprising omissions in the musical field – no Bach or Beethoven, for example – which suggests that even the sound of a name can affect its suitability as an eponymic word.

There are three main groups of eponymic words: those derived from mythological or fictitious names; those which are descriptive of a person or his works (as, for example, Shakespearian or Shavian); and the 'true' eponymic words which have become part of the language in a fuller sense and are taken from the names of people who actually exist or once existed. The examples in this dictionary are taken from the last group.

The aim of the selection has been to present a variety of eponymic words with relevant and interesting information concerning the men and women who have given their names to the words. It is, of course, the human association of these words which gives them their uniqueness and other peculiar attraction. Some areas have been avoided. Engineering eponyms – apart from a few included because of common usage or particular interest of subject – have been ignored. They are comprehensively dealt with in C. P. Auger's *Engineering eponyms* (second edition, Library Association, 1975). Horticulture and botany, also, have been generally avoided because of the proliferation of eponymic species – roses alone would fill a volume. Makes of motor cars (Rolls-Royce, Ford, Benz, etc.) are excluded because they are not truly eponymic.

Words of doubtful origin are not included. 'Lynch', for instance, has been variously ascribed to James Fitzstephen Lynch, a mayor of Galway, who tried and executed his own son in 1493; an eighteenth-century Virginian farmer, Charles Lynch; and a number of other Lynches, to say nothing of Lynch's Creek in both North and South Carolina.

It is hoped that, in addition to satisfying the curiosity of the casual reader with a general interest in eponymous persons, this book may answer some specific enquiries about eponyms. The subject index is intended to facilitate this aspect of use.

Some eponyms are instantly created as the result of an invention or a discovery; others gain acceptance more slowly. A dictionary of eponyms a generation from now would certainly include new examples of both types. Perhaps this author's own name may appear there as a synonym for 'axing', or a word for 'ruthless cutting or pruning of unprofitable services', after Lord Beeching who, as Dr Richard Beeching, became well-known for such activities during his term of office as Chairman of the British Railways Board.

New Malden   C. L. B.
Surrey   September 1978

Introduction to the Second Edition

In the compilation of this revised edition of the *Dictionary*, well over 100 eponyms have been added to those which comprised the main body of the first edition. There are also certain alterations and corrections to the original entries: for example, the guillotine as an instrument for inflicting capital punishment is no longer in use in France. And yet while the scope of the *Dictionary* has been considerably widened to embrace a greater choice of eponyms, the initial intention of confining these words to the category derived from 'the names of people who actually exist or once existed' has been adhered to.

It is perhaps necessary to explain the addition of the relatively large number of eponyms connected with medicine and surgery. At least one critic has drawn attention (not unfairly) to the inconsistency of including *Parkinson's disease*, but not *Bright's*, or *Addison's*, etc. It was not originally intended to do more than indicate the validity of the medical eponym (surely to include Parkinson of 'the law' to the exclusion of Parkinson of 'the disease' was untenable?); and even with these additions, there is no question of attempting a comprehensive list of diseases, etc., but rather a selection of the more important names in medicine and especially those with some particular human interest of the kind which gives the eponym its peculiar attraction.

The subject index, which has apparently been most helpful to the browser (and at least one reviewer), has been extended in this edition; and though the men and women of science have again furnished a generous proportion of the eponyms, there are many new subjects included. It would seem, in fact, that there is hardly any field of human activity which has not given us an eponymic word. Also, it is interesting to note (as indeed it *was* noted in a BBC World Service broadcast concerning this dictionary) how many of the eponyms in the English language originate from foreign nationals.

The hope that the *Dictionary* would have a comparatively wide appeal has perhaps been confirmed by the interest shown on the one hand by the eminent dramatic critic, the late Mr Philip Hope-Wallace (who kindly devoted his *Guardian* column to a review of the first edition), and on the other hand by the enthusiastic broadcast comments of the BBC's Mr Terry Wogan. Other writers and broadcasters whose helpful criticisms or comments I wish to acknowledge include Mr Eric Hiscock of *The Bookseller*, Mr Magnus Magnusson, Mr Brian Redhead, Mr Robert Robinson,

Mr David Jacobs, Mr Bob Holness, Mr Doug Case (of the BBC World Service programme 'Speaking of English') and Mr Steve Race, whose interest in eponyms is by no means confined to his special subject of music.

New Malden
Surrey

C. L. B.
December 1982

Introduction to the Third Edition

It is a measure of the greatly increased scope and size of this third edition of the *Dictionary* that it includes more than 30 additions to the subject index, ranging varyingly (and bizarrely) from 'satire' and 'sewers' to 'preaching' and 'nagging'. Updating and correcting a number of the original entries has also entailed the addition of much new material: inevitably, some of the eponymists still living at the time of the publication of the previous edition have since died; while such items as the total number of Derby wins achieved by the jockey Lester Piggott have had to be brought up to date.

Some information from readers' suggestions and helpful criticism has been incorporated in a number of new and original entries. Much of this has emanated from readers outside Great Britain; and as it was noted in the previous introduction, a large proportion of eponyms in the *Dictionary* originate from foreign nationals. In fact, they constitute some 50% of the total listed in this book and involve more than 20 countries.

Since the publication of the previous edition, several eponymous words have come to general notice: one particular example is 'Becquerel', which has been frequently referred to in the media following the nuclear power station disaster at Chernobyl, in the USSR, in 1986. 'Salmonella' and 'Listeria' are two other eponyms which have increasingly come into everyday use in recent times in connection with the contamination of our food supplies. This emphasizes the fact that there are scores of eponyms familiar to 'the man in the street', even though he may be unaware of their eponymous origins. One of the aims of this dictionary is, of course, to draw attention to this fact; as well as to supply relevant and interesting information associated with these particular and unique words in our language.

New Malden   C. L. B.
Surrey   February 1989

Note on Proprietary Terms
This book includes some names which are or are asserted to be proprietary names or trade marks. Their use does not imply that they have acquired for legal purposes a non-proprietary or general significance, nor is any other judgement implied concerning their legal status.

A

1 AARON'S BEARD   AARON'S ROD

Aaron was the founder of the Jewish priesthood and the brother of Moses (q.v.). At least two eponyms come from him.

Aaron's beard is the name for various plants, especially St John's Wort ('It is like the precious ointment upon the head, that ran down upon the beard, even Aaron's beard; that went down to the skirts of his garments' Psalms 133:2), while *Aaron's rod* is the mullein, or certain other plants with tall flowering stems ('. . . behold the rod of Aaron for the house of Levi was budded, and brought forth buds, and bloomed blossoms, and yielded almonds' Numbers 17:8). It is also one of the names for a divining rod, a forked twig for locating concealed water or metal.

2 ADAM

Robert Adam (1728–92) and his brother, James Adam (1730–94), were Scottish architects who introduced and gave their name to the neoclassical *Adam style* of architecture and furniture design. They were sons of the architect William Adam, whose two other sons, John and William, were also architects.

As a young man, Robert Adam visited Italy to study the classical style of architecture at first hand, and this was to have a strong influence on the eventual Adam style of architecture. In 1762, he was appointed architect to George III (q.v.) and after six years, James Adam succeeded him in the post. It was with his brother James that Robert Adam designed the special furniture for the Adam houses, which was light and decorative in style, ornamented with paint and inlaid designs featuring the wreath, the fan, and the honeysuckle. They also produced a number of impressive interiors for their houses, with particularly fine ceilings and mantlepieces.

In 1769, the four brothers acquired a plot of land known as Durham yard (it was formerly the site of the Bishop of Durham's palace), lying between the Strand and the Thames, and began developing the area in the Adam style. They renamed the plot as the Adelphi, from a Greek word meaning 'brothers'. The venture was not successful financially, but the Adelphi district became very fashionable for a time. Modern development has virtually obliterated the original buildings and streets, though there are many surviving examples of Adam architecture and interior decoration to be seen in London and elsewhere, with Robert Adam's screen and gate for the Admiralty in Portland Place probably being the best known.

3 ADDISONIAN TERMINATION

Joseph Addison (1672–1719) is remembered as the founder of *The Spectator* (with Sir Richard Steele) and the creator of Sir Roger de Coverley, 'a gentleman of Worcestershire, of ancient descent, a baronet'. Eponymously he is remembered by way of his tendency to end the occasional sentence with a preposition (e.g. from his essay *Sir Roger at the play*: 'Why, there is not a single sentence in this play that I do not know the meaning of.'). This was noted by one Bishop Hurd (1720–1808), a bishop of Worcester, who duly coined the term *Addisonian termination* to describe this 'offence'.

It should be pointed out, however, that Bishop Hurd was clearly being less than fair in singling out Addison, who was by no means the worst (nor for that matter the first) offender. In fact there is hardly an English writer of note, from Chaucer onwards, who has not at some time made use of this now generally accepted device.

Yet the pedants still oppose those who argue for the flexibility of the English language and the *effectiveness* of any given Addisonian termination as justification for its employment. Perhaps Winston Churchill could be said to have summed up the whole matter in his famous comment on a certain state document: 'This', he wrote, 'is the sort of English up with which I will not put.'

4 ADDISON'S DISEASE

Thomas Addison (1739–1860) is remembered as the discoverer of a glandular disease named after him as *Addison's disease*. This disease affects the adrenal or suprarenal glands (the glands located above the kidneys) and is marked by wasting effects, tiredness and a brownish pigmentation of the skin in those suffering from it.

Addison studied medicine at Edinburgh and was a physician at Guy's Hospital, in London, where he made his famous discovery at the comparatively advanced age of 62.

5 ADLERIAN

Alfred Adler (1870–1937) gives his name to the *Adlerian* school of philosophy. This departs from the Freudian theory (q.v.) in

2

its conception of the 'inferiority complex' as an explanation of various forms of human behaviour, as opposed to Freud's emphasis on the importance of sexual factors. According to Adler, we are all affected by an innate inferiority of one kind or another and our reactions to this condition decide the kind of person we become: e.g. the physically small or inadequate might well develop into a dominating type; or, alternatively, someone unsuccessful in coping with life's difficulties could become a hypochondriac, albeit unconsciously.

Adler was born in Vienna and was at first a disciple and close friend of his fellow-countryman Freud. He was also a friend and contemporary of the Swiss psychiatrist Carl Gustav Jung, another Freudian who eventually broke with the 'master' to found his own school of psychoanalysis.

6 ADMIRABLE CRICHTON

James Crichton (1560? – 82) was a Scottish prodigy who, it is said, was outstandingly gifted both as a scholar and an athlete. During his short life he travelled widely and met many of the leading scientists and philosophers of his day, who were greatly impressed by his learning and his fluency in some 12 languages, to say nothing of his skill as a swordsman. He is believed to have been little more than 21 years of age when he was killed in a brawl in Mantua.

Crichton was eulogized as 'The Admirable Crichton' by the Scottish writer Sir Thomas Urquhart (1611 – 60) and this term has since been applied to anyone who excels in various arts and sciences, or a polymath. *The Admirable Crichton* was also the title of one of the best-known plays of another Scottish writer, Sir James Barrie.

7 ALBERT

Prince Albert (1819 – 61), Consort of Victoria (q.v.), Queen of Great Britain and Ireland, has been commemorated by monuments, buildings, bridges, street names and names of pubs, etc. – all too numerous to mention. And, inevitably, many of these have long since disappeared, for one reason or another. Names too have been changed. What was formerly Lake Albert is currently Lake Mobutu Seso in Zaire, for example. But the prince-consort also gave his name to something more durable – a word in the English language. An *albert* is a short kind of watch-chain, named after Prince Albert Francis Charles Augustus

Emmanuel of Saxe-Coburg-Gotha – as any customer in the public bar of *The Royal Albert* or *The Albert Arms* must know.

An award for gallantry in life-saving, the *Albert medal*, was instituted in 1866 to commemorate the prince.

8 ALZHEIMER'S DISEASE

Alois Alzheimer (1864 – 1915) gives his name to a disease affecting the brain cells, *Alzheimer's disease* or *Alzheimer's syndrome*. Alzheimer, a German neurologist born in Breslau (now Wroclaw, in Poland), identified the characteristic features of the disease circa 1900.

Although sufferers from Alzheimer's disease display the common symptoms of senility (e.g. increasing loss of memory, vagueness, and difficulty in performing everyday tasks), the condition can occur in a patient in the 40 – 50 age group, when it is sometimes known as pre-senile dementia.

There is no known cure for the disease, but the Alzheimer's Disease Society, a registered charity based in London, provides specialized help and advice for sufferers and their families.

9 AMBROSIAN CHANT   AMBROSIAN MODES   AMBROSIAN RITE

Saint Ambrose (340 – 397) was Bishop of Milan from 374, and is particularly remembered for his great influence on the music and rituals of the Christian Church. He restored order into church music with the introduction of the *Ambrosian chant*, based on four scales, or modes (*Ambrosian modes*), and this remained as the principal form of church music for some 200 years.

St Ambrose also introduced a form of religious service, or liturgy, named after him as the *Ambrosian rite*, which is one of the few exceptions to the Roman rite used in the Roman Catholic Church, and this is still in use in Milan. And in 1609, the name of St Ambrose was honoured again, when Cardinal Borromeo, Archbishop of Milan, bequested his private library to the use of the public and named it after his famous predecessor as *The Ambrosian Library*.

10 AMPERE

André Marie Ampère (1775 – 1836), the French scientist, is one of three men (the other two being the Italian, Volta, and the Scotsman, Watt (qq.v.)) whose names are almost certain to be found in just about every house, office, shop, or factory – in fact, any place where electricity is used for lighting, heating, or running machines and appliances.

Ampère made a number of important discoveries in the field of magnetism and electricity, and his name has been given to the unit of electric current (usually abbreviated to *amp*), as well as a law, *Ampère's law*, formulated by him, which forms the basis of the study of electrodynamics.

11 ANDERSON SHELTER

Sir John Anderson, later Viscount Waverley (1882–1958), was a civil servant who entered Parliament in 1938, and became Chancellor of the Exchequer from 1943 to 1945. His name is best remembered, however, by the *Anderson shelter*, which he introduced in 1939 when he was Home Secretary and Minister of Home Security.

Faced with the urgent task of providing air-raid shelters for the civilian population in the impending war, Anderson had turned to his old friend and fellow-Scotsman, William Paterson (later Sir William Paterson), a distinguished engineer, who produced a design for a partly prefabricated shelter which could easily be erected by the non-expert in his own back-garden. Some three million Anderson shelters were built during the war and they undoubtedly saved many lives.

12 THE ANDREW

Andrew Miller was the name of one particularly notorious press-gang operator who 'recruited' for the Royal Navy in the Portsmouth area, *circa* 1800. Such was his reputation that any impressed man was said to have gone into 'the Andrew' and the term subsequently became synonymous with the Royal Navy itself.

At the height of the French Revolutionary and Napoleonic Wars, as many as half of the crew of any Royal Naval ship could be made up of impressed men and the press-gangs continued to operate up to the 1830s. It is a common but mistaken assumption that the press-gang takes its name from its victims being 'pressed' (i.e. forced) into service, whereas the word is really derived from the French *prêter*, 'to lend', or the 'imprest' money loaned to a newly enlisted man.

13 ÅNGSTROM

Anders Jonas Ångstrom (1814–74) was the Swedish astronomer and physicist who gave his name to the unit used for measuring the wavelengths of light, ultraviolet rays, X-rays (q.v. under Röntgen), etc., the *angstrom*. Ångstrom was a student and later a professor at the University of Uppsala, and carried out a number of original researches in connection with light, including an analysis of the spectrum of aurora borealis.

14 ANTHONY EDEN

Sir (Robert) Anthony Eden, later the Earl of Avon (1897–1977), is remembered as the British Prime Minister at the time of the ill-fated 'Suez adventure', in 1956, when Anglo-French forces invaded Egypt. He is also remembered for his resignation as Foreign Secretary in the Chamberlain government, following the Munich Conference, in 1938; and he was Foreign Secretary in Churchill's wartime government.

But Anthony Eden (as he was best known) is remembered in the English language somewhat less controversially, through a type of black felt Homburg hat he used to wear, which became known after him as an *Anthony Eden*. Eden was Foreign Secretary for the first time (in 1935) when his distinctive hat began to catch the imagination of the British public, and Anthony Edens enjoyed quite a vogue for a time.

15 APPLETON LAYER

Sir Edward (Victor) Appleton (1892–1965) discovered and gave his name to the upper region in the ionosphere, approximately 150 miles up, which acts as a reflector of radio waves, the *Appleton layer*. Appleton's researches had an important bearing on the development of radar, among other things. He was knighted in 1941, and in 1947 was awarded the Nobel prize (q.v.) for physics.

16 ARCHIMEDES' PRINCIPLE
ARCHIMEDEAN SCREW
ARCHIMEDEAN SPIRAL

Archimedes (*circa* 287–212 BC) is reputed to have said, 'Give me but one firm spot on which to stand, and I will move the earth'. He was of course referring to his discovery of the principle of the lever, which was just one of numerous discoveries and inventions attributed to this celebrated Greek mathematician and inventor.

Eponymously, he is remembered for the *Archimedean screw*, a water-raising device; the *Archimedean spiral*, concerning the measurement of curved areas; and the principle of specific gravity, the famous *Archimedes' principle*.

Concerning the latter, Archimedes is said to have jumped out of his bath exclaiming, 'Eureka!' ('I have found it!'), when he suddenly realized that the amount of water he had displaced on getting into the bath must be equal to the *bulk* (not the *weight*) of his body. This discovery eventually enabled him to determine the amount of gold in the crown of King Hiero II, which the king had suspected was not of pure gold.

Archimedes was born in Syracuse and died there at the hands of a Roman soldier, after the city had fallen to forces of the Roman consul Marcellus. He had played an active part in organizing the defences of Syracuse during the siege which had preceded its capture; and at one stage it appears that he devised a method of setting fire to the Roman ships by using lenses.

There is a sad irony in the fact that the death of Archimedes came about through the sheer single-mindedness of his genius. Marcellus had issued instructions stating that the great man must be brought to him unharmed; but when Archimedes was found and ordered to go to Marcellus, he refused, explaining that he was at that moment occupied with a certain geometrical proposition ('Wait till I have finished my problem'). This so exasperated the Roman soldier that he duly put Archimedes to the sword.

17 ARISTARCH

Aristarchus of Samothrace (*circa* 220 – *circa* 145 BC) was an eminent Greek grammarian and critic and the chief librarian of the celebrated Alexandrian Library for some 30 years. He edited the works of numerous Greek authors and in particular the Homeric epics, *The iliad* and *The odyssey*, which he arranged in 24 books. From his name, we have the eponym *Aristarch*, meaning a pedantic or severe critic.

Aristarchus of Samothrace is not to be confused with the renowned astronomer and mathematician Aristarchus of Samos (died *circa* 280 BC), who developed the Pythagorean system (q.v.) of the universe and is credited with discovering that the earth rotates on its own axis and revolves around the sun.

18 AUGUSTAN AGE

Gaius Julius Caesar Octavianus Augustus (63 BC – AD 14) was the nephew of Julius Caesar (q.v.) and the first Roman emperor. His reign lasted from 27 BC until his death, and was notable for its comparative peace and such great writers as Virgil, Horace, and Ovid. The period has come to be known as the golden age of Latin literature, or the *Augustan Age*, but the term is also used to describe any similar age in the literature of later times and in other countries. In England the reign of Queen Anne (q.v.) is generally taken to be the Augustan age, while in France it is usually the slightly earlier period of Louis XIV (q.v.).

19 AUJESZKY'S DISEASE

Aladár Aujeszky (1869 – 1933) gives his name to a disease of cattle and, especially, pigs, *Aujeszky's disease*. Aujeszky, a Hungarian pathologist born in Budapest, identified the disease in 1902.

It is also known as pseudo-rabies (from certain similarities in the behaviour of infected animals to that of rabid beasts) and infectious bulbar paralysis. Cattle affected by Aujeszky's disease rub themselves against trees excessively to alleviate intense itching. Pigs up to three weeks old are most likely to be killed by the disease, and many of the survivors die prematurely. A policy of preventive slaughter of infected animals on a national scale has been advocated by a majority of Britain's pig farmers as the best method of controlling the disease.

20 AVOGADRO'S LAW   AVOGADRO'S CONSTANT

Count Amedeo Avogadro (1776 – 1856) gave the scientific world an important new law when, in 1811, he announced his hypothesis stating that equal volumes of all gases at identical temperatures and pressures contain equal numbers of molecules. *Avogadro's law* (or *Avogadro's hypothesis* as it is sometimes called) was of particular importance in relation to the atomic theory developed by the Englishman John Dalton (q.v.) in 1803.

Avogadro was born in Turin and became a professor at the city's university. He also gives his name to *Avogadro's constant*, or *Avogadro's number*: the number of atoms or molecules in a mole of any substance.

B

21 BAILEY BRIDGE

Sir Donald (Coleman) Bailey (1901 – 85) invented and gave his name to the *Bailey bridge,* one of the outstanding inventions of the Second World War. The bridge was made up from prefabricated girders, could be fairly easily transported and erected by a relatively small number of men, and was strong enough to take the weight of some of the heaviest vehicles, such as tanks and trains. It was first used in the North African campaign, 1942 – 43, and played an important part in the Allied advance in the latter half of the war.

Like so many inventions and discoveries which come about through the needs of a nation at war, the Bailey bridge has also been successfully adapted for non-military purposes. And appropriately, perhaps, its inventor was knighted in 1946, the first full year of peace after the Second World War.

22 BAILY'S BEADS

Francis Baily (1774 – 1844), an English astronomer, gave the first full description of the phenomenon known after him as *Baily's beads.* This occurs during an eclipse of the sun, when a crescent of bright spots resembling a string of beads is briefly visible just before the total eclipse.

Baily described this effect in 1836, with the explanation of its cause as the sun shining between mountains on the moon. He also wrote an important account of John Flamsteed (1646 – 1719), the first English astronomer royal, and was a founder of the Royal Astronomical Society.

23 BAKELITE

Leo Hendrik Baekland (1863 – 1944) was a Belgian chemist who emigrated to the USA in 1889 and became well-known through his invention of a new kind of photographic paper (which he also manufactured) and a synthetic resin, which was given the trade name of *Bakelite.*

Bakelite (named from Baekland) was particularly effective for electrical insulation and was first used commercially in 1907. Baekland is often regarded as the founder of the modern plastics industry, through the practical application of his discoveries.

24 BALTIMORE

George Calvert, first Baron Baltimore (1580? – 1632), gives his name to the *Baltimore oriole*, a bird of the starling family, common throughout North America, whose black and orange colouring resembles the Baltimore coat of arms.

Baltimore was granted proprietorship of the territory which was later to be known as Maryland (after Henrietta Maria, Queen consort of Charles I of England) in the year of his death. He had previously been a secretary of state and proprietor of Newfoundland.

The Baltimore oriole is also known as the *fire-bird*, or simply the *Baltimore*.

25 BANTING

William Banting (1797 – 1878) was a London undertaker with a personal overweight problem. After trying various remedies (Turkish baths, strenuous exercises, etc.) without success, he turned to a diet prescribed by a Dr Harvey, an ear specialist, which denied him virtually all carbohydrates. Not only was the dieting successful, it attracted a great deal of publicity and a new word, *banting* (meaning slimming by means of a diet), was added to the English language.

Banting was well past middle-age when he started 'to bant' in earnest – and he lived on into his eighties. It has been suggested, however, that Banting did not turn to banting for health reasons alone. After all, the image of an overweight undertaker must have been almost as professionally undesirable as that of a hairless hairdresser, or a dentist with bad teeth.

26 BEAUFORT SCALE

Sir Francis Beaufort (1774 – 1857) was the English admiral and hydrographer who devised and gave his name to a scale of wind velocity, the *Beaufort scale*, or *Beaufort's scale*. The scale ranges from nought (i.e. calm, or conditions in which smoke rises vertically) to 12 (hurricane force winds above 75 mph).

Beaufort devised his scale in 1805 (the year of the Battle of Trafalgar) and became the official hydrographer to the Royal Navy in 1829.

27 BECQUEREL   BECQUEREL RAYS

Antoine Henri Becquerel (1852–1908) was the best known of a famous French family of physicists. And it was his work in conjunction with Marie and Pierre Curie (q.v.) which led to the award (shared with the Curies) of a Nobel prize (q.v.) and his discovery of what came to be named after him as *Becquerel rays*, the rays emitted by a radioactive substance.

On 26 April 1986, the disaster at the Russian nuclear power station at Chernobyl suddenly brought the name of Becquerel into common usage, as the world-wide concern over the effects of radioactivity on food was expressed through the media in *Becquerels* (or *Becquerel counts*).

28 BELCHER

James (known as 'Jem' or 'Jim') Belcher (1781–1811) gave his name to a kind of handkerchief or neckerchief, blue in colour with white blue-centred spots, a *belcher*. Belcher was an English pugilist, and a successful one until he lost an eye.

Like many other British boxers, Jem Belcher became a publican on retiring from the ring. But he stands apart as the only professional pugilist to have given his name to an accepted word in the English language – and had he not sported his *belcher*, he would now be quite forgotten to all but the historians of 'the noble art of self-defence'.

29 BELISHA BEACON

Sir Leslie Hore-Belisha (1893–1957) was Minister of Transport, 1934–37, and Secretary of State for War, 1937–40; but his name would be largely forgotten today, had it not been for the *Belisha beacon*, which he introduced in his first year as transport minister.

The now familiar amber-coloured beacon marking its studded road-crossing was the cause of a considerable amount of interest at the time; not least among the street-urchins who, when they were not painting faces on the glass (as they originally were) globes or throwing stones at them, were more than likely to be chanting a new jingle:

> A little dog walked down the road,
>   And not a tree in sight;
> But thanks to Hore-Belisha, now
>   That little dog's all right.

It is doubtful whether these lines were ever published in any anthology of verse, but the name of Hore-Belisha is certainly to be found in most English dictionaries.

30 BELLARMINE
Roberto Francesco Romolo Bellarmino, usually referred to as Cardinal Bellarmine or St Bellarmine (1542 – 1621), was the most controversial Italian theologian of his time and a great defender of Roman Catholic dogma. He gives his name to a large beer-mug or jug, bearing a rough likeness of the cardinal with a bearded face and a large belly. The *bellarmine* was first produced in Flanders by Dutch Protestants in mockery of Cardinal Bellarmine and was also known as a *greybeard*, from the cardinal's beard of course, or a demijohn, which is similarly shaped.

31 BELL'S PALSY
Sir Charles Bell (1774 – 1842) was an eminent Scottish surgeon who described and gave his name to *Bell's palsy*, paralysis of the facial nerve. The paralysis affects the muscles on one side of the face which is given a marked appearance of lopsidedness.

Bell was the author of numerous publications on neurology and also gives his name jointly (with the French physiologist François Magendie) to the *Bell-Magendie law* concerning neurology. His eldest brother, John, was a surgeon and the author of two works (both in three volumes) on anatomy and surgery.

32 BENEDICTINE
Saint Benedict of Nursia (*circa* 480 – *circa* 543) founded and gave his name to the *Benedictine* order of monks, also known as the 'Black Monks' from their garments. The abbey at Monte Cassino, in Italy, became the chief centre for the Benedictines and today it is the oldest monastic house in Europe, having survived occupation and destruction by the Lombards, in 585, the Saracens, in 884, and the Germans and the allied forces during the Second World War. On this last occasion, Monte Cassino was the focus for one of the hardest-fought battles of the war, when it was bombarded and attacked for over three months before falling to Polish troops in May 1944.

The Benedictines continue to observe the strict rule of their founder and combine religious duties and study with teaching and various kinds of manual work and crafts. The Benedictine nuns regard St Benedict's sister St Scholastica as their founder;

and it was during the post-war restoration of the abbey at Monte Cassino that an urn was rediscovered which is said to contain the remains of St Scholastica and St Benedict.

St Benedict also gives his name (albeit somewhat indirectly) to the liqueur *Benedictine*, which was originally produced by monks at the Benedictine abbey at Fécamp, in Normandy. Bottles of the liqueur carry the initials DOM, which stand for *Deo optimo maximo* (to God, best and greatest).

33 BENJAMIN
Benjamin was the youngest of the 12 sons of Jacob (q.v.) and his father's favourite (Genesis 42:3 – 4). From his name therefore we have the meaning of a youngest or specially favoured child.

An overcoat known as a *benjamin*, popular in the early years of the nineteenth century, was probably named after a tailor, with perhaps an allusion to Benjamin's brother Joseph (q.v.) and his 'coat of many colours'.

34 BERKELEIANISM
George Berkeley (1685 – 1753) gives his name to a system of idealistic philosophy known as *Berkeleianism*. This was evolved from a reaction to the materialistic philosophy of John Locke (1632 – 1704) and was first propounded by Berkeley in his *Essay towards a new theory of vision* and expanded upon in *A treatise concerning the principles of human knowledge*.

Berkeley was born in Ireland and became Bishop of Cloyne, in Cork. He lived in England and America for a number of years and was associated with such men of literature as Swift (who presented him at court), Pope and Addison (q.v.). In 1752 he retired to Oxford, where he died the following year. His chief work was *Alciphron, or the minute philosopher*, a series of seven dialogues in the manner of the Greek writer Alciphron.

Berkeleianism asserts that our so-called material world only exists through our senses. 'All the choir of heaven and furniture of earth – in a word, all those bodies which compose the mighty frame of the world – have not any subsistence without a mind'.

35 BERTHON BOAT   BERTHON'S LOG
Edward Lyon Berthon (1813 – 99) invented and gave his name to a collapsible lifeboat for use aboard ships, the *Berthon boat*. This was one of a number of inventions which Berthon was associated

with, though recognition of his work was long delayed.

He was one of the first to adapt the Archimedean screw (q.v.) to steam propulsion at sea with his design for a two-bladed propeller, but this was rejected by the British Admiralty in favour of a later invention of Francis Pettit Smith. Another of Berthon's ideas to be turned away by the Admiralty was a speed indicator, *Berthon's log*, which utilized a pipe underneath a ship with a mercury column attachment.

The Berthon boat seemed set to suffer a similar fate until the intervention of Samuel Plimsoll (q.v.) who was especially interested in its potential as a life-saver for seamen; and it was eventually adopted in considerable numbers. The boat was basically constructed of painted canvas on a wooden frame and could be easily folded and stowed on the smallest of craft. While the invention of the inflatable dinghy rendered the Berthon boat largely obsolete, there are still modified versions of it in use.

36 BERTILLONAGE   BERTILLON SYSTEM

Alphonse Bertillon (1853–1914) was a French anthropologist and criminologist who devised and gave his name to a system of identifying criminals by measurements, the *Bertillon system* or *Bertillonage*. This was the first scientific method of positive identification of the person and Bertillon must therefore be regarded as one of the founders of forensic science.

In spite of having received no formal scientific training, Bertillon became the founder and first chief of the department of identification in the Paris préfecture of police and was responsible for creating a unique accumulation of anthropometric measurements and photographs in support of his system. Bertillonage, correctly applied, proved to be all but infallible, but identification by fingerprints (and in particular the *Henry system*, devised by the English criminologist Sir Edward Henry) was eventually to supersede Bertillon's system. Nevertheless, criminal investigation was greatly advanced by the systematic methods of Bertillon.

37 BESSEMER PROCESS   BESSEMER CONVERTER

Sir Henry Bessemer (1813–98) revolutionized the manufacture of steel with his invention of a process (named after him) for converting cast iron into steel by means of a blast of air. The *Bessemer process* (using the *Bessemer converter*) greatly reduced costs of production and steel became more widely used.

An American, William Kelly, invented a converter independently of Bessemer, but the patent for his invention was issued after Bessemer's. So the 'Kelly converter' – unhappily for its inventor (and also unhappily for the English language, from the point of view of lovers of alliteration) – came to be named after the Englishman.

38 BEVIN BOYS

Ernest Bevin (1881 – 1951), as Minister of Labour and National Service in Churchill's wartime government, was responsible for an emergency measure, requiring a certain number of young men (eligible for military service) to work in the coal mines. These men – chosen at random from all walks of life – came to be known as *Bevin boys*, after the minister.

Bevin himself had come to be known as 'the dockers' KC', following his renowned defence of the London dockers' case at a court of enquiry in 1920. In the following year, he became the first general secretary of the Transport and General Workers' Union.

At the end of the Second World War, the new Prime Minister, Clement Attlee, appointed Bevin as Secretary of State for Foreign Affairs, and he remained in that office up to a few weeks before his death, at the age of 70.

39 BIG BEN

Sir Benjamin ('Big Ben') Hall, Baron Llanover (1802 – 67), was Minister of Works, 1855 – 58, and it was during his term of office that the famous hour bell in the clock tower of the Houses of Parliament was cast. The bell, weighing 13½ tons, was named after him as *Big Ben*; for Sir Benjamin was, in fact, a large man, and the bell first came into use in 1859 – the year in which he was raised to the peerage.

The chimes of Big Ben were first broadcast on New Year's Eve 1923, and soon became well known to everyone in Britain who listened to the radio, including a great number who had never been to London. And during the Second World War, its reassuring sound was probably as great a boost to the morale of the British people as were the speeches of Winston Churchill. Yet, oddly enough, there are few people, including musicians, who can accurately hum, sing or whistle that familiar tune leading up to the booming of the famous hour bell.

40 BIG BERTHA

Frau Berta (or Bertha) Krupp (1886–1957) was the granddaughter of Alfred Krupp (1812–87), the founder of the famous German armaments factories at Essen. She gave her forename to more than one large calibre gun produced by the Krupp factories during the First World War and named by the French as *Big Berthas*. One particular gun, which was also known as the *Kaiser Wilhelm geschutz*, had a range of some 75 miles and was used to shell Paris in the last year of the war. Berta Krupp took control of the Krupp Works on the death of her father, Friedrich Alfred Krupp (1854–1902), and in 1906 she married Gustav von Bohlen und Halbach, who obtained official consent to change his name to Gustav Krupp von Bohlen und Halbach. After the Second World War, Gustav Krupp was indicted as a war criminal at the Nuremberg Trials, but because of his physical and mental condition the Tribunal decided that he could not be tried. Berta Krupp's son, Alfred, was also tried for war crimes and sentenced to 12 years imprisonment in 1948.

In America, *Big Bertha* is an expression sometimes used to describe a fat woman.

41 BIG WILLIE

Sir William (Ashbee) Tritton (1875–1946) was the joint-inventor (with Major W. G. Wilson) of the first tank to be used in action, in 1916, which was named after him as *Big Willie*. In 1915, a smaller machine (*Little Willie*), had been officially tested and approved, following the appointment of a 'Landships committee' by Winston Churchill, at that time First Lord of the Admiralty. It was eventually decided to put 100 Mark I machines (the Big Willie) into production, and the word *tank* was adopted to preserve the secrecy of the new weapon.

The first of these tanks went into action on the Somme, on 15 September 1916, but largely due to the small number of machines available, their effect was relatively limited. The Big Willie was superseded, however, by a lighter, faster tank, the *Whippet*; and in November 1917, some 450 massed tanks were sent into action at Cambrai and succeeded in breaking through the German lines.

It has been argued that the tank played little part in the final outcome of the First World War, yet had its development and production been advanced by three or four years, there can be little doubt that the whole strategy of the war would have been quite different. And the appearance of Big Willie on the Somme battlefield in 1916 can now be seen as the beginning of a revolution in modern warfare.

Tritton was knighted in 1917, and at the end of the war, Sir William Tritton and Major Walter Gordon Wilson, CMG, were among those who received official recognition for their contribution to the evolution of the tank.

42 BING BOYS

General Julian Hedworth George Byng, first Viscount Byng of Vimy (1862 – 1935), was the commander of the Canadian Army Corps for the greater part of the First World War; and it was from this that the Canadian troops became known as the *Bing Boys*. Byng joined the British army in 1883 and served in the Soudan and the Boer War before taking command of the 9th Army Corps in Gallipoli where he conducted a skilful withdrawal from the Dardenelles in 1915. Commanding the Canadians he led the successful assault on Vimy Ridge in 1917; and later in that year, the Hindenburg line was breached under his command at the battle of Cambrai, when tanks were used *en masse* for the first time.

General Byng was governor-general of Canada (1921 – 26) and Commissioner of the Metropolitan Police (1928 – 31). He was made a viscount in 1926 and a field marshal in 1932.

43 BIRO

László Biro (1900 – 85) was a Hungarian journalist who in 1938 invented the first practical ball-point pen, the *biro*. Biro was obliged to leave Hungary with the rise of Nazism, preceding the Second World War, and eventually settled in Argentina, where in 1943 he took out a patent for his invention.

Biro's pen was first put to a really practical use by British Royal Air Force navigators who found they were able to use the biro at high altitudes, where conventional pens were unreliable or simply failed to function. A few years after the war, the ball-point became the most popular kind of pen on the market; but its original inventor had not had the foresight to take out patents in other countries, and other men in those countries grew rich from the enormous sales. Yet the ball-point pen is still commonly referred to as a biro, in the same way that we speak of refrigerators of various kinds as *frigidaires*, or vacuum cleaners as *hoovers* (q.v.).

44 BLOODY MARY

Mary I, or Mary Tudor (1516–58), was Queen of England and Ireland from 1553 until her death. During these five years, some 300 of her subjects were put to death as heretics (including the former Queen of England, Lady Jane Grey, and her husband, and the Archbishop of Canterbury, Thomas Cranmer) and many more were imprisoned and persecuted. Not for nothing then was the queen nicknamed 'Bloody Mary'.

And it is in no way a justification of Mary's cruelty to argue (as it can be argued) that her reign was no more 'bloody' than those of many of her predecessors, to say nothing of some who came after her.

Nonetheless, it is through Mary's nickname that we find her in the English dictionary. A *bloody Mary* is a cocktail, made basically from vodka and tomato juice.

45 BLOOMERS

Mrs Amelia Bloomer (1818–94) was one of the pioneers of the movement for women's rights in America. Born Amelia Jenks, in Homer, in the state of New York, she was married in 1840; and as Mrs Amelia Bloomer, she became well-known as a writer and lecturer on education and social reform. She also advocated reform in women's dress and took to wearing a new costume, consisting of a jacket, a skirt, and full Turkish-style trousers. These trousers came to be named after her as *bloomers*.

However, it appears that the original design of the *bloomer suit* came from another American lady, a Mrs Elizabeth Smith Miller, and not Mrs Bloomer. Mrs Bloomer's name, of course, is now firmly established in the English language – and it would be difficult to imagine that there would have been all those jokes (to say nothing of the picture post-cards) about bloomers, had 'bloomers' been called 'millers'.

46 BLÜCHER

Gebhard Leberecht von Blücher, Prince of Wahlstatt (1742–1819), was a Prussian soldier who gave his name to a kind of strong leather boot, or a shoe extending just above the ankle. He is best remembered, of course, for his part in the battle of Waterloo, when his late yet timely arrival was to deal the *coup-de-grace* to Napoleon (q.v.).

Blücher had seen plenty of action in his long military career and was nicknamed 'Marschall Vorwarts' (Marshal Forward). He was in his 73rd year at the time of Waterloo.

The boot named after Blücher is virtually unknown compared to the one named after Wellington (q.v.), just as his part in the victory at Waterloo is so often forgotten. But a remark reputedly made by him on a visit to London, in the year before Waterloo, must stand alongside the many remarks reputedly made by Wellington: 'Was für plündern!' (What a place to plunder!).

47 BOANERGES

The apostles James and John, the sons of Zebedee, were named *Boanerges* by Jesus Christ (q.v.) because they offered to 'command fire to come down from heaven' (Luke 9:54) to consume the Samaritans. (' . . . and he surnamed them Boanerges, which is, The sons of thunder:' Mark 3:17).

Boanerges has subsequently come to describe a noisy or shouting preacher, or any public speaker who rants and raves.

48 BOBBY   PEELER

Sir Robert Peel (1788 – 1850), as Chief Secretary for Ireland, was responsible for instituting the Irish constabulary (named after him as *peelers*). Then, in 1829, as Home Secretary in Wellington's (q.v.) government, he introduced a bill with the purpose of reorganizing London's police force; and on 29 September, in the same year, the first *bobbies* appeared on the streets of London. (The word is of course taken from the familiar form of Peel's Christian name.)

Peel was only 21 when he entered Parliament and was twice prime minister. He was still active in politics at the time of his death, in 1850, which occurred a few days after he was thrown from his horse in Hyde Park.

There can be few other men (let alone prime ministers) who have given both their Christian name and their surname to words in the English language.

49 BOEHM SYSTEM

Theobald Boehm (1793? – 1881) was a German flute-player who invented a system of fingering his instrument by the use of keys, which was named after him as the *Boehm system*. Boehm's invention enabled the player to perform with much greater facility than the earlier system of stopping the holes had allowed,as well as removing the restriction of having the holes cut in the instrument in other than the ideal acoustical positions.

Flute playing in fact was revolutionized by Boehm; and other wood-wind instruments (notably the clarinet and the oboe) were soon adapted to employ the Boehm system, which has now come to be adopted almost universally.

50 BOLIVAR
Simon Bolivar (1783–1830) is remembered and revered as 'El Libertador' (the Liberator), the revolutionary leader of the South Americans against the Spanish rule. In 1819 he founded the Republic of Colombia (now Colombia, Panama, Ecuador and Bolivar's native Venezuela) and six years later he established Upper Peru as a separate state which was named after him as Bolivia.

He also gives his name (uniquely) to the standard monetary unit of Venezuela, the *bolivar*.

51 BOLLANDIST
John Bolland (1596–1665) gives his name to a company of Belgian Jesuits dedicated to the writing of a series of books on the lives of the saints, entitled *Acta sanctorum*. These scholars are known as *Bollandists*.

John Bolland (also known as Jean de Bolland) edited the first volumes of the *Acta sanctorum* in 1643, in accordance with plans laid down by another Jesuit hagiographer, Heribert Rosweyde. More than 60 volumes have been published since that time.

52 BOOLEAN ALGEBRA
George Boole (1815–64) was an English mathematician who devised and gave his name to a method of applying mathematics to logic, known as *Boolean algebra*. Boole elaborated his method in his book *An investigation of the laws of thought on which are founded the mathematical theories of logic and probabilities*, and his work has influenced a number of eminent mathematicians, including Bertrand Russell, as well as being important in computer studies.

Boole's wife was a niece of Sir George Everest (q.v.).

53 BOSIE
Bernard James Tindal Bosanquet (1877–1936) was the Middlesex and England cricketer who gave his name to the *bosie*, which he is generally considered to have invented. The bosie, better known

as the 'googly' or the 'wrong-un' (Australian cricketers refer to it as the bosie mostly), is a delivery which turns the opposite way to what the batsman normally expects; and when it was introduced into cricket at the turn of the century, many of the world's best batsmen were completely puzzled by it. Even the great W. G. Grace failed to master it, though it must be said that he was very near the end of his long career in cricket at that time.

B. J. T. Bosanquet would not be judged by many as one of the game's greatest performers, though he was a good all-rounder, with two separate hundreds in one match on two occasions to his credit, as well as one 'double' (i.e. the feat of scoring 1,000 runs and taking 100 wickets in one season of first-class cricket). He stands alone, however, as the only player to have given his name to the language of cricket.

'Bosie' was also Oscar Wilde's pet name for his friend Lord Alfred Douglas, a son of the eighth Marquis of Queensberry (q.v.).

54 BOSWELLIAN   BOSWELLIZE   BOSWELLISM

James Boswell (1740 – 95) gives his name to the English language through his famous biography of his friend Dr Johnson, the *Life of Samuel Johnson*. *Boswellian* describes not just the literary style of Boswell in the biography, but any observant and devoted writing of that kind; and from this we have the verb and the noun *Boswellize* and *Boswellism*.

Boswell was born in Edinburgh where he studied law. His studies took him to London and it was there, in 1763, that he first met Dr Johnson who was then 53. Johnson died in 1784 and the biography was published in 1791. The historian Lord Macaulay (in what might be described as a good example of Boswellism) wrote '*The Life of Johnson* is assuredly a great, a very great work. Homer is not more decidedly the first of heroic poets, Shakespeare is not more decidedly the first of dramatists, Demosthenes is not more decidedly the first of orators, than Boswell is the first of biographers.'

55 BOUCH   BOTCH

Sir Thomas Bouch (1822 – 80) is remembered as the engineer of the first bridge to be built over the estuary of the River Tay, in Scotland, which was blown down as a train was passing over it on 28 December 1879, killing all the 70 or more people on the train. Ironically, had it not been for the Tay Bridge disaster, the name of Sir Thomas Bouch would be mostly forgotten; and certainly his name would not have become eponymous. It was in fact the revelation of shoddy workmanship and inadequate inspection in the building of the bridge which led to the name of Bouch coming to be used in Scotland as a synonym for work carried out unskilfully, or bungled, *Bouched*. And it is believed that from the Scottish pronunciation of the word that we have the better known 'botch', a word of course with the same meaning.

Sir Thomas Bouch had come to be regarded as one of the leading experts in the construction of railways and railway bridges in Great Britain and was knighted for his services to railway engineering in 1878, the year in which the Tay Bridge was opened. Although he was not held to be fully responsible for the collapse of the Tay Bridge, it was clearly the tragic event on that Sunday night in December 1879 that hastened his early death in October the following year.

56 BOWDLERIZE   BOWDLERISM

Thomas Bowdler (1754 – 1825) was an Edinburgh doctor of medicine who turned to publishing, and produced heavily expurgated editions of Shakespeare and other authors. In his *Family Shakespeare*, published in 1818, he altered or cut out passages which could not, in his opinion, 'with propriety be read aloud in a family'. Dr Bowdler, then, could be said to be the spiritual forebear of today's would-be censors of books, plays and films, whose judgements are biased by their own ideas of what is moral and what is not. To use the word which is derived from Bowdler's name, such people would undoubtedly be in favour of *Bowdlerizing*.

Thomas Bowdler died in 1825, yet *Bowdlerism* is often referred to as a product of Victorian England. Victoria (q.v.) did not begin her reign, of course, until 1837.

57 BOWIE KNIFE

James Bowie (1799 – 1836) was the reputed inventor of the *bowie knife* – a strongly made dagger with a one-edged blade of some 12 inches in length and curving to a point – which was named after him.

Like one of his contemporaries, Davy Crockett (q.v.), Bowie has acquired something of a legendary status in American folklore; and the numerous stories of his exploits are, not surprisingly, of varying credibility. It does seem reasonably certain, however, that he once killed a man in a fight, using a one-edged weapon made out of a blacksmith's rasp, and that this weapon was the prototype of the bowie knife.

Bowie was born in Burke County, Georgia, and settled in Texas, which at the time was a part of Mexico. He became a Mexican citizen, but was strongly opposed to the central Mexican government and was one of the leaders of the Texan rebellion in 1836. He had joined the Texas army in 1835, becoming a colonel; and on 6 March 1836, he was killed at the Alamo, where fewer than 200 Texans (including Davy Crockett) had held out against some 3,000 Mexicans for 13 days.

Colonel Bowie was confined to his sick-bed when the gallant defenders of the fort were finally overwhelmed, yet along with the others it seems that he died fighting bravely. Alamo, in fact, has come to be known as the 'Thermopylae of America'.

The bowie knife – largely no doubt through the reputation of the man who gave it its name – was in such demand at one time that a number were manufactured in England for sale in America: a fact which sounds almost as unlikely as one of those stories about James Bowie himself!

58 BOWLER HAT

Thomas and William Bowler (or perhaps Beaulieu) were nineteenth-century hat makers who apparently gave their name to the *bowler-hat*, or the *bowler*, the hard roundish-brimmed hat known in the United States as the derby (q.v.).

It seems that the bowler was first made to the special order of one William Coke, of the well-known Coke family of Holkham, in Norfolk, who required a sturdy, low-crowned hat for his favourite sport of shooting. The hat was supplied through James Lock & Co, the London hatters, who preferred (and still prefer) to call it a *coke*, though *bowler* has persisted as the generally accepted name.

We also use the verb *bowler-hat* in reference to the discharge of a commissioned officer from the services, when his military headgear is exchanged for such as a bowler (the bowler, in fact, is still the regulation off-duty hat in certain British regiments). And more recently, the expression *golden bowler* came into use when, as a result of cuts in UK defence expenditure, large numbers of serving officers were encouraged to resign their commissions prematurely, with the inducement of a generous lump-sum payment.

59 BOYCOTT
Charles Cunningham Boycott (1832–97) was a captain in the British army who, on retiring, was employed as an agent for Lord Erne's estates in County Mayo, Ireland. He became the particular target for organized agitation by the Irish Land League, who attempted to shut him off from all social and commercial activities, and the word *boycott* was coined from his name.

60 BOYLE'S LAW
Robert Boyle (1627–91), the seventh son of the first Earl of Cork, was one of the principal founders of modern chemistry and physics. He is remembered especially for *Boyle's law*, which states that, at a constant temperature, the volume of a given quantity of any gas is inversely proportional to the pressure on that gas. Boyle's law is also known as *Mariotte's law*, from the French physicist Edme Mariotte (1620?–84) who confirmed Boyle's principle quite independently of the British scientist.

In addition to his scientific work, Boyle was much concerned with theology; and in this respect he gives his name to *The Boyle Lectures*, a series of eight sermons in defence of Christianity (q.v.) and given annually. These were endowed in his will and first given in 1692.

61 BRADBURY
Sir John Swanwick Bradbury, later first Baron Bradbury of Winsford (1872–1950), gave his name to a once common expression for a £1 note, a *bradbury*. Sir John Bradbury (he became Lord Bradbury in 1925) was joint Permanent Secretary to the Treasury from 1913 to 1919, and his signature was on all the £1 notes issued between 1914 (when the first notes appeared) and 1918. Nowadays, genuine bradburies could be worth as much as £100.

Less well-known than bradburies were the later *fishers*, notes bearing the signature of Bradbury's successor at the treasury, Sir Norman Fenwick Warren Fisher (1879–1948).

62 BRAIDISM
James Braid (1795?–1860) was a Scottish surgeon who became noted in the medical profession for his special study of mesmerism (q.v.). In the course of his investigations, he found it desirable to invent a new word, *neurohypnotism* (later *hypnotism*), to describe

24

the particular sleeplike state of a mesmerized subject. Hypnotism (Hypnos is the Greek god of sleep) is also known after Dr Braid as *Braidism*.

Dr Braid (or *Brade* as he was also known) practised in Manchester where he gave demonstrations of hypnotism.

63 BRAILLE
Louis Braille (1809–52) invented and gave his name to an alphabet and a system of reading and writing for the blind. Braille, a Frenchman, became a teacher of the blind at the age of 19 and soon afterwards (in 1829) published his first book in *Braille*, in Paris. He also used his skill as a musician (he played the organ in a Paris church) to adapt his system to the special needs of music.

Braille's system consisted basically of six raised points on a flat surface in various combinations and was far superior to previous methods, which had concentrated in the main on the use of raised type. Nowadays, Braille is used and taught in schools for the blind throughout the world; and books and literature of all kinds are reproduced in Braille in considerable quantities.

But this great benefactor of mankind, who invented the system named after him, died at the early age of 43, long before Braille had become accepted or even recognized as the remarkable invention it undoubtedly is. Moreover, Louis Braille never in fact saw any of his own books in Braille – he had been blind from the age of three.

64 BRIGHT'S DISEASE
Richard Bright (1789–1858) was one of the remarkable team of young physicians under the direction of Sir Astley Paston Cooper at Guy's Hospital, in London, during the first half of the nineteenth century. The others were Thomas Addison and Thomas Hodgkin (qq.v.) and they all came to make important contributions to medical science.

Bright became particularly noted for his work on disorders of the kidneys and *Bright's disease* (or nephritis) relates to inflammation of the kidneys. His description of this disease was published in 1827 and he was also the first to describe many other diseases and conditions.

65 BROUGHAM

Henry Peter Brougham, Baron Brougham and Vaux (1778–1868), was one of the leading legal reformers of the nineteenth century. He is best remembered for his defence of Queen Caroline at her trial against her husband, George IV, who had tried to obtain a divorce when he became king, in 1820.

Brougham, a Scotsman, was Lord Chancellor from 1830 to 1834; and it was during this period that the bill abolishing slavery in the British Empire became law. With William Wilberforce and others, Brougham had for many years been in the forefront of the campaign against slavery.

Brougham was also an ardent advocate of education for many people, maintaining that 'Education makes a people easy to lead, but difficult to drive; easy to govern, but impossible to enslave'. He was a founder of London University.

The *brougham*, a one-horse closed carriage, was named in honour of Lord Brougham. Both the family name and the carriage are pronounced 'broom'.

66 BROWNING

John Moses Browning (1855–1926) invented and gave his name to a variety of firearms. Born in Utah, the son of a gunsmith and a Mormon, his first inventions were manufactured by established firearms companies such as Colt and Winchester (qq.v.). But with his brothers, Matthew and Edmund, he eventually established his own gunmaking firm, producing the *Browning automatic pistol*, the *Browning machine-gun* and the *Browning automatic rifle*. Browning firearms were used by the Allies in both World Wars and are still in official use with the military and the police in various countries.

67 BROWNISTS

Robert Browne (1550–1633) was born in Rutland and, after graduating at Cambridge, became a schoolmaster and preacher. He attacked the Established Church and was the leader of a separatist movement based on congregational principles. His followers were called *Brownists*.

He became reconciled to the Church and, in 1591, was appointed rector of Achurch in Northamptonshire. There, when over 80 years of age, he assaulted the parish constable and was taken to Northampton Gaol, where he took ill and died.

The Brownists are generally regarded as the predecessors of the Independents or Congregationalists in England.

68 BRUCELLA   BRUCELLOSIS

Sir David Bruce (1855 – 1931) was a British army physician and bacteriologist who specialized in tropical diseases. In this latter connection he is best known for discovering that the tsetse fly was the carrier of sleeping sickness, the potentially fatal disease prevalent in tropical Africa; and that the tsetse also caused a disease of horses and cattle, nagana. Eponymously, it is through another disease of animals that he is remembered, *Brucellosis*, also called contagious abortion. This can be communicated to humans, when it is known as undulant fever, or Malta fever. (Sir David had in fact traced the bacterium to the milk of Maltese goats.)

Born in Melbourne, Australia, David Bruce joined the Royal Army Medical Corps in 1883. He served in South Africa during the Second Boer War and was present at the Siege of Ladysmith, after which he was decorated and promoted to the rank of lieutenant-colonel. In 1908 he was knighted and retired from the army with the rank of major-general.

69 BUCHMANISM

Frank Nathan Daniel Buchman (1878 – 1961) was an American evangelist whose activities gave rise to the word *Buchmanism*. He preached that a change in the minds of men could lead to 'world-changing through life-changing', and a lecture to undergraduates at Oxford, in 1921, resulted in the founding of his 'Oxford groups' of followers.

In 1938, Buchman launched a new campaign for 'Moral Re-Armament' (MRA), which attracted a considerable following and (it is claimed) exerted some influence internationally. Buchmanism tended to decline, however, after the death of its founder, whose personal magnetism had clearly played an important part in the movement's popularity over the years.

70 BUDDHISM   BUDDHIST

Gautama Buddha (*circa* 560 – 480 BC), the Indian philosopher and founder of *Buddhism*, was originally known as Prince Siddhartha (or Sakyamuni) Gautama. Legend has it that he experienced the great change in his life as he sat under a pipal tree (the sacred Bo tree) at Buddh Gaya, and subsequently took the title of Buddha (meaning, 'the Englightened') from his experience at that place.

Buddhism has influenced a number of other Oriental religions, and has led to the founding of sects such as *Zen Buddhism*. And the influence of especially the meditative aspect of Buddhism has become noticeable in the Western world in recent times.

Buddha was a contemporary of Confucius (q.v.), but the worldliness of Confucianism has little in common with the mystical awareness of Buddhism. Buddha, like Confucius, however, left behind no written record of his philosophy.

71 BUNSEN BURNER

Robert Wilhelm Bunsen (1811 – 99) invented and gave his name to a burner for use in laboratories, the *bunsen burner*.

Bunsen, a German, was a professor at Heidelberg, where he established his reputation as one of the leading chemists of his day. Much of his greatest work was accomplished in collaboration with the physicist Kirchoff, and it was with Kirchoff, in 1860, that he discovered the elements caesium and rubidium.

It was some five years earlier, however, that Bunsen had discovered that a certain mixture of coal-gas and air could produce a smokeless flame of great heat. He then proceeded to invent the bunsen burner. And of all Bunsen's numerous discoveries and inventions, the bunsen burner remains the one which he is best remembered for – or even (to many people) the only thing he is remembered for at all.

72 BURIDAN'S ASS

Jean Buridan was the fourteenth-century French schoolman (i.e. a teacher of philosophy and theology of the Middle Ages) who gave his name to the hypothetical *Buridan's ass*. It is argued that the ass, placed exactly between two equally inviting meals, would be unable to decide which one it should eat and would consequently die of starvation.

Thus, anyone displaying indecision, or a fatal hesitancy in making a choice, can be likened to Buridan's ass.

73 BURKE

William Burke (1792 – 1829), the notorious murderer, and his accomplice, William Hare, suffocated their victims after getting them drunk, and sold the bodies to a Dr Robert Knox, an Edinburgh anatomist. It was in Edinburgh that Burke and Hare, both Irishmen, first met and where they committed their numerous crimes. (Not all their victims were accounted for, but it is likely that they murdered some 20 people over a period 12 months or so.)

When they were eventually arrested and charged with the murders, Hare turned King's evidence and Burke was convicted and hanged. His body was dissected at a public lecture and his name went into the English language as a verb. (*To burke* is to murder by smothering or stifling and, figuratively, to suppress quietly or 'hush up'.)

Hare changed his name and retired into obscurity south of the border.

C

74 CAESAR   CAESARIAN   JULIAN

Gaius Julius Caesar (100 – 44 BC), carried out two successful invasions of Britain, in 55 and 54 BC; he could also be said to have invaded the English language with equal success. We use the word *Caesar* for an absolute monarch, or a dictator, while *kaiser* and *csar* (or *tsar*) are derived from the surname of the famous Roman general too. And Julius Caesar is commonly supposed to have given his name to the *Caesarian operation* (the delivery of a child by means of cutting through the walls of the abdomen), since he was apparently born by this means.

In 46 BC, Julius Caesar introduced and gave his name to the *Julian calendar*, the *Julian year* being calculated at 365¼ days. To effect the necessary adjustment, the year 46 BC was made to consist of 445 days and became known as the 'year of confusion'. The Julian calendar was in use in Britain and the Colonies until 1752 when it was replaced by the Gregorian calendar (q.v.) although the *New Style* had been in effect in France, Italy, Portugal and Spain since 1582. Russia was one of the last countries to abandon the *Old Style* (Julian) calendar – in the year of the revolution, 1917, by which time there was a difference of 13 days between the *Old Style* and the *New Style*. According to the Gregorian calendar, the revolution began on 7 November, but it is still referred to as the 'October Revolution' – since the date according to the Julian calendar was 25 October.

75 CALIXTIN(E)

Georg Calixtus (1586 – 1656) was a German Lutheran (q.v.) theologian who urged reconciliation or syncretism (a word especially associated with his name) of the various Christian churches and was accused of apostasy.

Followers of Calixtus were known as *Calixtins* or *Calixtines*; and present day advocates of unification of the Christian churches could be given this name. They were also linked with the Hussites (q.v.) under the joint name of *Utraquists* (from the Latin *utraque specie*, or 'under each kind'), because of their assertion of the right to take both wine and bread in the Holy Communion.

76 CALLIPPIC PERIOD
Calippus (or Callippus) was a Greek astronomer of the fourth century BC who claimed to have corrected the Metonic cycle (q.v.) by quadrupling Meton's period of 19 years and deducting one day. But his own calculations were not strictly accurate. It was subsequently shown that the *Callipic period* was short of a whole day every 553 years.

77 CALVINIST CALVINISTIC CALVINISM
John Calvin (1509 – 64), the religious reformer and originator of *Calvinism*, was born in Picardy, in France. His name originally was Jean *Chauvin* (sometimes spelt *Cauvin*). He broke with the Roman Catholic Church and left France for Switzerland where, at Geneva, he eventually established himself as the virtual dictator of a regime of strict morality, which dealt severely with heretics and other offenders. It was at Geneva, in 1553, that the Spanish theologian and physician, Michael Servetus, was burned at the stake. It was also at Geneva that the Scottish reformer, John Knox (an ardent *Calvinist*), wrote his famous *First blast of the trumpet against the monstrous regiment of women*, which so offended Queen Elizabeth I (q.v.).

Nowadays, the word *Calvinistic* has come to be used more generally, or outside its strictly religious meaning, in the sense of strict, severe, or excessively moral.

78 CAMERONIAN
Richard Cameron (1648? – 80) founded and gave his name to a religious sect of Reformed Presbyterians, the *Cameronians*. His church refused to accept the allegiance to Charles II (q.v.) and Cameron became the ringleader of a group of 'persecuted Presbyterians' who took to arms to defend their rights. A battle took place at Airds Moss, near Auchinleck, in Ayrshire, in which Cameron was killed. His head and hands were cut off and fixed on the Netherbow Port, at the Canongate, in Edinburgh.

Some of the Cameronians who survived the battle, however, were amnestied and then regrouped to form the nucleus of the British army's famous Cameronian regiment (the 26th Foot and later the First Battalion of Scottish Rifles).

79 CARDIGAN
James Thomas Brudenell, seventh Earl of Cardigan (1797 – 1868), was the English soldier who led the Light Brigade in their famous

charge at the battle of Balaclava in 1854. And as we all know (even if we have only seen the film or read Tennyson's poem), Lord Raglan (q.v.), the commander of the British troops, had given certain orders but 'some one had blunder'd'; and Lord Lucan had ordered Cardigan and his 'Noble six hundred' to charge the Russian guns.

> 'Their's not to make reply,
> Their's not to reason why,
> Their's but to do and die:
> Into the valley of Death
> Rode the six hundred.'

Cardigan, it is said, was the first man to reach the Russian lines, and he managed to ride back unscathed; which is remarkable, considering that more than half of his men were killed or wounded in the charge. It is remarkable, too, that the battle of Balaclava and those involved in it gave no fewer than three new words to the English language – all describing articles of clothing. The noble earl himself gave his name to a woollen waistcoat with long sleeves, the *cardigan*, in fact.

And almost a part of the English language is the well-known remark made by the French general, Bosquet, who watched the charge of the Light Brigade from a ringside seat: 'C'est magnifique, mais ce n'est pas la guerre.' (It is magnificent, but it is not war.)

80 CAROLINGIAN   CARLOVINGIAN
Charlemagne, or Charles the Great (742–814), gave his name to a dynasty of Frankish kings, the *Carolingian*, or *Carlovingian*, dynasty which began in 751 with Pepin le Bref (Pepin the Short), the father of Charlemagne, and ended with the death of Louis V, in 987. (*Carolingian* is taken from the Latinized form of his title, Carolus Magnus, and *Carlovingian* from the German, Karl der Grosse.)

Charlemagne became king of the Franks in 768, with the death of his father, and in 800 he assumed the title of Emperor of the West, and was crowned Carolus Augustus, Emperor of the Romans, by Pope Leo III, becoming the first of the Holy Roman emperors, with an empire comprising Gaul, Italy, and much of Spain and Germany.

While Charlemagne is remembered as a great warrior, his reign was also marked by wise rule and patronage of the arts and sciences, and he was undoubtedly the outstanding ruler of the Carolingian dynasty.

81 CARTESIAN

René Descartes (1596–1650) founded and gave his name to the school of philosophy known as *Cartesian*.

Descartes was eminent both as a mathematician and a philosopher; and his method of reasoning, with its rejection of traditional ideas ('I think, therefore I am'), greatly influenced the development of philosophy and science. His major work, *Le discours de la méthode*, contains a number of frequently quoted passages (including the above example), such as: 'Common sense is the most widely distributed commodity in the world, for everyone is convinced that he is well supplied with it'; and 'The reading of all good books is like a conversation with the finest men of past centuries.'

Descartes was born at Touraine in France, but lived the latter part of his life mainly in Holland. He died in Sweden, shortly after arriving there at the invitation of Queen Christina.

A once popular scientific toy known as the *Cartesian devil*, or the 'Bottle-imp', was also named after Descartes. This consisted of a transparent container with a floating object which dived when the top of the container was pressed.

82 CASANOVA

Giovanni Jacopo Casanova de Seingalt (1725–98) was the author of 12 volumes of memoirs (*Mémoires écrites par lui-même*) which describe with great frankness the intimate details of a life seemingly devoted to lechery and intrigue. And from these memoirs, the name of *Casanova* has come to be synonymous with that of the legendary Don Juan, the great lover and womanizer.

Casanova was born in Venice, the son of an actor. It would seem that he inherited more than a little acting ability, for over the years he played the parts of a soldier, a priest, a quack doctor, a gambler, a musician – and many more, as he travelled from one European capital to another, making and losing fortunes and friends on the way. And among his friends, he numbered some of the most famous of his day: the Empress Catherine, Voltaire, Madame de Pompadour (q.v.) and even the Pope.

But there are many details in Casanova's account of his life which are open to doubt – especially those concerning his supposedly numerous affairs with women. And it could well be that the man whose name has passed into the language as the great lover, should really be named as the great confidence trickster.

83 CATHERINE-WHEEL
CATHERINE-WHEEL WINDOW

Saint Catherine of Alexandria, the patron saint of wheelwrights, was apparently a virgin princess who, in 307 AD or thereabouts, was executed for her Christian beliefs. It is said that she miraculously survived attempts to torture her on a fiendish machine with spiked wheels and was eventually beheaded, her body afterwards being taken by angels to Mount Sinai. The convent of St Catherine was founded to commemorate her supposed resting place, and 25 November is held as her feast day.

The *catherine-wheel* has become the symbol of her martyrdom, and the *catherine-wheel window* (a round window with radial divisions, or a rose-window) is named after her. The *catherine-wheel* is also the name given to a sideways somersault and, of course, a rotating firework.

84 CATILINE

Lucius Sergius Catilina (*circa* 108 – 62 BC) was a Roman noble who conspired to assassinate the consuls and destroy Rome. His plans were foiled by Cicero (q.v.) who denounced him in a series of Orations, which led to the arrest of a number of the conspirators and the passing of a death sentence on Catilina. He fled to Etruria, but was killed there soon afterwards at the battle of Pistoria.

A *Catiline* has since become a word used to describe any daring but reckless conspirator.

85 CELSIUS THERMOMETER

Anders Celsius (1701 – 44) invented and gave his name to the *Celsius thermometer*, also known as the *centigrade thermometer*. The scale on the Celsius thermometer is a simplification of the earlier Fahrenheit scale (q.v.), showing the freezing point of water at zero and the boiling point at 100 degrees. (The original thermometer constructed by Celsius in 1742 showed the *freezing* point at 100 and the *boiling* point at zero, but this was reversed to the present scale in 1750.)

Celsius was born at Uppsala, in Sweden, and became a professor at Uppsala University, where his uncle, Olaf Celsius, had been a teacher of Linnaeus (q.v.), the famous botanist. He was a leading astronomer of his time (he built the observatory at Uppsala) and one of the first to advocate the adoption of the Gregorian calendar (q.v.) in Sweden.

86 CHARLES'S LAW
Jacques Alexandre César Charles (1746 – 1823) is remembered as the inventor of the hydrogen balloon, in which he made the first ascent on 1 December 1783, just ten days after the first manned ascent of the Montgolfier brothers' hot-air balloon.

Eponymously, he is remembered for his law concerning the expansion of gases, *Charles's law*, which states the effect of temperature changes on the volume of a gas. The studies of J. A. C. Charles anticipated the findings of another Frenchman, Joseph Louis Gay-Lussac (1778 – 1850), and Charles's law is also known as *Gay-Lussac's law* in consequence of this.

87 CHASSEPOT
Antoine Alphonse Chassepot (1833 – 1905) invented and gave his name to a rifle, the *Chassepot*. This was manufactured at the Paris arsenal where Chassepot worked, and was officially adopted by the French army in 1866.

88 CHATEAUBRIAND STEAK
Vicomte François René de Chateaubriand (1768 – 1848) is remembered as a distinguished statesman and a gifted and original writer. His political career was one of many vicissitudes, culminating in his appointment as ambassador to Great Britain (where he had at one time lived in exile from France) and afterwards, Minister of Foreign Affairs. As a writer, he is regarded as one of the leaders of the French romantic movement, especially with his *Le génie du Christianisme*.

Chateaubriand is remembered in the English language, however, as a gourmet, from one of his favourite dishes, named after him as a *Chateaubriand steak* − a grilled steak cut from the thick end of the fillet.

89 CHAUVINISM   CHAUVINIST   CHAUVINISTIC
Nicolas Chauvin was a soldier in the French Revolutionary Army who later served under Napoleon (q.v.). Although he was decorated for his courage in battle, Chauvin's wildly exaggerated patriotism and unquestioning adoration of Napoleon eventually made him an object of ridicule among his comrades. He was caricatured by various writers and from his name came the word *chauvinist* to describe anyone who is blindly devoted to his own country. The use of the word has been extended to apply to

anyone unthinkingly committed to a particular cause – e.g. *male chauvinist* for one committed to male supremacy.

90 CHEKHOVIAN

Anton Pavlovich Chekhov (1860 – 1904) has for many years been the best known Russian author outside of his country of birth. He is generally regarded as one of the most original writers of short stories, while his plays are regularly performed at the leading theatres in Europe and the English-speaking world. The *Chekhovian* influence on other writers has also been considerable, but the adjective carries a broader meaning than a description of Chekhov's style of writing: it has come to epitomize the virtually hopeless plight of the cultured yet unworldly person becoming overwhelmed by the pressures of a changing and mercenary society. And though Chekhov was writing about the declining middle classes in the Russia of his day, his work gives us a portrait of the ordinary, unambitious man or woman of any place or time.

Chekhov was of humble origin (his grandfather was a serf), but he studied medicine at Moscow University and qualified as a physician. He practised his profession for only a short time, following his early success in writing, which included sketches for vaudeville and French farces as well as his better known short stories and plays. Of the latter, the best known are *The Seagull, Uncle Vanya, The Three Sisters* and *The Cherry Orchard*; this last play being written in the year of his death, from tuberculosis, at the age of 44. Three years earlier he had married the actress Olga Knipper, who became celebrated for her interpretations of many of the characters in her husband's plays.

91 CHESTERFIELD

Philip Dormer Stanhope, the fourth Earl of Chesterfield (1694 – 1773), gave his name to a kind of long overcoat and a large, well-padded sofa.

Chesterfield was a wealthy and influential man, a successful politician and diplomatist, and an impressive orator in Parliament. But he is particularly remembered (apart from the overcoat and the sofa) for his *Letters*, addressed to his natural son, Philip Stanhope, and his godson of the same name. They are, in effect, instruction in eighteenth-century 'one-upmanship' for the young men, and are written in a witty, epigrammatical style, which lends itself to random quotation. A well-known example is contained in a letter written on 29 January 1748: 'Advice is seldom welcome;

and those who want it the most always like it the least'.

Lord Chesterfield is also remembered in another, less-flattering literary connection, and again in the form of a letter. He incurred the wrath of the formidable Dr Johnson by his belated and patronizing recognition of the famous *Dictionary*, which the author had (some seven years earlier) dedicated to Chesterfield. Johnson had completed the massive work under great difficulties and completely ignored by his 'patron'; and the letter he wrote to Chesterfield is a classic of its kind and typically 'Johnsonian'. It contains the much-quoted passage: 'Is not a Patron, my Lord, one who looks with unconcern on a man struggling for life in the water, and, when he has reached ground, encumbers him with help? The notice which you have been pleased to take of my labours, had it been early, had been kind; but it has been delayed till I am indifferent, and cannot enjoy it; till I am solitary, and cannot impart it; till I am known, and do not want it'.

Johnson had earlier said of Chesterfield: 'This man, I thought, had been a Lord among wits; but, I find, he is only a wit among Lords!' And there is clearly a strong reference to the fourth earl in Johnson's *Dictionary*, under 'patron', which he defines as, 'commonly a wretch who supports with insolence, and is paid with flattery'.

92 CHIPPENDALE

Thomas Chippendale (1718? – 79) designed and gave his name to an elegant style of drawing-room furniture, which became very fashionable in the eighteenth century and was extensively copied.

The aptly named Chippendale came to London from Yorkshire, setting up shop in St Martin's Lane, Charing Cross. He published his designs in *The gentleman and cabinet maker's director*, and in fact devoted more and more of his time to designing rather than making furniture, which suggests that far from all the 'genuine' *Chippendale* originated from Chippendale's shop.

93 CHRISTIAN   CHRISTIANITY   CHRISTENDOM   JESUITRY

Jesus Christ, also known as Jesus of Nazareth (*circa* 4 BC – *circa* AD 30), founded and gave his name to *Christianity*. He has also given his name to numerous other words (without doubt more than any other man) including *Jesuitry, Christendom, christening, Christmas, Christolatry, christophany,* etc.

94 CICERONE

Marcus Tullius Cicero (106 – 43 BC), the great Roman statesman and philosopher, is said to have acquired his name through having a wart (in Latin, *cicer*) on the end of his nose. In turn, his name has been given to a word for a guide, or anyone who draws the attention of strangers to objects of local interest, in the manner of an orator, like Cicero, a *cicerone*.

It was Cicero's great strength as an orator that brought about his death, when following the assassination of Julius Caesar (q.v.) in 44 BC, he launched an attack on Mark Antony in what was known as his *Philippic* orations. He was subsequently proscribed by the new triumvirate of Mark Anthony, Marcus Aemilius Lepidus and Gaius Octavius (q.v. under *Augustus*) and put to death.

95 CLARENCE

William IV, formerly the Duke of Clarence (1765 – 1837), gave his name to a type of closed four-wheeled carriage with seating for two or more passengers, a *clarence*.

William was the third son of George III (q.v.) and succeeded his brother, George IV, as King of Great Britain, in 1830. He was known as 'the Sailor-King', largely through having served as a midshipman at the battle of Cape St Vincent in 1780. He was also known as 'Silly Billy', apparently from his light-hearted attitude towards his duties as king, though it is doubtful whether he gave his name to that particular expression.

96 CLERIHEW

Edmund Clerihew Bentley (1875 – 1956) originated and gave his second Christian name to a particular kind of four-line verse, the *clerihew*. The first clerihews appeared in 1905 in a book entitled *Biography for beginners*. The verses were illustrated by G. K. Chesterton, and the author used the name 'E. Clerihew'. He gave the following explanation in an introductory verse:

> The art of Biography
>   Is different from Geography.
> Geography is about maps,
>   But Biography is about chaps.

Bentley also wrote a very successful piece of detective fiction – *Trent's last case* – under his real name. But it is by his clerihews that E. C. Bentley will be best remembered. This simple verse-form has been imitated (often badly) by numbers of writers, including the distinguished poet W. H. Auden. Bentley's peculiar humorous versifying is typified by his best-known clerihew:

> Sir Christopher Wren
> Said, 'I am going to dine with some men.
> If anybody calls
> Say I am designing St Paul's.'

97 COCKER ACCORDING TO COCKER

Edward Cocker (1631–75) was the author of a highly successful book on arithmetic, *Arithmetick*, which has given us the word *Cocker* as a synonym of accepted standards of accuracy and correctness.

Cocker was an engraver and a teacher of arithmetic and writing who lived in London. For all the popularity of his book – which ran to more than 100 editions – Cocker would probably be forgotten, were it not for a play by an Irish actor and playwright, Arthur Murphy. In this play, *The apprentice*, Murphy introduced the phrase, 'according to Cocker', which has become a part of the language. Murphy, too, would probably be forgotten, but for that phrase.

98 COLBERTINE

Jean Baptiste Colbert (1619–83) was one of the outstanding French statesmen of his time. As minister of finance under Louis XIV (q.v.) he carried out wide ranging reforms, greatly increasing state revenue and extending trade overseas. The French navy was virtually created through his efforts. His general popularity, however, was never high with the French people, largely as a result of the oppressive taxes, for which he was held to blame.

Nonetheless, Colbert is also remembered as a great patron of the arts, and it is in this connection that his name is noted in the language, from a kind of lace which is named after him as *Colbertine*.

99 COLT COLT REVOLVER COLT .45

Samuel Colt (1814–62) invented and gave his name to a pistol with a revolving magazine, the *Colt revolver*.

Colt was born in Hartford, Connecticut, and after an early spell as a seaman, returned to his home town where he established an arms factory for manufacturing his inventions. He patented his first *Colt* in 1835, but it was more than ten years before an improved model was adopted by the US army.

There had been attempts at inventing a revolver as early as the seventeenth century. Colt's 'six-shooter', however, was the first really serviceable firearm of this kind; and subsequent inventions were largely based on his revolver. The Mexican War of 1846–48 proved the effectiveness of the Colt, and in 1854 it was issued in Britain to the Royal Navy. A .45 calibre version of the Colt was used by US forces in both World Wars.

But, like the Thompson submachine-gun (q.v.) in later years, the Colt also became one of the favourite weapons of the law-breakers. The so-called 'Wild West' period in the history of America has become almost as synonymous with the Colt as the names of such as Jesse James, 'Billy the Kid', and the Clantons; to say nothing of those on the other side of the law – Wyatt Earp, 'Wild Bill' Hickock, *et al*.

The tremendous popularity of the 'Western' has, of course, over-glamorized and exaggerated the importance of the period (it lasted some 25 years, from the end of the Civil War) and its characters; but there is no doubt that the revolver and the rifle played an important part as the weapons used by both the men who flouted or upheld the law. It was said that 'he who lived by the gun, died by the gun'. And more often than not, the gun was a Colt revolver.

100 COMSTOCKERY
Anthony Comstock (1844–1915) was the secretary of the New York Society for the Suppression of Vice from 1873 until his death. During these years he conducted a campaign of strict censorship of books, plays and works of art supposed to be immoral and corrupting. His activities gave rise to the word *comstockery* (coined by the dramatist George Bernard Shaw) as a synonym for prudery.

Comstock served in the Union army during the American Civil War; and the raids he conducted on bookshops and publishing houses were indeed of a military nature in their execution. He wrote a number of books concerned with his obsession about public morals and was particularly severe on nudity in art.

101 COMTISM   COMTIST
Isidore Auguste Marie Francois Comte (1798–1857) was a French mathematician and philosopher who founded the philosophical

system known as positivism or (from his name) *Comtism*. This propounded a new arrangement of the sciences, recognizing only positive facts through the observation of phenomena and their sequence and disregarding metaphysical and theological ideas. One of the foremost disciples of positivism was the English philosopher Frederic Harrison (1831–1923) who established the movement in England. Another English philosopher and *Comtist* was John Stuart Mill; and it was largely through the financial support of Mill and others that Comte continued his work until his death (he died insane) in 1857.

102 CONFUCIANISM

Confucius (551?–478 BC), the great Chinese philosopher, was originally known as K'ung Futzu or Kung Futse, meaning philosopher Kung. There is no written record of his teachings, but the sayings of Confucius, recorded by his followers, are well-known in China and elsewhere. A typical example of the *Confucian* philosophy is, 'Do not unto others what you would not wish unto yourself'.

Confucianism was developed from the ideals of Confucius some time after his death, and became one of the main religions in China, although Confucius had never presented himself as a religious teacher. Today, in the People's Republic of China, Confucius is seen largely as a reactionary.

103 CONGREVE   CONGREVE ROCKET

Sir William Congreve (1772–1828) invented and gave his name to the first rocket to be used in warfare by the British, the *Congreve rocket*. He was also the inventor of a type of friction match, known as a *Congreve*, which preceded the modern friction match, or lucifer-match.

Congreve's rocket was first used to effect in an attack on Boulogne on 8 October 1806, and remained in service for more than half a century. A British rocket brigade played an important part in the defeat of Napoleon (q.v.) at 'the Battle of the Nations' at Leipzig, in 1813; and in the following year the rocket was immortalized in Francis Scott Key's poem *The star-spangled banner* (later of course to become the national anthem of the USA) when he wrote of 'the rocket's red glare' as the British bombarded Fort McHenry.

Sir William Congreve became Comptroller of the Royal Laboratory at Woolwich in that same year, when he succeeded his father (the first baronet) in the post. His other inventions included a naval gun.

104 COPERNICAN SYSTEM

Nicolas Copernicus, sometimes spelt Koppernik, etc. (1473–1543), originated and gave his name to the *Copernican system*, which stated that the earth revolves about the sun.

Copernicus was born in Torun, in Poland (then Prussian Poland), and became canon of the cathedral at Frauenburg. His novel theory of the planets (including the earth) revolving around the sun was propounded in his book *De revolutionibus orbium coelestium* (*On the revolution of the celestial orbs*); but Copernicus feared the official reaction to his (at that time) revolutionary ideas, and the printing of his book was delayed for a number of years and completed only just before the author died.

The notion that the sun, the planets, and the stars revolved around the earth, had been accepted since the second century, and was not to be finally rejected for more than another hundred years. And in 1633, the great Italian astronomer and mathematician, Galileo, was forced by the Inquisition to repudiate the Copernican theory, though it is said that after recanting he muttered 'E pur si muove' ('Yet it does move').

105 COUEISM

Emile Coué (1857–1926) was a French chemist who devised a system of psychotherapy, named after him as *Couéism*. Coué's patients were persuaded to believe that, 'Every day, in every way, I am getting better and better'. But such methods are no longer confined to the clinics, and brainwashing of one kind or another (e.g. high-powered advertising) is now an accepted fact in our modern society; and not least in the world of professional sport, where the high rewards and the accompanying prestige which await the successful competitor have brought him or her to realize that it is not necessarily enough merely to be fitter, faster, or stronger, or better equipped in technique than one's opponent. It is necessary to *believe* in one's ability to win.

Perhaps the best-known exponent of what might be termed *psychological gamesmanship* was the world heavyweight boxing champion Muhammad Ali (or Cassius Clay as he was formerly known), who virtually mesmerized (q.v.) his opponents (to say nothing of his public) into believing that he was 'the Greatest', before he had even climbed into the boxing-ring.

106 CROESUS

Croesus was the last king of Lydia, in Asia Minor, who reigned from 560 to 546 BC, when he was overthrown by Cyrus 'the Elder', King of Persia. He was reputed to have been the richest man in the world and from this we have the eponym *Croesus*, meaning an extremely wealthy man.

It is said that Croesus was once told by Solon, the renowned Athenian statesman, that we should 'call no man happy till he dies, he is at best but fortunate'. He was recalling these words as he was about to be burnt alive by the Persian soldiers, when Cyrus intervened and demanded an explanation of what Croesus was saying. And it seems he was sufficiently impressed to reprieve his victim and to become his friend.

107 CROMPTON'S MULE

Samuel Crompton (1753–1827) was the inventor (in 1779) of a cotton-spinning machine known as a mule, since like that animal it was a hybrid, owing something to both Sir Richard Arkwright's water-frame and James Hargreave's spinning-jenny.

Crompton's mule, or the spinning-mule, brought small reward to its inventor, a Lancashire weaver who was too poor to patent it, though the House of Commons did award him £5000 in 1812.

108 CURIE CURIUM CURIE POINT
CURIE'S LAW CURIETHERAPY

Marie Curie (1867–1934) and her husband, Pierre Curie (1859–1906), became famous for their discovery of radium in 1898. Mme Curie was also famed as the first woman to be awarded a Nobel prize (when she shared the 1903 prize for physics with her husband and the French scientist A. H. Becquerel (q.v.)) and the first person to receive two Nobel prizes. (She won the 1911 prize for chemistry individually.)

Marja Sklodowska (as she was before her marriage) was born in Warsaw, where she studied under her father, a professor of physics. She continued her studies in Paris, at the Sorbonne, where she met Pierre Curie. After his death (in a road accident), she succeeded him as professor of physics at the Sorbonne. One of their daughters, Irène, became a physicist, and married another physicist, Frédéric Joliot (who later changed his name to Joliot-Curie), with whom she shared the Nobel prize for chemistry in 1935. Another daughter, Eve, distinguished herself as a concert pianist and a writer (including work as a war correspondent) and wrote a biography of her mother.

Pierre and Marie Curie have given their name to a number of words in our language: *curium*, the element of atomic number 96, and *curietherapy*, the treatment of certain diseases with the use of radium, are named after them jointly; while Mme Curie gives her name to the measure of the activity of a radioactive substance, the *curie*, and Pierre Curie has the *Curie point* (or the *Curie temperature*), the temperature for a given ferromagnetic substance, named after him, as well as *Curie's law*, which states that the magnetic susceptibility of a paramagnetic substance is inversely proportional to the absolute temperature.

The element of atomic number 84, *polonium*, was discovered by Mme Curie and named in honour of her country of birth.

109 CUSHING'S SYNDROME

Harvey Williams Cushing (1869–1939) is remembered both as a brilliant surgeon and an eminent scientist. His name is given to a disorder of the chemistry of the body, *Cushing's syndrome* or *Cushing's disease*. This is caused by either a malfunction of the adrenal glands (the glands beside the kidneys), resulting in the over-production of certain hormones, or through deliberate treatment with such hormones. The symptoms include obesity in the face and the trunk and high blood pressure.

Cushing was born in Cleveland, Ohio, and graduated at Yale and Harvard. He became one of America's leading specialists in brain surgery; and in the First World War, served with distinction in the Army Medical Corps on the Western Front. Among his many publications was a biography of the distinguished Canadian physician Sir William Osler, for which he was awarded a Pulitzer prize in 1925.

110 CYRILLIC   CYRILLIC ALPHABET

Saint Cyril, or Constantine of Thessalonica (827–69), and his brother, Saint Methodius (826–85), were the reputed inventors of the *Cyrillic alphabet*, named after St Cyril. This is a version of the Greek alphabet and one of the two Slavonic alphabets, the other being the Glagolitic.

The brothers are also said to have translated the gospels and various liturgical books into Old Slavonic.

44

D

111 DAGUERREOTYPE

Louis Jacques Mandé Daguerre (1787 – 1851), invented and gave his name to the first photographic process of practical use, the *daguerreotype*. Daguerre's process employed the action of sunlight to produce permanent pictures on metal plates and reduced the exposure time for taking the photograph from some eight hours to about 15 minutes.

Daguerre was a landscape painter, and a scene painter for the opera before he turned to photography. He had already been involved in inventing and exhibiting the Diorama (a method of exhibiting pictures with the use of dramatic lighting effects) when in 1829 he met the physicist J. N. Niepce, who three years earlier had taken the first photograph to be permanently fixed. The two Frenchmen worked together up to Niepce's death in 1833, after which Daguerre continued experimenting alone until, in 1839, he produced his *daguerreotype* process. But at the same time, an Englishman, William Henry Fox Talbot, was perfecting a negative-positive process which was to become the real basis of modern photography, rendering the daguerreotype obsolete.

Nonetheless, it was Daguerre's invention that really aroused the public interest in photography, and his cameras were the first to be manufactured for sale. And it is perhaps ironic that it was not Daguerre the painter, but Daguerre the inventor who had the greater influence on painting. Photography revolutionized the world of art in many respects (and portrait painting in particular), but artists such as Degas, and, later, Magritte, saw the camera as a positive aid to their work.

Photography today, of course, is regarded as an art in itself; and yet modern technology has now made it possible for almost anyone to obtain a camera capable of taking a photograph *and* developing it in a matter of seconds.

112 DALTONISM

John Dalton (1766 – 1844), the English chemist and mathematician, is best remembered for his atomic theory, but he has given his name to something quite different. Dalton (and his brother) suffered from colour-blindness. At the time, there had been very little scientific study of this condition, so Dalton decided to investigate his own particular case. In 1794, he gave the first detailed description of colour-blindness, which is now named after him as *Daltonism*.

'Daltonism' is also the word used to describe a method of education in schools (also called the Dalton plan), which allows the pupil considerable freedom in choosing and studying his subjects and encourages him to work separately from the traditional group, or class. This method was first tried in Dalton, Massachusetts, in 1920. The town was named after John C. Dalton (1825–89), who was born in Massachusetts.

113 DAMOCLEAN   SWORD OF DAMOCLES

Damocles was a courtier of Dionysius the Elder of Syracuse, who reigned from 405 to 367 BC. Cicero (q.v.) tells of Damocles being invited to a great banquet by Dionysius, but then being made to sit beneath a sword suspended by just one hair. This was intended to remind Damocles (in the most obvious way) of the danger attending the richest and happiest of lives, following his flattery of Dionysius and his good fortune.

From this, we use the word *Damoclean* to describe imminent or 'overhanging' danger.

114 DANIEL

Daniel, the Hebrew prophet chronicled in the Old Testament book of Daniel, gives his name to the English language as a wise judge through the Apocryphal book, The History of Susannah. The young Daniel proves Susannah innocent of adultery; and Shakespeare uses his name eponymously in his *Merchant of Venice*, when Shylock declaims: 'A *Daniel* come to judgment! yea, a *Daniel*! / O wise young judge, how I do honour thee!'

115 DANIELL CELL

John Frederic Daniell (1790–1845) was an English chemist who invented and gave his name to one of the earliest practical electric batteries, the *Daniell cell*. This was a development of the Voltaic pile (q.v.), having two plates, one of copper and one of zinc, in dilute sulphuric acid and connected by a wire.

Daniell also invented and gave his name to a type of hygrometer, an instrument for measuring the humidity of air and other gases, and wrote extensively on meteorology.

116 DARBYITE

John Nelson Darby (1800–82) was one of the founders of the Plymouth Brethren, also known after him as *Darbyites*, though the eponym is more specifically applied to an 'Exclusive' division of the sect.

Darby was a minister of the Protestant Church in Ireland, where he formed an association with a former Roman Catholic, Edward Cronin, who shared Darby's disillusionment with the established churches which they regarded as corrupt. The 'Brethren' set up their first centre at Plymouth, in Devon, in 1830, and have since been known as the Plymouth Brethren. In 1849, however, the sect split into two distinct divisions, the 'Open Brethren' and the 'Exclusives', of which Darby was the leader.

The present day 'Exclusives' (or Darbyites) represent a minority of the sect and observe strict rules concerning fraternization with 'Sinners', or non-members (members being known as 'Saints'). Overall, the Brethren believe in the desirability of 'direct' communication with God and see no need of an organized ministry.

117 DARWINISM

Charles Robert Darwin (1809–82) revolutionized the world of science and greatly offended Christian believers with his works *On the origin of species by means of natural selection*, and *The descent of man*. *Darwinism* asserted that 'man still bears in his bodily frame the indelible stamp of his lowly origin'.

Darwin was born in Shrewsbury, England and was educated for the ministry at Edinburgh and Cambridge. But, while at Cambridge, he became interested in natural history and, in 1831, he embarked on a scientific expedition to South America and Australia. (Darwin, in Australia, is one of a number of places named after Charles Darwin.)

He returned to England five years later, with many specimens and a vast amount of information on the flora, fauna and geology of the places he had visited. But it was not until 1859 that *The origin of species* was published.

After his death in 1882, Darwin was honoured by burial in Westminster Abbey; but *Darwinism* was still bitterly opposed by a number of religious bodies. As late as 1925, John Thomas Scopes, a schoolmaster of Dayton, Tennessee, was charged with violating a state law by teaching Darwin's theory of evolution in a public school. The ensuing trial became known as the 'monkey trial' and attracted a great deal of attention, partly because Scopes was defended by the famous lawyer, Clarence Darrow. Despite Darrow's brilliance, Scopes was convicted, but fined only a nominal sum and the conviction was later reversed by another court.

Yet the controversy over Charles Darwin's theory of evolution continues to this day.

118 DAVIS ESCAPE APPARATUS

Sir Robert Henry Davis (1870 – 1965) was the inventor of a device for assisting escape from a sunken or damaged submarine, named after him as the *Davis escape apparatus*.

The advent of the submarine as a weapon of war had brought its problems both to the men under the water and their potential victims on the surface. But even in peacetime conditions, the risks run by the submariner were very high, and numerous lives were lost for the lack of an adequate means of escape from a submerged vessel. The Davis apparatus was made available in 1929, and two years later it served to enable six men to escape from a British submarine which had sunk off the coast of China.

In addition to the Davis escape apparatus, Sir Robert Davis invented numerous devices for the use of deep-sea divers and submariners, and all 'those in peril on (and under) the sea' have good reason to be thankful for men of his kind.

119 DAVY CROCKETT HAT

David Crockett, known as Davy Crockett (1786 – 1836), is one of the most famous of American folk heroes. His various exploits – as a fearless bear hunter, an Indian scout, a deadly marksman and a colourful and outspoken politician – have been recounted in any number of stories, songs and motion pictures; and his name has been given to the *Davy Crockett hat*, a fur hat with a distinctive 'tailpiece' of the kind he used to wear.

Davy Crockett ('King of the wild frontier') ended his life as bravely as he had lived it, when, with Colonel James Bowie (q.v.) and a gallant band of less than 200 Texans, he was killed at the battle of the Alamo, defying a Mexican army of some 3,000 men.

120 DAVY LAMP

Sir Humphry Davy (1778 – 1829) invented and gave his name to the *Davy lamp*, the safety-lamp used in coalmines. The knowledge of chemistry was greatly advanced by his numerous discoveries (potassium, sodium, calcium, etc.) and it was Davy who discovered the exhilarating effect of nitrous oxide when inhaled, which has given it the name of 'laughing gas'.

It has been said, however, that 'Sir Humphry Davy's greatest discovery was Michael Faraday' (q.v.).

121 DECIBEL   BEL

Alexander Graham Bell (1847–1922) gave his name to the measure for comparing the intensity of sound, the *bel*; more frequently expressed in its tenth part, the *decibel*. Bell's name is associated by most people, of course, with the invention of the telephone, though there were others, it has been claimed, who anticipated his invention; notably the German physicist Reis, who died some years before Bell's patent was granted in 1876, and an American inventor, Elisha Gray.

Bell became a naturalized US citizen in 1882. He was born in Scotland and emigrated to the USA in 1871 to work as a teacher of the deaf. His invention was patented on 9 March 1876; and on the following day, at a house in Boston, Massachusetts, he made his historic telephone call to his assistant Thomas Watson: 'Mr Watson, come here, I want you'.

122 DELLA-ROBBIA

Luca della Robbia (*circa* 1400–82), the Florentine sculptor famed for his work in terracotta, gives his name to a particular kind of enamelled terracotta with white figures against a (usually) blue background.

There are examples of *Della-Robbia* in most of the world's leading art galleries, but his native Florence has retained a large proportion of his work. Luca della Robbia's nephew and pupil, Andrea, and his sons, Giovanni and Girolamo, were also sculptors of note.

123 DERBY

Edward Stanley, twelfth Earl of Derby (1752–1834), instituted and gave his name to the *Derby stakes*, the famous one-and-a-half-mile horse race for three-year-old colts and fillies, held annually since 1780. Other races have since come to be named after the Derby (in particular, the Kentucky Derby) and the word is also used to describe any sporting event with a strong local interest.

The first winner of the Derby Stakes was a horse named *Diomed*, owned by Sir Charles Bunbury; and two years later, Lord Egremont's *Assassin* was the first of his five Derby winners, a record which has only been equalled by the late Aga Khan. Another successful owner (and one of the most colourful) was the Liberal prime minister Lord Rosebery, who had a Derby winner in each year he was in office (1894 – 95) and a third in 1905; and it was Disraeli who gave the Derby its other name of 'the blue ribbon of the turf'. In fact, until 1891, parliament used to adjourn on Derby Day.

Not surprisingly, many famous jockeys have ridden Derby winners, but the remarkable record of Lester Piggott in this race must stand alone. In 1976 he broke the long-standing record of six Derby winners, held jointly by Robinson and Donoghue; and his final total of wins was nine, when he rode *Teenoso* in 1983 at the age of 47, some two years younger than the late Sir Gordon Richards, who was almost 50 when he rode his first and last Derby winner in 1953, the year before Piggott's first success in the Derby at the age of 18.

The British Royal Family have long been associated with horse-racing and not least the Derby. But in 1913, this association became part of a tragedy when a young suffragette, Emily Davison, threw herself under the king's horse, *Anmer*, as the riders approached Tattenham Corner, and died from her injuries shortly afterwards. Yet even two World Wars have failed to stop the Derby being run, though from 1915 to 1918 and again from 1940 to 1945, the race was held at Newmarket instead of its original home on the Epsom Downs, in Surrey.

Derby is also the name for the bowler-hat (q.v.) in America (where it is pronounced 'durbi').

124 DERRICK

Derrick was the name of a seventeenth-century hangman who employed a hoisting apparatus which came to be named after him. One of his most famous 'customers' was the former favourite of Queen Elizabeth (q.v.), the second Earl of Essex, who was executed on Tower Hill in 1601. On this occasion, however, Derrick used an axe – with ghastly results, by all accounts.

Derrick mostly plied his 'trade' at Tyburn. The notorious Tyburn gallows stood near what is now Marble Arch – and there can surely be few places in London with so many grim associations with the past, and fewer men who have had more grisly qualifications for getting their names in the dictionary than Derrick the hangman.

125 DERRINGER

Henry Deringer (1786–1868) was an American small arms manufacturer, especially remembered for his invention of a small short-barrelled pistol, named after him (with a slight alteration in the spelling) as a *derringer*.

The pistol was small enough to be easily concealed in a pocket, or even in the side of a boot.

126 DEWAR-FLASK

Sir James Dewar (1842–1923) invented and gave his name to the *Dewar-flask*, the prototype of the modern thermos or vacuum flask. When the Dewar-flask was demonstrated in 1892, its inventor was already well-known in scientific circles, especially for his experiments with gases. He was the first man to produce liquid hydrogen.

Another distinguished chemist, Sir Frederick Abel, a leading authority on explosives, worked with Dewar to produce a new propellant which would be suitable both for small arms and heavy artillery. Their subsequent joint invention – a smokeless explosive in the form of plastic sticks – came to be known as *cordite*.

Dewar was a Scotsman, but he was not directly related to the well-known family of distillers, John Dewar & Sons.

127 DEWEY CLASSIFICATION

Melvil Dewey (1851–1931) devised the library classification system known as *Dewey Decimal Classification*. Many libraries all over the world, particularly public libraries, are classified by *Dewey*.

Dewey was a student at Amherst College, Massachusetts, when he devised his classification system and it was first adopted by the college library there. He became a founder of the American Library Association, and the founder and first director of the New York State Library School.

Two other Americans devised library classification systems: Henry Evelyn Bliss, and Charles Ammi Cutter. Bliss's *Bibliographic Classification* is used in some special libraries and Cutter's *Expansive Classification* is still used a little in the United States, but hardly at all elsewhere.

128 DICKENSIAN

Charles John Huffman Dickens (1812–70) gave us many eponyms through the characters in his novels: *gamp* (umbrella) from Mrs

Sarah Gamp in *Martin Chuzzlewit; Micawberish*, from Wilkins Macawber in *David Copperfield; Scrooge*, from Ebenezer Scrooge in *A Christmas Carol*; and numerous others. We also have *Dickensian*, from his own name, which is more than just a description of his style of writing. The word is used to describe the England of Dickens's time, with particular reference to the social conditions associated with that period, or at least how we imagine things to have been through reading his novels. And a *Dickensian Christmas* is usually intended to indicate an agreeably old-fashioned Christmas.

It is a mistaken assumption, however, that phrases such as *what the dickens, to play the dickens* and *the dickens only knows*, are derived from Charles Dickens. The 'dickens' referred to here is another name for the devil or Old Nick and was in use long before the nineteenth century. Shakespeare certainly uses it in *The merry wives of Windsor* (III, ii) when Mistress Page (referring to Sir John Falstaff) says: 'I cannot tell what the dickens his name is . . .'

129 DIESEL

Rudolf Diesel (1858–1913) gave his name to a type of internal combustion engine which has become known as the *Diesel engine*.

Diesel, a German who was born in Paris, patented his engine in 1892; and after five years, the firm of Krupp (q.v. under Big Bertha) produced the first successful *diesel*. But some years earlier (in 1890 in fact), a British engineer, Herbert Akroyd-Stuart, had patented a similar kind of compression-ignition engine, which was effectively the prototype of the modern diesel engine.

The word 'diesel', however, is so well established in the English language that it is very unlikely to be replaced by one so 'alien' as 'Akroyd-Stuart'.

130 DIOGENIC   DIOGENES CRAB
DIOGENES CUP

Diogenes (412?–323? BC) is remembered as the Greek philosopher who lived in a tub, or a large earthenware jar. From this he gives his name to the *Diogenes crab*, a hermit-crab which makes its home in an empty shell.

Diogenes was the best known of the Cynic sect, a school of philosophers founded by Antisthenes, a pupil of Socrates (q.v.) and the teacher of Diogenes; and the adjective *Diogenic* is sometimes used as a synonym of 'cynical'.

One of his most fulsome admirers was Alexander the Great,

who is said to have remarked that were he not Alexander, he would wish to be Diogenes. It is also recorded that Alexander asked the philosopher whether he could do anything for him and was told that he might stand aside to allow the sun to shine on him!

The *Diogenes cup* is another name for the simplest kind of drinking-vessel, namely the cupped hands, which could conceivably have been preferred by the austere-living Diogenes.

131 DOBERMAN(N) PINSCHER

Louis Dobermann was a dog-breeder in Apolda, a town in Germany, during the latter half of the nineteenth century. He successfully bred (or 'manufactured') a large terrier, suitable for work as a guard-dog and named after him as the *Dobermann pinscher*. Dobermann was also a night-watchman and his dog was ideally equipped to assist him in this capacity. Strongly built, fierce, agile, yet well disciplined and loyal with good training, the Dobermann could be said to represent the ideal dog for the law-enforcer. Yet Dobermanns have also been used as guide-dogs for the blind.

The Dobermann stands some 26 inches high, and has a short haired, soft coat in various colours. It has long, strong forelegs.

132 DONAT

Aelius Donatus was a teacher of grammar and rhetoric in Rome, in the middle part of the fourth century. He wrote a Latin grammar, *Ars Grammatica*, which achieved such popularity in Western Europe in the Middle Ages that the *Donat* (or *Donet*), from his name, became synonymous for a grammar or any such text-book.

133 DONATIST   DONATISM

Donatus Magnus, or Donatus the Great, Bishop of Carthage (*circa* 312), gave his name to a Christian sect in North Africa, which came about from a dispute over the election of a new bishop. The *Donatists* were extreme puritanicals, maintaining that theirs was the one truly pure and holy church. Their schism from the rest of the church lasted for more than a century.

134 DOPPLER'S PRINCIPLE   DOPPLER EFFECT DOPPLER SHIFT

Christian Johann Doppler (1803 – 53), the Austrian physicist and mathematician, published a paper in 1842 in which he stated a principle concerning the change of wavelengths, known after him as *Doppler's principle*. This explained the apparent increase and decrease in pitch of the sounds emitted by an object (e.g. the whistle of a moving railway engine) as it approaches or goes away from a stationary observer.

Doppler's observations of these changes – the *Doppler effect* – enabled astronomers to calculate the velocity of stars of distant galaxies, since the light emitted from a moving object also appeared to change in a similar way; the colour of a receding star seeming to become more red or to undergo a 'red shift', the *Doppler shift*. And the Doppler effect has also been applied to radar as a means of identifying stationary and moving targets.

135 DOUBTING THOMAS

Saint Thomas was '. . . one of the twelve, called Didymus' (John 20:24). He doubted the word of the other disciples when they told him they had seen the resurrected Jesus, saying, 'Except I shall see in his hands the nails, and put my finger into the print of the nails, and thrust my hand into his side, I will not believe' (John 20:25). And though he eventually came to confess his belief, Thomas had said enough to give his name to the phrase *doubting Thomas*, which we apply to anyone who doubts or disbelieves, or has little faith in the word of others. An extreme example of such a person could be said to be a Pyrrhonist (q.v.).

There are various legends concerning St Thomas and from one of these he has become known as the Patron saint of architects and masons. It is said that when an Indian king commissioned him to build a palace, he created a 'palace in heaven' by spending the money he had been provided with on the poor and needy.

136 DOULTON

Sir Henry Doulton (1820 – 97) invented and gave his name to the distinctive art pottery, *Doulton ware*. Doulton had already achieved success with his stoneware drainpipes and other sanitary ware, when he began manufacturing decorative pottery. The production of Doulton ware utilized certain features of the seventeenth century Italian *sgraffito ware*, in which a colouring effect is obtained by the removal of pieces of outer layers.

Nowadays, Doulton stands with Wedgwood (q.v.) as one of the leading names in modern pottery.

137 DOVER'S POWDER

Thomas Dover (1660–1742) was an English physician who prescribed and gave his name to a powder for easing pain, *Dover's powder*. Dr Dover's preparation included opium and the root of the Brazilian plant ipecacuanha and was intended to induce sweating. It became well known, but there were a number of imitations.

Dover was also renowned as a privateer and in particular for his rescue of the marooned Alexander Selkirk from one of the Juan Fernandez Islands, in 1709, as he was returning to England on a captured Spanish man-of-war. Accounts of this incident inspired Daniel Defoe to write his classic tale *Robinson Crusoe*. On another occasion, Dover applied his medical skills to curing some 170 of his sailors of the plague.

138 DOW-JONES INDEX

Charles Henry Dow (1851–1902) was an American financial journalist who with his partner, Edward D. Jones (1856–1920), produced the first index of US stock prices, which have since become internationally famous as the *Dow-Jones averages*.

Dow and Jones came together in 1882, when they founded Dow Jones & Co., providing a delivery service of bulletins to the finance houses in Wall Street, the financial centre of New York. And after two years, the company began compiling their indexes of price movements, based on representative groups of stocks and shares. They also supplied news sheets, which proved to be very popular with the financiers; and in 1889, the news sheets appeared as the *Wall Street journal*, with Dow as its first editor.

139 DOWN'S SYNDROME

John Langdon-Down (1828–96) was an English doctor who described and gave his name to *Down's syndrome*, or mongolism. This is a genetic defect of mental development, commonly identified with certain physical characteristics of the people of Mongolia, the Mongols (or Tungus), such as a round, flattish face and half-hooded or seemingly slanted eyes.

While mongolism is congenital, recent research has done much to establish its causes. It must be said, too, that most mongoloids are of a friendly and loving disposition and relatively self-sufficient.

140 DRACONIAN

Draco was the name of an archon (or chief magistrate) in Athens, in the latter half of the seventh century BC. He is remembered for his code of laws (the first written laws for Athens) which were severe in the extreme, with almost every named crime carrying the death sentence. Consequently, we use the word *Draconian* as a synonym for severe, or extremely severe.

141 DUCHENNE'S MUSCULAR DYSTROPHY

Guillaume Benjamin Amand Duchenne (1806–75) was a French physician who gave the first accepted description of a hereditary disease of the muscles named after him as *Duchenne's muscular dystrophy*. This disease causes progressive wasting of various muscles from an early age and eventually affects the muscles regulating breathing and the heart muscle.

Duchenne (known as Duchenne of Boulogne) was also one of the first to realize the possibilities of using electricity in diagnosing and treating certain diseases.

142 DUNCE   DUNSE   SCOTIST

John Duns Scotus (*circa* 1265–1308) was a Franciscan friar and a noted schoolman (*see* Buridan's ass), known as Doctor Subtilis, or the Subtle Doctor, on account of his skill in reasoned argument on theology and philosophy. He took his name from the burgh of Duns, his supposed birthplace in the county of Berwickshire, in Scotland, and his followers came to be called *Dunses*, or *Dunsmen*, or more commonly *Scotists*.

The Scotists became strongly opposed to the followers of Thomas Aquinas, the Thomists (q.v.), and were reluctant to accept any new theological ideas. This led to their eventual decline and the word *dunce* was coined from the name of their founder to describe a stupid or dull person, or anyone reluctant to learn or consider new things.

Alexander Pope utilized the word for the title of his famous satirical poem *The Dunciad* (or 'dunce-epic'), first published in 1728, in which he holds up to ridicule a number of his fellow-authors, including the Poet Laureate Colley Cibber in a later edition, depicted as 'King of Dullness'.

143 DUPUYTREN'S CONTRACTURE

Baron Guillaume Dupuytren (1777–1835) was a French military surgeon who made many improvements to operating techniques and invented a number of surgical instruments. He is remembered eponymously for his description of a progressive thickening of the tissues under the skin of the palm, which (if untreated) can cause deformity of the fingers. This is known after him as *Dupuytren's contracture*. His name is also given to a fracture of the radius, the thicker and shorter bone of the forearm, with the dislocation of the lower end of the ulna, the inner and larger bone.

The name of Dupuytren has come into popular notice in recent times with the British Prime Minister Margaret Thatcher and the US President Ronald Reagan having to undergo operations for Dupuytren's contracture. The cause of the contracture is not known, though it does occur most commonly to elderly men.

E

144 EDWARDIAN   TEDDY BOY

Edward VII, King of Great Britain and Ireland, known as 'the Peacemaker' (1841 – 1910), was the eldest son of Queen Victoria (q.v.). He was king from 1901 until his death in 1910, and it is this period which we refer to as *Edwardian* and not the reigns of the other seven English kings named Edward. Sometimes the Edwardian age is taken to mean the early years of the present century up to the start of the Great War: a period generally depicted as one of reaction to the strictness of the Victorian age, as well as one of peace and prosperity before the eruption of 1914.

It was the Edwardian age, of course, which gave the name to that phenomenon of the 1950s, the *Teddy Boy* or the *Ted*, who adopted a pseudo-Edwardian style of dress. But for the most part, the Teddy boy was anything but Edwardian in his general behaviour; while his idol was the 'king' of rock'n'roll, Elvis Presley, rather than King Edward VII. In fact, to the majority of older people in Britain the Teds (or the *Neds* in Scotland) were only distinguishable from any other young louts by their clothes – and even these were regarded as deplorable. Yet, within a few years, the conventional men's fashions in clothes began to reveal certain characteristics of the original Teddy boys' garb, albeit suitably toned down!

Unlike Queen Victoria, King Edward would no doubt have been rather amused by all this.

145 EINSTEINIUM   EINSTEIN SHIFT

Albert Einstein (1879 – 1955) is remembered for his theory of relativity, concerning the nature of space and time, which dramatically refuted the long-held theory of Sir Isaac Newton (q.v.). His name has been honoured eponymously through the element of atomic number 99, *einsteinium*; and he also gives his name to his discovery of a displacement of the lines of the solar spectrum, the *Einstein shift*, for which he gave the explanation.

Einstein was born in Germany of German-Jewish parents, but spent much of his early life in Switzerland and became a naturalized Swiss. He was a professor at Zurich, Prague, Berlin and eventually Princeton, New Jersey, after being forced to flee from Germany by the Nazis in 1933. In 1921, he had been awarded the Nobel prize (q.v.) for physics; and it was Einstein, at the outset of the Second World War, who was nominated to write to US President Franklin D. Roosevelt as the spokesman for a number of eminent scientists, warning him of the possibilities of an atomic bomb.

Albert Einstein was a cousin of Alfred Einstein (1880–1952), the distinguished musicologist, and was himself an accomplished amateur musician. There is a story told of the composer Stravinsky who, on hearing the comment of another musician regarding Einstein's excellent sense of rhythm, is said to have remarked that it was surely not surprising that one of the greatest mathematicians of our time should be able to count 'one, two, three, four . . .'.

146 ELIZABETHAN

Elizabeth I (1533–1603) was in her 26th year when she became Queen of England on the death of her half-sister Mary (q.v. under Bloody Mary) in 1558. Over the following 45 years there was a great upsurge of creativity in England, especially in poetry, music and the theatre. The *Elizabethan age* was notable too for its adventurers and discoverers, with Raleigh and Drake leading the way.

But Elizabeth's reign had its dark side as well – the persecution of the Catholics, culminating in the execution of Mary Queen of Scots, and the rebellion in Ireland.

Yet the prevailing impression of Elizabethan England is that of the achievements of the poets and musicians, and one of them in particular – William Shakespeare. He dominated poetry and drama as no one man dominated Elizabethan music, although William Byrd, John Bull and John Dowland, for example, were all outstanding musicians of their time. Elizabeth herself was, it is said, a fine player of the virginals – a small, oblong-shaped harpsichord; and a mistaken belief that the 'Virgin Queen' gave her name to this instrument still persists. Virginals were, in fact, in existence before Elizabeth was born.

The word *Elizabethan* is sometimes used to refer to the reign of Elizabeth II (1926–   ) who, coincidentally, was also in her 26th year when she became Queen. But early attempts to attach the term *New Elizabethan age* to her reign were soon abandoned.

147 EMINENCE GRISE   (GREY EMINENCE)

Francois Le Clerc du Tremblay, known as Père Joseph or *l'Eminence Grise* (1577–1638), was private secretary and confidant to the French statesman Cardinal Richelieu. His nickname referred to both the colour of his habit and the power he exercised over Richelieu from behind the scenes; and from this, *éminence grise* has come to be used in a general way (and usually in the original French) to describe a grey or shadowy influence in the background.

Richelieu, in his turn, completely dominated the French King, Louis XIII, and personally directed the domestic and foreign affairs of France with ruthless efficiency, while aided and abetted by the trusty Père Joseph. As a cardinal, Richelieu wore a red habit and was known as *l'Eminence Rouge*.

148 EPICURE   EPICUREAN   EPICURISM

Epicurus (342? – 270 BC) founded and gave his name to the *Epicurean* school of philosophy, which held the truly virtuous life to be one of refined pleasure, giving peace of mind and freedom from pain. From this we have the *epicure* – a person of exquisite taste, especially in regard to food and wine.

The Reverend Sydney Smith, the noted wit and something of an epicure himself, wrote:

> Serenely full, the epicure would say,
> Fate cannot harm me, I have dined today.

Opponents of Epicurus (or Epicurus of Samos as he is sometimes called, from the place where he was born or brought up) attempted to misrepresent his teaching as the selfish pursuit of the sensual pleasures of life. Very little of the writings of Epicurus have survived him, but his philosophy is notably expounded by the Roman poet Lucretius in his poem, *De Rerum Natura*.

149 ERASTIANISM

Thomas Erastus (1524 – 83) gives his name to the doctrine of the control of church affairs by the state, *Erastianism*. It is a mistaken belief, however, that Erastus subscribed to this doctrine in its fullest sense.

Erastus (whose real surname was Lieber, or Liebler) was a German-Swiss physician and theologian and a follower of Zwingli (q.v.). He strongly opposed the right of the church to inflict excommunication and other punishments and was himself to suffer excommunication.

Erastian has been used to indicate *a certain degree* of state involvement in affairs of the church. The Church of England, for example, is sometimes referred to as Erastian.

150 EUCLIDEAN GEOMETRY
Euclid was a Greek mathematician of the third century BC, but little more is known of his life. His name has become immortalized, however, through his *Elements*, his great work on elementary geometry in 13 books.

It can be said that Euclid's name is synonymous with geometry; and *Euclidean geometry* has certainly provided the basis for the teaching of that branch of mathematics for generations. His definition of a line as 'length without breadth' would be hard to improve upon for its sheer preciseness.

151 EUSTACHIAN TUBE
Bartolommeo Eustachio (1520–74), the eminent Italian anatomist, gave his name to a number of discoveries concerning the ear, the heart and other parts of the human body. The best known of these are the *Eustachian tube*, the passage between the middle and the back of the nose, and the *Eustachian valve*, the rudimentary valve in the heart.

Eustachio gave the first detailed description of the ear and is regarded as one of the founders of modern anatomy.

152 EVEREST
Sir George Everest (1790–1866) gave his name to the highest mountain in the world, Mount Everest. He was the surveyor-general of India, 1830–43.

The word *Everest*, though not to be found in many dictionaries, has come to be part of everyday language: for example, we speak of the 'Everest' of so-and-so's achievement, in the sense of the 'highest point'.

Since 1921, expeditions had set out to conquer Everest without success and with considerable loss of lives. Then, in 1953, an expedition led by Colonel John Hunt (later Lord Hunt) was organized; and on 29 May of that year, the New Zealander, Edmund Hillary (later Sir Edmund Hillary), and the Sherpa, Tensing Norkay, became the first men to reach the summit.

And it was a remarkable coincidence that the news of this great achievement was first received in Britain on 2 June 1953 – the very day of the coronation of Elizabeth II.

F

153 FABIAN

Quintus Fabius Maximus Verrucosus (died 203 BC) was known as Cunctator (the delayer) from the defensive strategy he employed in saving Rome from the military might of Hannibal. By skilful manoeuvring, he managed to avoid the direct conflict of a pitched battle, which would almost certainly have resulted in defeat for the Romans. *Fabian tactics* have since been used by a number of generals, notably George Washington in the American War of Independence.

The Fabian Society, a society of Socialist intellectuals founded in London in 1884, took its name from Fabius Maximus. The Fabians advocated a gradual approach to socialism, as opposed to revolutionary methods. George Bernard Shaw was a prominent Fabian.

154 FAHRENHEIT

Gabriel Daniel Fahrenheit (1686–1736) was a German, born in Danzig (now Gdansk, Poland), who spent most of his life in Holland and England. He invented a thermometer (using mercury instead of alcohol) with a new scale, named after him. The *Fahrenheit scale* has the freezing-point of water marked at 32 degrees and the boiling point at 212.

Fahrenheit's scale was the one most used in Britain, and other English-speaking countries, and the USA, for many years; but, by and large, this has now been superseded by the centigrade scale (q.v. under Celsius). The word *Fahrenheit*, however, is firmly established as part of the English language – even though it is named after a German who was born in Poland and died in Holland. (He did at least live in England at one time.)

155 FALLOPIAN TUBES

Gabriello Fallopio, or Gabriel Fallopius (1523–62), was the Italian anatomist who is credited with discovering the function of the tubes or oviducts leading from the ovary to the womb, and named after him as the *Fallopian tubes*.

From recent experiments, a technique has been developed known as *embryo transfer*, which enables a woman with a malfunction of her Fallopian tubes to give birth to a baby hitherto denied to her. The egg is taken from the mother for fertilization with the father's sperm and is eventually reimplanted in the mother's womb, effectively 'by-passing' the natural function of the Fallopian tubes. The first so-called test-tube baby was born by means of embryo transfer on 25 July 1978 at a hospital in Oldham, in the north of England. And in 1982 a second child was given birth to by the same mother, by the same means.

156 FANNY ADAMS SWEET FANNY ADAMS
Fanny Adams was the name of a little girl who was murdered in a hop-garden at Alton, in Hampshire, probably in the year 1812. The body of the poor child (she was only seven or eight years old) was discovered in a river, cut into small pieces.

The tragic tale of Fanny Adams did not end there, however, for some years later her name came to be used as a description of the tinned mutton which was being issued to the Royal Navy. A sailor (it is said) found a button in one such tin and with macabre humour named its contents *Fanny Adams*. From this was evolved the expression *Sweet Fanny Adams* (meaning anything of little substance or 'nothing at all') and then the ambiguous abbreviation SFA.

Perhaps the fate of poor Fanny is best summed-up in the words of a barrack room ballad:

> All that is left now
> Of Sweet Fanny Adams
> Is S-F-A!

157 FARAD FARADAY FARADIC FARADIZE FARADISM
Michael Faraday (1791–1867) has been described as 'Sir Humphry Davy's greatest discovery' (q.v.). Faraday, the son of a blacksmith and apprenticed as a bookbinder, certainly owed a good deal to the great man who, in 1812, engaged him as his assistant at the Royal Institution in London, where he was professor of chemistry. In the following years, Faraday fully justified Sir Humphry's faith in him, making many important contributions to virtually all branches of physical science. And, in 1833, he succeeded his old master as professor of chemistry at the Royal Institution.

Faraday eventually became known in his own right as the founder of the science of electromagnetism and gave his name to the unit of electrical capacity, the *farad*; and to a unit of quantity of electricity, the *faraday*. Other words named after him in this connection are *faradic*, *faradization*, *faradize*, and *faradism*.

The international telephone exchange in Blackfriars, London, is also named after him.

158 FEBRONIANISM
Johann Nikolaus von Hontheim (1701–90) was a German Roman Catholic prelate who used the pseudonym *Justinus Febronius* to propound a doctrine, known as *Febronianism*. This opposed the supremacy of the Pope and asserted the independence of national churches in the management of their affairs. Febronianism could therefore be seen as a form of Congregationalism or independency.

159 FERMI   FERMION   FERMIUM
Enrico Fermi (1901–54), the Italian physicist, was one of the great pioneers in the field of atomic energy and the subsequent development of the atomic bomb. He gives his name to the *fermi*, a unit of length in nuclear physics, equal to 10^{-5} angstrom (q.v.); a group of subatomic particles, *fermions*; and the element of atomic number 100, *fermium*. (And it was Fermi who synthesized *transuranium*, element of atomic number 93, by bombarding uranium with neutrons.)

Fermi was awarded the Nobel prize (q.v.) for physics in 1938 (the first Italian to win the physics prize outright); and in the following year, he went to live in America. The first American nuclear reactor was built under his direction.

160 FORSYTHIA
William Forsyth (1737–1804) gives his name to the genus of spring-flowering shrubs, *Forsythia*. This popular shrub with its bright yellow bell-shaped flowers was brought to England from China.

Forsyth was the botanist in charge of the Royal Gardens at St James's and Kensington during the reign of George III (q.v.).

161 FORTEAN
Charles Hoy Fort (1874–1932) occupies a unique place in American literature, though his work remains relatively

unknown. He was a journalist and an embalmer of butterflies before he acquired sufficient financial independence to devote himself to his overriding passion of compiling detailed accounts of strange phenomena. His work attracted such attention from other writers that in 1931 a *Fortean Society* was formed, with Theodore Dreiser, Ben Hecht, Booth Tarkington and Alexander Woollcott among its members; and largely through the society's publications, the word *Fortean* came to be applied to the study of strange phenomena.

Fort had three books published in his lifetime: *The book of the damned, New lands* and *Lo!* A fourth book, *Wild talents*, appeared shortly after his death in 1932. He was single-mindedly painstaking in his researches and quest for knowledge and as a young man had travelled around the world, returning to London in 1921 for a number of years, to study at the British Museum. *Forteans* have described him as 'the apostle of the exceptional' and 'the prophet of the unexplained'.

162 FOSBURY FLOP

Richard Fosbury (1947–   ) is an American athlete who originated a style of high jumping named after him as the *Fosbury flop*. This is a technique in which the jumper approaches the jump head-first with the face upwards and literally lands on his back. It has virtually superseded earlier styles such as the 'straddle'.

Fosbury was comparatively unknown before he competed in the Olympic Games in 1968, when he won a gold medal with a jump of 7'4½" (2.24 metres), employing the Fosbury flop.

163 FRED KARNO'S ARMY

Fred Karno (1866–1941) was well-known in the British music-halls in the early years of the century as the impresario of a troupe of slapstick comedians. In fact, the general public's association of Karno's name with the zany type of comedy he presented was such that, with the outbreak of the First World War, any group of clearly untrained recruits was mockingly labelled *Fred Karno's army*, after the seemingly disorganized antics of Karno's comedians.

Then somebody wrote a song, which was sung by the troops to the tune *Aurelia* (best known by the hymns, *The Church's one foundation* and *From Greenland's icy mountains*). The lyric began:

> We are Fred Karno's army,
> The Ragtime Infantry . . .

Inevitably, the variations were numerous and often highly colourful and were not confined to the army.

Fred Karno (whose real name was Westcott) must also be remembered for introducing such famous artists as Charlie Chaplin and Stan Laurel to the larger public. His personal success came to an end, however, with the failure of an enterprise to promote a Thames-side resort which was to have been named after him as 'Karsino'.

164 FREUDIAN   FREUDIAN SLIP

Sigmund Freud (1856 – 1939) is generally regarded as the inventor of psychoanalysis. *Freudian* theories have greatly increased our awareness of the complexities of the human mind, and Freud has undoubtedly had an immense influence on the thinking of twentieth-century man.

Freud was born at Freiburg in Moravia, of a Jewish family, and studied medicine in Vienna, specializing in neurology. He became interested in the work of the Austrian physiologist, Joseph Breuer who, in his use of hypnosis for the treatment of certain illnesses, had observed that patients were apt to recall long forgotten emotional experiences. The two men worked together for some time, but Freud proceeded to explore the wider implications of the special power of the unconscious part of the human mind. He developed a new method of treatment, replacing hypnosis with a 'normal' doctor-patient discussion and encouraging 'free association of ideas'. His first major work, *Traumdeutung* (*The interpretation of dreams*), was published at the turn of the century.

Nowadays, psychoanalysis has become widely accepted, and not only as a treatment for the mentally ill or disturbed person. But Freud's influence has not been confined to the areas of medicine and science: modern art and poetry have reflected his ideas, especially those relating to dreams and their apparent connection with repressed desires. There can be few other men of recent times who have linked the arts and the sciences in this way.

A *Freudian slip* is the description we give to the subconscious use of a word or expression similar to that which we intend to use when our mind is half-thinking of something else. A typical example (quoted by Freud) is that a woman who is anxious to have children will say *storks* when she means *stocks*.

Freud was professor of neuropathology at the University of Vienna from 1902 until 1938, when the Nazi invasion forced him to leave Austria. He spent the last year of his life in London.

165 FROEBELISM   FROEBEL SYSTEM

Friedrich Wilhelm August Froebel (1782–1852) originated and gave his name to the kindergarten system of education known as the *Froebel system*. Froebel reasoned in effect that encouragement rather than instruction of young children, by means of games and constructive activities, constitutes the best preparation for later education, and leads to the fuller development of the individual and the greater appreciation of life.

Froebel was born in Germany, and was a forester's apprentice and an architectural student before going to Switzerland to study and work with the educational reformer, Pestalozzi (q.v.), who had a great influence on his later life. After military service, he opened his own school and, in 1837, the first kindergarten (or *garden of children*), at Blankenburg. *Froebelism*, as Froebel's method came to be called, was condemned by most of the traditionalists in educational circles, and he was attacked both on religious and political grounds. Nowadays, of course, pre-school or nursery education based on Froebel's system has become an accepted part of most modern education systems.

166 FUSCHIA

Leonhard Fuchs (1501–66) was the German naturalist and botanist who gave his name to the genus of South American flowering shrubs, *Fuchsia*. Fuchs was a professor of medicine at the University of Tübingen and compiled a book of medicinal plants, which became a standard work. The fuschia was named in his honour in 1703.

G

167 GALENICAL

Claudius Galen (circa AD 129 – 99) has been called 'the Prince of Physicians' and was certainly the most influential physician of his day and for more than 1,000 years after his death. His name survives in the language through the noun *galenical*, any pure vegetable drug (such as opium) used as a medicinal remedy.

Galen was born at Pergamum, in Asia Minor (now Bergama, in Turkey), of Greek parents. He studied philosophy before turning to medicine, becoming famous as the personal physician to the Roman emperor Marcus Aurelius. And although many of his theories have come to be discounted, his biological experiments and his descriptions of his findings were important landmarks in early medicine.

168 GALLIO

Junius Annaeus Gallio was a Roman proconsul of Achaia in the first century. He is remembered in the English language through his refusal to pass judgment on St Paul at Corinth in 52 AD. (' ... I will be no judge of such matters.' Acts 18:15)

Consequently we have the noun *Gallio* for someone (especially an official) who avoids trouble by distancing himself from affairs outside his province by disclaiming responsibility.

169 GALLUP POLL

George Horace Gallup (1901 – 84) founded the American Institute of Public Opinion with the purpose of conducting public opinion polls. He devised and gave his name to the *Gallup Poll* and achieved considerable success in predicting election results, etc. by his original methods.

Public opinion polls were being organized in America early in the last century, but Dr Gallup's method of representative sampling gave the opinion poll a new scientific respectability and most modern systems are now based on Gallup. It could even be said that the Gallup Poll has become synonymous with the public opinion poll.

Nowadays, statistics and surveys have become part of our lives, with computerized information on scores of subjects (from what we eat and drink to who our favourite politician is) being pushed at us from morning to night. And it has been argued that in certain circumstances, an opinion poll could actually influence the result of an election.

170 GALVANIZE GALVANISM GALVANIC GALVONOMETER

Luigi Galvani (1737–98), of Bologna, is remembered as the discoverer of electricity produced by chemical action. *Galvanism* is the word from his name used to describe this.

Galvani's other researches led him to deduce that the twitching of muscles in a frog's legs, when it was brought into contact with certain metals, was due to animal electricity – hence the word *galvanize*, to shock or spur into action. It was his fellow-countryman, Volta (q.v.), who later provided the correct explanation. Nevertheless, Galvani's contribution to the understanding of electricity was considerable. The *galvanometer*, an instrument for measuring electric currents, was also named after him.

Galvani was professor of anatomy at his native Bologna, but in 1797 he refused to take an oath of allegiance to the new Republic and was dismissed from the university. He died the following year in considerable distress. Posterity, at least, has been kinder to him; and it could be said that Galvani's researches *galvanized* those who came after him to greater efforts.

171 GARIBALDI

Giuseppe Garibaldi (1807–82) gave his name to a type of loose-fitting blouse – and the *Garibaldi biscuit*. In his day, of course, Garibaldi was the great popular hero of the *Risorgimento* (the national movement for liberating and unifying Italy), and his name became an inspiration both to his countrymen and freedom fighters everywhere, when in 1860, his volunteer force of little more than 1,000 – the celebrated 'red-shirts' – inflicted crushing defeats on armies of many times their number.

The famous red shirts of Garibaldi's followers, however, were originally adopted out of convenience (it seems that they just happened to be the only ones available at the time) rather than any romantic notion of inspiring confidence in their wearers, or frightening the enemy. And it appears unlikely, too, that Garibaldi was even the originator of the well-known biscuit named after him, though apparently he was particularly fond of any kind of pastry with layers of currants cooked into it.

Nonetheless, it would seem to be appropriate that the man who gave his name to the Garibaldi biscuit should have been born in Nice.

172 GATLING-GUN   GAT

Richard Jordan Gatling (1818–1903) invented and gave his name to the *Gatling-gun*, the best-known and most successful of the early machine-guns. As early as the fourteenth century, there had been attempts to construct guns capable of firing a number of shots in quick succession; and in 1721, a gun employing a revolving chamber was manufactured by an Englishman, James Puckle. But until the appearance of the *Gatling*, in the 1860s, machine-guns were generally regarded as little more than novelties that sometimes worked.

Gatling was born in Hertford County, North Carolina, but lack of technical resources in the Southern states frustrated his ambitions as an inventor and he moved north to Indiana. He was granted a patent for the Gatling-gun in 1862, and four years later it was adopted by the US army. Orders from Britain, Russia, and other countries soon followed, largely due to Gatling's own astuteness as a business man, though the Gatling was undoubtedly the most reliable machine-gun of its time. And had Colonel Custer placed more confidence in the Gatlings he possessed (which, it seems, he deliberately left behind at his headquarters), the massacre of his men at the Battle of Little Big Horn (Custer's Last Stand) might never have occurred.

The advent of the Maxim (q.v.), the first fully automatic machine-gun, spelt the end for the Gatling, which was hand-cranked. But *Gatling*, abbreviated to *gat*, has since become a slang term for any automatic pistol – as, of course, anyone who has read a detective paperback or seen a gangster film must know.

173 GAULLISM   GAULLIST

Charles André Joseph Marie de Gaulle (1890–1970) was the first president of the Fifth Republic of France, 1958–69. His followers were known as *Gaullists*, and, two decades after his death, *Gaullism* is still an active force of the right wing in French politics.

Charles de Gaulle distinguished himself as a soldier in the First World War and by the start of the Second World War had risen to the rank of general. When France fell to the Germans in 1940, it was under de Gaulle's leadership that the fight for his country was carried on in England. ('France has lost the battle but she has not lost the war.') He was an interim President of France from 1945–1946, but it was not until 1958, when he was in his 69th year, that de Gaulle made his major bid for political power. And after five years in office, he said, 'I myself have become a *Gaullist* only little by little'.

174 GAUSS   DEGAUSS
(Johann) Karl Friedrich Gauss (1777–1855), the German mathematician and astronomer, is known as the founder of the mathematical theory of electricity, and for his research with W. E. Weber (q.v.) in connection with magnetism and electricity. The unit of magnetic flux density, the *gauss*, was originally named after him.

The name of Gauss also came to be used for another word, coined in the Second World War. It was in the first months of the war that a new German weapon, the magnetic mine, began taking its toll of British shipping. These mines were sunk to the sea-bottom and detonated by a device which reacted to the magnetism of an approaching ship. Once the nature of the weapon had been established, equipment was speedily designed to protect, or *degauss*, a ship against a magnetic mine by neutralizing the ship's magnetic field. And, by March 1940, *degaussing* equipment was already being fitted to British ships.

175 GEIGER COUNTER
Johannes Hans Wilhelm Geiger (1882–1945) gave his name to an instrument for detecting and measuring radioactivity and cosmic rays, the *Geiger counter*.

Hans Geiger (as he was usually known) came to England from his native Germany and worked first with Rutherford (q.v.) and then his fellow-countryman, Wilhelm Muller, in inventing and developing the Geiger counter, which is sometimes referred to as the *Geiger-Muller counter* or the *Geiger-Rutherford counter*. Since its introduction, in 1928, the use of the Geiger counter has become increasingly widespread, and the name of Geiger is just as familiar to the man-in-the-street as to the scientist, nowadays.

176 GEISSLER TUBE
Heinrich Geissler (1814–79) was the inventor of an original piece of scientific apparatus, named after him as the *Geissler tube*. This consists of a sealed glass tube filled with rarefied gas, with a

platinum electrode at each end. Electricity is passed through the tube to demonstrate the luminous effects on the gas.

Geissler, a German, made his tube and many other kinds of scientific equipment in his workshop at Bonn, his birthplace. He also gave his name to the *Geissler pump*, a mercury pump.

177 GEORGIAN

George III (1738–1820), King of Great Britain and Ireland, was the grandson of George II and the great-grandson of George I. His reign (the longest of any king of Great Britain) lasted from 1760 until his death in 1820, when he was succeeded by his son, George IV. This period is known as *Georgian*, especially in regard to architecture and furniture, etc., though the term Georgian is also applied to the reigns of any of the other Georges. (Georgian poetry, for example, is usually understood to be the poetry of a group of English poets, active during the reign of George V.) The term Georgian is again used to describe someone from the State of Georgia in the USA, or the constiuent republic of Georgia (or Gruziya) in the USSR. The former American President Jimmy Carter is a *Georgian* – and so was Joseph Stalin (q.v.).

George III was perhaps the least popular of the Hanoverian Georges, though none of them was particularly likeable, according to the poet Walter Savage Landor:

> George the First was always reckoned
> Vile, but viler George the Second
> And what mortal ever heard
> Any good of George the Third?

George III certainly seems to have attracted his share of abuse, not least in respect of the American War of Independence. ('George III lost America and then lost his wits', was a popular saying of the time.) And in the words of the well-known clerihew (q.v.):

> George the Third
> Ought never to have occurred.
> One can only wonder
> At so grotesque a blunder.

178 GERRYMANDER GERRYMANDERING

Elbridge Gerry (1744 – 1814) was a vice-president of the United States (1813 – 14) and one of the 56 men who had signed the Declaration of Independence in 1776. His name is remembered today, however, for another reason. Gerry was born in Massachusetts and became governor of the state in 1810. And it was during his second term of office that Gerry resorted to the device of rearranging the electoral boundaries in favour of his own party. This was not by any means a new practice, neither was it illegal; but on this occasion, the redrawn map of a particular district happened to catch the observant eye of the famous portrait-painter, Gilbert Charles Stuart, who was amused to notice that the outline of the district was similar to that of the lizard-like salamander. He pointed out this novelty to a newspaper editor, who thought that a better description would be *Gerrymander* – and a new word was coined.

And while Governor Elbridge Gerry's *gerrymandering* may have caused him some loss of face, it certainly won him a place in the dictionary.

179 GILBERT

William Gilbert (1540 – 1603) was physician to Elizabeth and James I (qq.v.), but is remembered not so much for his contribution to medical science, as for his great pioneering work on magnetism and electricity. His treatise *On the magnet*, or *De magnete* (it was first published in Latin), was the first book on science of real importance to be published in England; and Gilbert was the first to use such terms as 'electric force' and 'magnetic pole'. He has become known as 'the father of electricity', and the unit of magneto-motive force, the *gilbert*, is named after him.

180 GILBERTIAN

Sir William Schwenck Gilbert (1836 – 1911) began his famous association with the composer Sullivan (later Sir Arthur Sullivan) in 1871, when Gilbert wrote the libretto and Sullivan the music for a burlesque, *Thespis*. Then, four years later, the impressario Richard D'Oyly Carte produced the first of the highly successful Savoy Operas by Gilbert and Sullivan, *Trial by jury*.

The rest of the story of their remarkable partnership is well known, though it is often forgotten that both Gilbert and Sullivan produced a considerable amount of work independently of each other and with other collaborators, which today is hardly ever performed. And had Gilbert not met Sullivan, it is unlikely that the word *Gilbertian* (relating to Gilbert's engagingly absurd type of humour, as it is often portrayed in the 'G & S' comic operas), would ever have found its way into the dictionary. Equally, had Sullivan not met Gilbert, who could say that Sir Arthur would not be remembered in the main (if at all) as the composer of the music for *The lost chord*?

181 GLADSTONE BAG   GLADSTONE CLARET GLADSTONE SHERRY

William Ewart Gladstone (1809–98) was 82 when he became British Prime Minister for the fourth time; and when he resigned, in 1894, he was in his 85th year. Not surprisingly then, he became known as the *Grand Old Man*, or the GOM. This term has since passed into the language as a description of anyone who achieves long and distinguished service in his particular calling: W. G. Grace, for example, is referred to as the GOM of English cricket.

The actual name of Gladstone, however, is preserved in the English language primarily by the *Gladstone bag*, a portmanteau named in honour of the GOM. Gladstone, as Chancellor of the Exchequer, had already given his name to *Gladstone claret* and *Gladstone sherry*, through his reduction in the duty on cheaper wines in the 1860 budget. Some future chancellor, perhaps, would do well to bring back these now largely forgotten names.

182 GLASSITE

John Glas, or Glass (1695–1773), founded and gave his name to a Scottish Christian sect, the *Glassites*. Glas, a minister of the Church of Scotland, was deposed for his denunciation of all national establishments of religion as 'inconsistent with the true nature of the Church of Christ'.

The influence of the sect spread to England and then America, where its followers became known as Sandemanians (q.v.) from the son-in-law of John Glas, Robert Sandeman.

183 GLUCKISTS

Christoph Willibald von Gluck (1714–87) occupies an important place in the history of music. He introduced a new dramatic element into the opera, which by the mid-eighteenth century had become little more than a show-case for the virtuoso singer; and may therefore be regarded as the precursor of his fellow-countryman Richard Wagner (q.v.).

Gluck (the 'von' in his name denotes a Papal knighthood), is remembered eponymously as the result of an intense rivalry which arose between admirers of his music (known as *Gluckists*) and those of the Italian composer Piccini (the *Piccinists*). Both composers had been invited to Paris by the respective champions of the German and Italian schools of opera; and the subsequent and rather foolish feud between the Gluckists and the Piccinists was eventually terminated by an unquestionably successful production of Gluck's opera *Iphigenia in Tauris*, in 1779.

The 'victory' of the Gluckists was more than a local affair, however, since, some 200 years later, Gluck's music (and especially his opera *Orpheus and Eurydice*) is still performed and enjoyed universally; whereas poor Piccini's operas and other works are (along with the Piccinists) all but forgotten.

184 GOBELIN

Gobelin was the name of a fifteenth-century French family of dyers and weavers, whose fame was honoured in the naming of a rich French tapesty, *Gobelin*.

Two brothers of the family, Gilles and Jean, first became renowned in introducing a method of dyeing in scarlet, before adding tapestry weaving to their skills. The family's works were eventually taken over by Louis XIV's minister, Colbert (q.v.), as a Royal establishment, with the artist Charles Le Brun as chief designer of the tapestries.

185 GOLDWYNISM

Samuel Goldwyn (1882–1974) was one of the American film industry's most successful producers and probably its most quoted (or even mis-quoted) character. He was especially noted for his unintentionally humorous remarks, which have come to be known after him as *Goldwynisms*. A typical example is 'A verbal contract isn't worth the paper it's written on'.

It has been suggested, however, that Goldwyn consciously cultivated his eccentricities and that a number of his sayings were not as spontaneous as they seemed. Certainly there is no proof that some 'original' Goldwynisms emanated from the man who gave his name to the word, in the same way that so many Spoonerisms (q.v.) have been wrongly attributed.

Goldwyn (his name originally was Goldfish), emigrated to the USA from Poland in 1896 and after six years became a naturalized

American. He began producing films in Hollywood from 1910 and organized Goldwyn Pictures Corporation, which in 1924 merged with Metro Pictures to become (the following year) the great Metro-Goldwyn-Mayer production company, *MGM*. But Goldwyn broke away from the organization to work independently and went on to produce scores of popular successes or films 'for the family'. He died in 1974 in his 92nd year.

Goldwynisms attributed to Samuel Goldwyn included: 'In two words: impossible'; 'Anybody who goes to see a psychiatrist ought to have his head examined'; 'If Roosevelt were alive he'd turn in his grave'; and perhaps the best-known of them all 'Include me out'.

186 GONGORISM
Luis de Gongora y Argote (1561–1627), the Spanish poet, originated and gave his name to a florid and extremely affected literary style, *Gongorism*. His writing has its counterpart in the English language in some of the works of his contemporary, the English dramatist John Lyly, whose romance *Euphues* brought the 'euphuistic' style into vogue.

187 GRAAFIAN FOLLICLES
Regnier de Graaf (1641–73), the Dutch physician and anatomist, discovered and gave his name to *Graafian follicles* (or vesicles), the small sacs of the ovary in which the ova are matured. He is also famed for his works on the pancreatic juice.

188 GRANGERISM   GRANGERIZE
James Granger (1723–76) was an English vicar who, in 1769, published a *Biographical history of England* with a number of blank pages for the addition of illustrations, prints, newspaper cuttings, or virtually anything more or less connected with the subject of the book. Granger's publication proved to be highly successful, and this new kind of collecting (or *Grangerism* as it became known) developed into a fad of the time.

Unfortunately, this seemingly harmless pursuit resulted in the mutilation of other books, including many of considerable value; and while individual *Grangers* continued to be regarded as collectors' items, *grangerizing* happily tended to fall out of fashion. Today, its practice is mostly confined to young children.

189 GRANNY SMITH

Maria Ann Smith, known as Granny Smith (died 1870), gave her name to an apple, the *Granny Smith*, which she cultivated in her home-town of Eastwood, in the state of New South Wales, Australia.

The Granny Smith is one of the most popular of apples. It is green-skinned, crisp and distinctively flavoured. And while generally eaten as a dessert apple, it is also ideal for cooking.

190 GRAVES'S DISEASE

Robert James Graves (1796–1853) was a physician of Dublin, in Ireland, whose description of the toxic goitre (or thyrotoxicosis) has come to be named after him as *Graves's disease*. This disorder of the thyroid gland (the gland in the front of the neck) may result in a protrusion of the eyeballs, or exophthalmic goitre.

A German physician, Karl von Basedow (1799–1854), described the toxic goitre in 1840, some five years after Graves's description but with no knowledge of the earlier account. This was, moreover, the first truly particularized description and in consequence Graves's disease is also known as *Basedow's disease*.

191 GREENGAGE

Sir William Gage of Hengrave, near Bury St Edmunds in Suffolk, is said to have imported a new kind of plum tree into England from France, in the early part of the eighteenth century. The fruit turned out to be greenish when ripe, and was apparently named after Sir William as the *greengage*.

In France, the greengage had long been known as *reine-claude*, after Queen Claude, wife of Francis I and daughter of Louis XII.

192 GREENOCKITE

Charles Murray Cathcart, 2nd Earl of Cathcart, known as Lord Greenock (1783–1859), was a distinguished soldier who served in a number of campaigns during the Napoleonic Wars and fought at Waterloo alongside his younger brother, Sir George Cathcart, who was aide-de-camp to Wellington (q.v.).

It is not, however, in a military capacity that Lord Greenock is remembered in the English language. He gives his name to a rare mineral, *greenockite*, or cadmium sulphide, which he discovered in 1841.

193 GREGORIAN CALENDAR

Pope Gregory XIII, born Ugo Buoncompagni (1502–85), gave his name to the *Gregorian calendar*, which he introduced in Italy in 1582. This replaced the Julian calendar which calculated the year at some 11 minutes longer than the astronomical year; and in 1582, Pope Gregory ordered that 5 October of that year should be called 15 October and ten days were 'lost to history'. Britain adopted the Gregorian (or New Style) calendar in 1752, by which time it was necessary to 'lose' 11 days, and 3 September 1752 became 14 September 1752. By the time the newly created USSR decided to 'go Gregorian', the difference between the Julian (Old Style) and the Gregorian calendars was 13 days. And, among other things, this meant that while someone born in Russia between 1900 and the introduction of the New Style had simply to add 13 days to his original date of birth to calculate his 'correct' birthday, someone born in Russia *before* 1900 had to add only 12 days, since 1900 was not a leap year according to the Gregorian calendar.

The composer Igor Stravinsky, born in Russia in 1882, but since 1945 an American citizen, forgot to take the missed leap year into account when he decided to make the necessary adjustment to his date of birth; and up to his death, in 1971, he continued to celebrate his birthday on 18 June. He was, in fact, born on 17 June, according to the Gregorian calendar.

194 GREGORIAN CHANT

Pope Gregory I, also known as St Gregory the Great (540?–604), is particularly remembered as the Pope who sent Augustine to England as a missionary, later to become the first Archbishop of Canterbury. And it was during his papacy that the *Gregorian chant*, which is named after him, was introduced into church music, superseding the Ambrosian chant (q.v.).

195 GREGORIAN TREE

Gregory Brandon and his son Richard ('Young Gregory') were seventeenth-century hangmen known as *the two Gregories*. The *Gregorian tree* – a common expression for the gallows at the time – was named after them. The two Gregories, first father and then son, were in business from the time of James I (q.v.) to 1649, the year of the death of Charles I (q.v. under King Charles's head). In fact, it could be said that Young Gregory *literally* ended the reign of Charles, since he actually cut off the King's head. He had previously beheaded the former right-hand man of Charles I, the Earl of Strafford (in 1641), and William Laud, Archbishop of Canterbury (in 1645).

Young Gregory did not long outlive his king, however. Full of remorse, it is said, he died of natural causes less than five months after the execution of Charles I.

196 GRESHAM'S LAW

Sir Thomas Gresham (1519? – 79) is particularly remembered for his well-known theory concerning coinage, *Gresham's law*. This maintains that when money of high intrinsic value is in circulation with money of lesser value, it is the inferior currency which tends to remain in circulation, while the other is hoarded or exported. Or in a phrase, 'bad money drives out good'.

Gresham certainly spoke with some authority, since he was a highly successful merchant and a financial adviser to four successive English sovereigns. He founded the Royal Exchange, and a public school which is named after him.

The original Royal Exchange was destroyed in the Great Fire of London, but Gresham College survives along with Gresham's law.

197 GRIMM'S LAW

Jacob Ludwig Carl Grimm (1785 – 1863) and his brother, Wilhelm Carl Grimm (1786 – 1859) are best known as the joint authors of *Grimm's fairy tales*, translated into English from the German *Kinder- und Hausmärchen* and originally published in England as *German popular stories*.

The Grimm brothers were, however, equally well-known in their day as philologists, and Jacob has given his name to the English language through *Grimm's law*, a law concerning the mutations of the consonants in the various Germanic languages and formulated in his *Deutsche Grammatik*. His theories were later revised by the Danish philologist, Karl Verner (q.v.). It was Jacob Grimm, too, who gave us the word *umlaut*.

198 GROG   GROGGY

Edward ('Old Grog') Vernon (1684 – 1757) was an English admiral noted for his grogram cloak (grogram being a kind of coarse cloth, usually of wool and mohair or silk), which he wore in rough weather. From this he was given the nickname of 'Old Grog'. Vernon's naval career was not particularly distinguished; and he would probably be quite forgotten today but for the fact that, in 1740, he ordered that his sailors' official issue of rum should be diluted with water. This mixture (and variations of it) came to be known as *grog*, after the admiral's nickname.

From the word *grog*, we have many others, the best-known being *groggy*; which originally referred to the effect of grog on someone drinking it (i.e. half-drunk, or not as drunk as one who's been drinking undiluted spirits), but now can be applied to a strict teetotaller feeling unwell, and having had nothing more intoxicating to drink than perhaps a Coca-Cola.

But the last chapter in the history of grog was surely written in 1970, when the traditional issue of rum to sailors in the Royal Navy was officially discontinued. Even 'Old Grog' couldn't have got away with that!

199 GROLIER   GROLIERESQUE
Jean Grolier (1479–1565), the French diplomat and bibliophile, gave his name to a kind of book binding, *Grolieresque*, characterized by geometrical patterns and leaf-sprays in gold.

Grolier collected over 3,000 copies of the best works available and personally supervized the bindings and decorations. His books carried the inscription 'Io. Grolieri et Amicorum'. (The property of Jean Grolier and his friends.)

The library was dispersed in 1675, but there are some 350 *Groliers* from the original collection which are known to exist.

200 GUILLOTINE
Joseph Ignace Guillotin (1738–1814) is frequently misrepresented as being the inventor of the *guillotine*. What Dr Guillotin (he was a physician) *did* do was to propose to the French National Assembly that all Frenchmen sentenced to death should be executed by means of a beheading machine, for humanitarian reasons. (At the time, only Frenchmen of high rank were granted the 'privilege' of being beheaded.)

A machine was designed by a colleague of Dr Guillotin, a Dr Louis, and was for a short time known as a 'Louisette'; but it soon came to be named after Dr Guillotin, and the word guillotine, as both a noun and a verb, is now part of the English language.

The first person to be guillotined in France was a highwayman, in 1792; and for the next two years, 'Madame La Guillotine' (one of the instrument's many macabre nicknames) was kept very busy, as thousands of victims of the French Revolution and the 'Reign of Terror' which followed it were pushed through the 'little national sash-window' (as one writer described the guillotine). Louis XVI, the King of France, and his wife Marie Antoinette, were guillotined in 1793; and in the following year, Robespierre and other leaders of the Revolution suffered the same fate. 'O Liberté! O Liberté! que de crimes on commet en ton nom!' (O Liberty! O Liberty! what crimes are committed in thy name!) are supposed to have been the last words of one victim, Madame Roland, before the now notorious oblique blade put an end to her life.

Nowadays, of course, the guillotine is the name of various kinds of machines for cutting paper, straw, etc., and the word also describes a means of ending a discussion by application of a specially drastic rule. But the guillotine as an instrument for inflicting capital punishment was, until recently, still in use in France.

It should be noted that there were instruments similar to Dr Louis's design in use as long ago as the fourteenth century, at least. And it is recorded that the inventor of one such machine, called 'the maiden', came to be executed by his own invention. Dr Joseph Ignace Guillotin, however, died of natural causes.

201 GUNTER'S SCALE   GUNTER'S CHAIN
Edmund Gunter (1581 – 1626) was the English mathematician who invented and gave his name to a scale, or slide-rule, for solving navigational problems, etc., *Gunter's scale*. Gunter's scale is also the name given to a type of rig with sliding rings, resembling the scale.

Another invention of Gunter's was the chain (*Gunter's chain*) – originally a chain of 100 links – for land surveying. And, 'according to Gunter' (the American equivalent generally of the English 'according to Cocker' (q.v.)), ten chains equal one furlong, and eight furlongs one mile.

202 GUPPY
Robert John Lechmere Guppy (1836 – 1916) was a Trinidad clergyman whom we remember eponymously from the *guppy*, a small brightly coloured fish, native in the main to the West Indies. The species was relatively unknown when the Reverend Guppy sent some specimens to the British Museum, yet it has since become one of the most popular with the home aquarist, being both hardy and prolific as well as attractive in appearance.

The guppy, or *Lesbistes reticulatus,* is viviparous (i.e. the young are produced in a very advanced stage of development) and the male of the species grows to some one-and-a-half inches in length, against the two inches of the less brightly coloured female. It is from the colouring of the male that the guppy is also known as the rainbow fish, while its high breeding rate has given it yet another name, *millions.* In its natural habitat it feeds on mosquito larvae and has been used by ecologists for the control of mosquitos.

203 GUY

Guy Fawkes (1570 – 1606) was probably the unluckiest as well as the most unfairly represented man to give his name to a word in the English language. The story of the Gunpowder Plot (the plan of a group of Catholics to blow up the House of Lords along with James I on the day of the opening of Parliament, 5 November 1605) is supposedly well known. Yet it is often forgotten that Fawkes, the one whose name we 'remember, remember . . .', was only one of a number of conspirators and not even their leader. And even though he was the 'technical expert', with the task of actually detonating the barrels of gunpowder – and presumably well aware of the likely consequences of the plot's success (to say nothing of the certain penalties attending its failure) – he could hardly have imagined that more than 300 years after his death, Englishmen (including Catholics) would still be celebrating the Fifth of November as Guy Fawkes Day with the burning of his effigy, the *guy.*

After all this time, of course, there can be few if any who bear any personal grudge against Guy Fawkes himself. But it is surprising that many people (according to a recent survey) believe that the original *Guy* was burnt at the stake – *and* on the fifth of November. He was in fact *hanged* for his crime – on 31 January 1606. And as a result of the terrible tortures he had suffered, he was apparently unable to mount the scaffold unaided.

H

204 HANSARD   HANSARDIZE

Luke Hansard (1752–1828) was a London printer who carried out work for the House of Commons, printing the *House of Commons' journals*. His eldest son, Thomas Curson Hansard (1776–1833), became a partner in his father's firm and in 1803 printed the first reports of parliamentary debates, written by the political journalist William Cobbett (who later became a Member of Parliament). The Hansard family continued to print these reports for the next 86 years, but subsequent reports were still known and referred to as *Hansard*.

Hansard has now become part of the English language; and there is even a verb, to *hansardize*, meaning 'to remind someone of what he *really* said'. In fact, many an embarrassed MP has been confronted with his own words – taken from *Hansard*. The late Lord Samuel, the Liberal leader (who must have had thousands of his own words recorded in its pages), said: 'Hansard is history's ear, already listening'. And since 3 April 1978 we have all been able to listen along with Hansard to the proceedings of the House of Commons and the House of Lords through broadcasting on radio.

205 HANSEN'S BACILLUS   HANSEN'S DISEASE

Armauer Gerhard Henrik Hansen (1841–1912) discovered and gave his name to the bacillus causing leprosy, *Hansen's bacillus*. Hansen, a Norwegian physician, made his discovery some years before Koch (q.v.) discovered the tubercle bacillus, which closely resembles the leprosy bacillus.

Leprosy itself is sometimes referred to as *Hansen's disease*, no doubt to counteract the traditional stigma attached to the leper, whose very name has become synonymous with an outcast.

206 HANSOM-CAB

Joseph Aloysius Hansom (1803–82) invented and gave his name to the light two-wheeled carriage known as the *hansom*, or the *hansom-cab*.

Joseph Hansom was born in York and qualified as an architect. He designed the Birmingham town hall (erected in 1833), but soon afterwards turned his attention to road-vehicle design with an emphasis on safety. The hansom in its original form was in fact named the 'Patent Safety Cab'.

A particular feature of the hansom was its rear seat for the driver, raised high enough to allow the reins to go over the roof of the cab. There were two passenger seats. Within a few years of its invention, the hansom became one of the most popular cabs in London, as well as in most of the other cities in the United Kingdom; and Disraeli referred to it as 'the gondola of London'.

There were still a number of hansoms plying for hire more than 30 years after the introduction of the first taxi-cabs. And, ironically, the first petrol-driven taxis to operate in London were, in effect, hansom-cabs with engines.

207 HAUSSMANNIZE

Baron Georges Eugène Haussmann (1809 – 91) was prefect of the Seine from 1853 to 1870, during which time he inaugurated and carried through vast improvements to and rebuilding of the roads, sewers, parks, bridges and other features of Paris. From his achievements we have (apart from the material benefits), the verb *haussmannize*, used in a general way to describe widening, opening out and rebuilding; yet in a more specific sense meaning the improvement of streets through widening.

The Boulevard Haussmann in Paris was named in Haussmann's honour; but the large sums of money incurred in his schemes eventually led to his dismissal from office.

208 HAVELOCK

Sir Henry Havelock (1795 – 1857) became famous for his heroism and inspired generalship during the first year of the Indian Mutiny, in 1857. His name was subsequently honoured by the *havelock*, the familiar white cover for the military cap of that time, with a flap to protect the back of the neck against the hot sun of India and other such countries.

Havelock had been in the British army since the time of Waterloo; and though he had not fought at that battle, he had seen much active service in India where he had spent most of his military career. He was well versed in both military history and the native languages and was a man of strong religious principles.

With the outbreak of the Indian Mutiny, Havelock first led his troops to recapture Cawnpore, where (unknown to him) all the Europeans, including the women and children, had been massacred by the mutineers. His next objective was Lucknow and, in spite of sickness among his men and the intense heat, he fought his way to the beleaguered garrison and held out against the mutineers for almost two months. Lucknow was eventually relieved by troops under the commander-in-chief in India, Sir Colin Campbell, but Havelock died from dysentery a week later, on 24 November 1857.

Havelock's son, Sir Henry Marsham Havelock-Allan, was also a distinguished soldier and, in 1858, was awarded the Victoria Cross (q.v.) for an act of bravery during the Indian Mutiny, while under the command of his father.

209 HEATH ROBINSON

William Heath Robinson (1872–1944) became famous for his humorous drawings of weird and complicated mechanical devices, which gave the impression of being unlikely actually to work. We now describe any such home-made type of machine as a *Heath Robinson* contraption.

For all his sense of humour, Robinson (Heath was in fact his second Christian name) was a serious artist, who illustrated numerous books of verse, etc. His drawings appeared in various publications, including the *Sketch*, the *Graphic*, the *Bystander*, and the *Strand magazine*, and he also designed scenery for stage productions. He was undoubtedly ahead of his time in his satirizing of twentieth-century man as the slave of his own inventiveness, and his ideas were most effectively translated to the cinema screen in Charlie Chaplin's *Modern times*, which depicted the little tramp as the powerless victim of 'Heath Robinsonism'.

210 HEAVISIDE LAYER

Oliver Heaviside (1850–1925) gave his name to a region in the earth's upper atmosphere, the *Heaviside layer*, also known as the *Kennelly-Heaviside layer*. It was in 1902 that Heaviside suggested the existence of such a region and its effect on radio waves; and in the same year, a professor at Harvard University, Arthur E. Kennelly (q.v.), announced similar findings.

Heaviside was born in London, and was largely self-taught as a scientist. He made a number of important contributions to the advancement of wireless telegraphy and devised his own operational calculus. He was a nephew of Sir Charles Wheatstone (q.v.).

211 HENRY

Joseph Henry (1797–1878) gave his name to the unit of inductance, the *henry*. Henry's discovery of the method of producing induced current coincided with a similar discovery by the Englishman, Michael Faraday (q.v.), though the two men were working quite independently. Henry was an American.

In 1846 he became the first director of the Smithsonian Institution (q.v.), Washington DC, where he established a weather-reporting system. Out of this was born the US Weather Bureau. Henry is therefore credited with initiating scientific weather reporting in the United States.

212 HENRY'S LAW

William Henry (1774–1836) was an English chemist who studied medicine at Edinburgh. He practised for a time in Manchester but soon devoted himself to chemistry. He formulated the law named after him as *Henry's law*. This states that the amount of gas absorbed by a liquid is directly proportional to the pressure.

213 HEPPLEWHITE

George Hepplewhite was an eighteenth-century cabinet maker who originated a style of furniture design, named after him as *Hepplewhite*. Hepplewhite's designs were of a more delicate and graceful kind than those of the earlier Chippendale (q.v.), and were notable for their painting and inlay work. His designs for chairs, too, were particularly outstanding.

Hepplewhite was apparently a Lancastrian who settled in London, where he ran his business in St Giles, Cripplegate, and died in 1786. Yet surprisingly little more is known of his personal life.

214 HERTZ   KILOHERTZ   MEGAHERTZ

Heinrich Rudolf Hertz (1857–94) was the German scientist who gave his name to the unit of frequency, the *hertz*. Electromagnetic waves, or radio waves, were also named after him, as *hertzian waves*.

Working from the electromagnetic theory of the Scottish scientist, James Clerk Maxwell (q.v.), Hertz demonstrated the existence of radio waves and revealed their peculiar properties. His discoveries played a major part in the development of wireless telegraphy.

In recent years, the name of Hertz has become familiar to millions of radio listeners through the introduction of the *kilohertz* (a measure of frequency equal to 1,000 cycles per second) in place of the metre, on most new radios.

215 HIPPOCRATIC OATH   HIPPOCRATIC LOOK

Hippocrates (460? – 377? BC) has become known as the 'Father of Medicine' and gives his name to the famous code of ethics of the medical profession, the *Hippocratic oath*. His name is also associated with other words and expressions, including the *Hippocratic look* (or *Hippocratic face*), the facial appearance of a dying person, observed and described by Hippocrates.

Few details of the life of Hippocrates are known to us, other than that he was born on the Greek island of Cos and achieved great eminence in his time as a physician and a surgeon. His name is sometimes given as 'Ypocras'; and Chaucer refers to him under this name in *The Canterbury tales*.

216 HOBBESIAN   HOBBESIANISM

Thomas Hobbes (1588 – 1679), the great English philosopher, is particularly remembered for his famous 'social contract' which he advocated in his chief work *The Leviathan, or the matter, form, and power of a commonwealth, ecclesiastical and civil.*

Hobbesianism (or *Hobbism*), the political philosophy of Hobbes, sees man as a naturally selfish creature whose life is 'solitary, poor, nasty, brutish, and short'; and the establishment of a sovereign power, a leviathan or a strong man, is therefore necessary to control man's 'condition or war of everyone against everyone'. *Hobbesian* philosophy also embraces Erastianism (q.v.) regarding the role of the church.

Hobbes was associated with many of the notable philosophers and men of science of his day, both in England and on the Continent, and was a mathematical tutor to the future Charles II (q.v. under King Charles spaniel). He was born in the year of the Spanish Armada and died in his 92nd year, his last words being, 'I am about to take my last voyage, a great leap in the dark.'

217 HOBDAY

Sir Frederick Thomas George Hobday (1869 – 1939) was a leading veterinary surgeon of his time and a principal of the Royal Veterinary College. He gave his name to the English language from an operation he performed on horses to cure a respiratory impediment known as 'roaring'; and such was his success with the operation that the cured horses were said to have been *hobdayed*.

Hobday served with distinction in the Army Veterinary Corps during the First World War, when the horse and other animals still played an important role. From 1912 he had been the veterinary surgeon to the royal household and he was knighted in 1933.

218 HOBSON'S CHOICE

Thomas Hobson (1544? – 1631) was a Cambridge carrier, whose insistence on hiring out his horses in strict rotation, and therefore presenting his customers with the choice of the horse nearest the stable door or no horse at all, gave rise to the well known expression *Hobson's choice* (i.e. the choice between one thing or nothing). Hobson was apparently a well known character in his day, and apart from having his name perpetuated in the English language, he is also remembered through two epitaphs written for him by none other than John Milton, who knew him as a young man.

In more recent times, the name of Hobson has been revived in a successful play by the English dramatist Harold Brighouse, entitled *Hobson's choice*, in which Hobson is not a Cambridge carrier but a Lancashire bootmaker, who is himself presented with Hobson's choice by his own daughter and son-in-law.

219 HODGKIN'S DISEASE

Thomas Hodgkin (1798 – 1866) was a physician at Guy's Hospital in London, and one of the outstanding pathologists of his day. He is particularly remembered for his description of a rare glandular disorder, named after him as *Hodgkin's disease*. This is probably a very unusual form of cancer, although it can be easily confused with a number of other quite different diseases.

With two other outstanding young physicians at Guy's, Richard Bright and Thomas Addison (qq.v.), Hodgkin was greatly influenced by the brilliant surgeon and anatomist Sir Astley Paston Cooper, who was one of the first to emphasize the importance of pathology in practical medicine.

220 HOOVER   HOOVERING

William H. Hoover, usually known as W. H. Hoover (1849 – 1932), did *not* invent the vacuum-cleaner, as many people assume. Yet the name of Hoover is so strongly associated with vacuum-cleaning that we speak of *hoovering* the carpet, and refer to any kind of vacuum-cleaner as a *hoover* (to the annoyance of the Hoover Company's rivals, no doubt).

In fact, W. H. Hoover was not an inventor at all, but he was an extremely astute businessman who foresaw the sales potential of a new type of vacuum-cleaner which had been constructed by one J. Murray Spangler, a caretaker in a department store in Ohio. Spangler's invention was, in effect, the prototype of the upright style of vacuum cleaner of today, with the exposed dust-bag. Hoover persuaded Spangler to sell his rights to his invention, and in 1908 the Hoover Suction Sweeper Company produced the first *hoover*, selling at $70. Four years later Hoover vacuum cleaners were being exported to Britain (where the vacuum cleaner had been invented at the beginning of the century) and the name of Hoover was well on its way to becoming an accepted word in the English language, in spite of W. H. Hoover's personal objection to his name being used eponymously and without a capital 'H'.

The name of Spangler, on the other hand, is all but forgotten; yet it could well be that, had the inventor of the *hoover* retained the rights of his invention, we would be speaking today of *spangling*, or *spanglering*, instead of hoovering the carpet.

221 HOTCHKISS

Benjamin Berkeley Hotchkiss (1826 – 85) was an American inventor whose name has been given to a number of firearms and in particular the *Hotchkiss machine-gun*. This employed a revolving barrel and was one of the first successful weapons of its kind. Developments of the Hotchkiss were widely used in the First World War by the Americans, the British and the French. And in October 1914, a French aeroplane, 'unofficially' armed with a Hotchkiss machine-gun, shot down a German aeroplane in the first decisive air-to-air combat.

Other inventions named after Hotchkiss include the highly successful *Hotchkiss magazine rifle*.

222 HOTSPUR

Sir Henry Percy, known as 'Hotspur' (1364 – 1403), was the eldest son of Sir Henry Percy, the first Earl of Northumberland. With his father, he at first supported the newly acclaimed Henry IV, but then revolted against him and was killed at the battle of Shrewsbury, on 21 July 1403. His fiery temper and rash behaviour have given us the word *Hotspur* as a synonym for a person such as Sir Henry Percy.

Hotspur figures in Shakespeare's *Henry IV, part I*, in which Sir John Falstaff pretends to have killed him after finding his corpse at the battle of Shrewsbury. And 'the Hotspur of debate' was the name given to Edward Stanley, later prime minister Lord Derby (q.v. under Prince Rupert's drops).

223 HOUDINI

Erich Weiss (1874–1926) was an American magician and escapologist who was known professionally as Harry Houdini. He took his stage-name from a famous French magician and illusionist, Jean Eugène Robert Houdin (1805–71), a maker of numerous mechanical devices for conjurers but one who was concerned to expose charlatans in his profession.

Harry Houdini (or just *Houdini* as he became known), achieved such fame from his feats of escapology (including underwater escapes from locked containers in which he was handcuffed and fettered) that his name became synonymous with an escapologist; and even the cat with its proverbial 'nine lives' has been referred to as a 'feline Houdini'.

Houdini's luck ran out, however, when an American student punched him in the abdomen (Houdini had claimed that he could 'take' such a punch) unawares. He declined medical treatment in order to fulfil one of his engagements and consequently died from peritonitis.

224 HUBBLE'S CONSTANT

Edwin Powell Hubble (1889–1953), the American astronomer, was one of the world's leading authorities on nebulae. He gave his name to a theory concerning the expansion of the universe, *Hubble's constant*, the hypothetical period of time since all the matter in the universe was located in one mass, on the assumption that the expansion rate has remained constant over that period.

Hubble worked at the Mount Wilson Observatory, at Pasadena, California, where with the aid of the 100 in. telescope, he made a number of important discoveries in the field of astronomy.

225 HUNTINGDONIAN

Selina, Countess of Huntingdon (1707 – 91), founded and gave her name to a Methodist sect with Calvanistic (q.v.) connections, known as *Huntingdonians*, or 'The Countess of Huntingdon's Connexion'. She had joined the Wesleyans (q.v.) in 1746, the year of the death of her husband, the ninth earl, but supported the evangelist George Whitefield in his separation from John Wesley, making him her chaplain.

The Countess supported many other preachers and built a number of chapels, most of which became identified with the Congregationalists.

226 HUNTINGTON'S CHOREA

George Huntington (1851 – 1916) was the American neurologist who described and gave his name to the rare hereditary disease, *Huntington's chorea*. This condition is characterized by involuntary twitching movements in the limbs, the neck and the face, as well as a gradual loss of mental powers.

The disease is also known as *chorea major*, as distinct from the much less serious *chorea minor*, or Syndenham's chorea (q.v.), and the majority of sufferers are over 35 years of age. And while there is no known cure, certain drugs are effective in relieving the symptoms.

227 HUSSITE

John Hus, or Huss (1373? – 1415), was a religious reformer from Bohemia, whose followers were known as *Hussites*. He was a disciple of the English theologian and reformer John Wycliffe (who initiated the first complete translation of the Bible into English); and it was his teaching of Wycliffe's doctrines which led to his excommunication in 1410.

Four years later, Hus was treacherously persuaded to stand trial for heresy by the Council of Constance. He was duly convicted and condemned to death and was burnt at the stake on 6 July 1415. The Hussites took up arms against their leader's persecutors in a series of conflicts known as the *Hussite War*.

The works of Hus, largely based on those of Wycliffe, were to become a considerable influence on Luther (q.v.).

228 HUTCHINSONIAN

Anne Hutchinson, née Marbury (1591 – 1643), was the daughter of an English clergyman who, with her husband, emigrated to

America in 1634. She established a sect in Boston, Massachusetts, and her followers, known as *Hutchinsonians*, were persuaded to believe in salvation through the grace of God in disobedience to the laws of the church and the state. Her activities eventually led to a trial for heresy and sedition and her expulsion from the colony.

After taking refuge in Rhode Island, Anne Hutchinson and her family settled in what is now Pelham Bay, New York, where they were murdered by Indians.

John Hutchinson (1674–1737) was an English philosopher and writer on theology whose *Thoughts concerning religion* affirmed that the Hebrew Scriptures contained a complete system of natural history, philosophy and religion. His small but articulate group of followers were known as *Hutchinsonians*, but were in no way connected with those named after the aforesaid Anne Hutchinson (q.v.).

229 HUTTONIAN

James Hutton (1726–97) was a Scottish geologist whose theories concerning the igneous origin of certain rocks gave rise to the word *Huttonian*. He maintained that the heat at the centre of the earth was the reason for the inequalities and other phenomena in the earth's crust. In this he is credited with originating the modern conception of the formation of the earth's crust, in opposition to previously accepted assumptions.

Hutton, born in Edinburgh, first studied medicine there and then at Paris and Leyden, eventually moving to the study of mineralogy and geology via agriculture and chemistry. His work exercised a notable influence on his fellow-countryman, the geologist Robert Jameson (q.v.).

I

230 IMMELMANN TURN   BLUE MAX

Max Immelmann (1890–1916) was one of the leading German fighter-pilots of the First World War. He is particularly remembered for a manoeuvre he devised, named after him as the *Immelmann turn*; and the 'Pour le Mérite' medal was also named in his honour as the *Blue Max*.

Immelmann employed his famous 'turn' to escape from a pursuing aircraft by performing a half-loop with a roll off the top, which then placed *him* in the attacking position. Many of his 15 recorded victories were apparently achieved by this means; and while his record appears modest when compared with the 80 victories credited to the legendary 'Red Baron', Manfred von Richthofen, it must be remembered that pilots such as Immelmann and Richthofen's mentor, Oswald Boelcke, were the real pioneers of the techniques of aerial combat. In fact, a 'rule book' of Boelcke's was still officially in use during the Second World War.

Like so many other 'aces' of the Great War – Ball, Boelcke, Guynemer, Hawker, McCudden, Mannock, Richthofen, Voss – Immelmann was not destined to survive the conflict. He was killed on 18 June 1916, when the Fokker aircraft he was flying inexplicably broke up in mid-air. (There is no reliable evidence to support accounts of Immelmann meeting his end as the victim of his own famous manoeuvre.)

231 IRVINGITES

Edward Irving (1792–1834) was a Scottish clergyman and one of the great preachers of his day. He came to London in 1822 as a minister of the Church of Scotland, but in 1833 he was excommunicated as a heretic.

About this time, Irving and his followers founded the Holy Catholic Apostolic Church and its members came to be known as *Irvingites*, though the name was rejected by them. *Irvingite* still persists, however, as the popular name for a member of the Holy Catholic Apostolic Church.

Irving had close friendships with a number of well known writers, including S. T. Coleridge, Charles Lamb, and Thomas Carlyle, his fellow-countryman. By a strange coincidence, Coleridge, Lamb, and Irving himself all died in 1834.

232 ISHMAEL

Ishmael, Abraham's son by his concubine Hagar, handmaiden of his wife Sarah, gives his name to the English language as an outcast, or someone at war with society. ('And the angel of the Lord said . . . thou art with child, and shalt bear a son, and shalt call his name *Ishmael* . . . And he will be a wild man; his hand will be against every man, and every man's hand against him.' Genesis 16:11 – 12)

Ishmael is regarded by the Arabs as their ancestor, and Mohammed (q.v.) claimed descent from him.

233 ISIDORIAN DECRETALS

St Isidore of Seville (*circa* 560 – 636) was archbishop of Seville and one of the leading scholars of his time. His teaching, stemming from a strict sense of Christian duty, exercised a great influence on both ecclesiastical and civil matters in Spain and formed the basis of the country's constitutional law. The *Isidorian decretals*, the decrees or ecclesiastical laws named from St Isidore, are not, however, those of his making; they are usually referred to in connection with forged documents published in the ninth century in France, claiming temporal power for the papacy.

J

234 JACK KETCH

John Ketch, known as Jack Ketch (died 1686), was one of the most notorious of English hangmen. He is believed to have been appointed as public executioner in 1663, in succession to 'Squire' Dun, who in turn had succeeded Richard Brandon, the executioner of Charles I (q.v. under Gregorian tree). After his death, the name of *Jack Ketch* became a popular synonym for a public hangman or executioner; and by the eighteenth century, his name was being used for the hangman in the newly introduced Punch and Judy puppet plays.

Ketch is particularly remembered for the execution of Lord Russell (a leading conspirator in the Rye House Plot to kidnap Charles II), in 1683, and the Duke of Monmouth, in 1685. On both occasions, he carried out the beheading in the most brutal and inept manner, employing, it is said, some eight blows of the axe to sever the head of the unfortunate Monmouth. It was Ketch, too, earlier in 1685, who supervised the barbarous flogging of the perjurer Titus Oates, who in the space of three days was twice whipped through the streets of London on a cart. (Incredibly, Oates survived his punishment.)

In the last year of his life, Ketch was dismissed from his post and imprisoned for insulting a sheriff. A butcher named Rose was appointed in his place, but after a few months the new hangman was himself convicted and hanged and Ketch regained his old post.

235 JACK RUSSELL

John Russell, known as Jack Russell (1795 – 1883), was an English country parson whose life-long passion for fox-hunting earned him the nickname of the 'sporting parson'. The *Jack Russell* terrier is named after him.

Russell became the perpetual curate of Swymbridge, in his native county of Devon, and a noted master of foxhounds. His love of hunting did not endear him to his bishop, but he performed his church duties conscientiously and was well liked by most people of his acquaintance, one of whom was the Prince of Wales, later Edward VII (q.v.). He continued to enjoy riding to hounds as an octogenarian and died at the age of 87.

The Jack Russell was originally bred as a working dog. There are considerable variations in its appearance and this has tended to label it as a 'strain' of terriers, rather than an accepted breed.

236 JACK-STRAW

Jack Straw(e) was one of the leaders of the English Peasants' Revolt in 1381, when peasants from the south-east of England, mainly Kent and Essex, marched on London to protest against taxes and other hardships. Under another of their leaders, Wat Tyler, the mob broke into the Tower of London and beheaded Simon of Sudbury, the Archbishop of Canterbury, who was largely held to blame for the economic troubles of the time.

Tyler's subsequent meeting with the 14 year old Richard II at Smithfield, and his death at the hands of William Walworth, the Lord Mayor of London, in the course of the negotiations, is well known; whereas Jack Straw's part in the affairs is somewhat obscure and apparently of relatively small importance. And this could well be one of the reasons for the description of someone of little substance or significance, or of no great importance, as a *Jack-straw*, or *jack-straw*.

There is a reference to Jack Straw the man in Chaucer's *The nun's priest's tale*.

237 JACOB'S LADDER

Jacob, son of Isaac and Rebekah and twin brother of Esau, gives his name to a rope ladder with wooden rungs, used on ships, a plant resembling a ladder, and a continuous chain of buckets on an elevator – all known as *Jacob's ladder*, from the ladder in Jacob's dream ('And he dreamed, and behold a ladder set up on the earth, and the top of it reached to heaven; and behold the angels of God ascending and descending on it.' Genesis 28:12).

Jacob's staff, a pilgrim's staff or a surveying rod, is also said to derive from Jacob ('. . . with my staff I passed over this Jordan.' Genesis 32:10), though it is more often credited to St James of Compostela (q.v. under Jacob's staff).

After wrestling with an angel, Jacob received the name of Israel ('Thy name shall be called no more Jacob, but Israel.' Genesis 32:28).

238 JACOB'S STAFF

Saint James of Compostela (or St James the Greater) was one of the 12 apostles, a son of Zebedee and the brother of the apostle

John. Tradition has it that, after being put to death by order of Herod, his body was miraculously borne to Compostela, in Spain, which became a place of pilgrimage for Christians. James is the patron saint of pilgrims, and one of his symbols in religious art is a staff. The pilgrim's staff, known as a *Jacob's staff*, is therefore probably named after him, from the Latin *Jacobus* for James.

A *Jacob's staff* is also the name for a surveyor's rod.

239 JACOBEAN   JACOBUS

James I (1556–1625) was King of Great Britain from 1603 until his death, and the word *Jacobean* (from the Latin 'Jacobus' for James) refers to his reign, or anything characteristic of that time. There was also a coin of the period, a *jacobus*, which was named after James I. It was originally worth about 20 shillings.

James was also King of Scotland, as James VI, becoming king when he was barely a year old, on the enforced abdication of his mother, Mary Stuart, Mary, Queen of Scots. And it was his immediate predecessor on the English throne, Elizabeth I (q.v.), who had signed the death-warrant for Mary in 1587.

But apart from the obvious difficulties of any Scottish king coming to rule a nation with a long history of hostilities against the Scots, James was not the most prepossessing or popular of men. The authors of *1066 and all that* (the well known light-hearted book on English history), declared that 'James I slobbered at the mouth and had favourites: he was thus a Bad King.' He certainly did slobber, as well as being short and misshapen and having a stammer. He was, however, an extremely erudite man, which apparently prompted his contemporary, Henri IV of France, to refer to him as, 'The wisest fool in Christendom.'

240 JACOBITE   JACOBITES

James II (1633–1701) was a son of Charles I and a grandson of James I (q.v.). He was king of England, Scotland, and Ireland from 1685 until his enforced abdication, in 1688, when he left England for France, where he died in exile. His supporters, who claimed that James was still the rightful king, became known as *Jacobites*, and at his death they named his son, James Francis Edward Stuart – known as 'The Old Pretender' – as 'James III'. The Old Pretender's son, Charles Edward Stuart ('Bonnie Prince Charlie', or 'The Young Pretender'), was later named 'Charles III' by the Jacobites.

In 1715, a Jacobite rising ended indecisively, as did a rising in the Highlands a few years later. But in 1745, led by 'Bonnie Prince Charlie', the Jacobites made what was to be their final attempt at returning the Stuarts to the throne, which ended with their defeat at Culloden on 16 April 1746. The battle was movingly commemorated by Robert Burns in his *Lament for Culloden*:

> The lovely lass of Inverness,
>   Nae joy nor pleasure can she see;
> For e'en and morn she cries, 'Alas!'
>   And aye the saut tear blin's her e'e:
> 'Drumossie moor, Drumossie day,
>   A waefu' day it was to me!
> For there I lost my father dear,
>   My father dear and brethren three.'

Jacobites are also members of a religious sect in Syria, who take their name from Jacob Baradai, or Jacobus Baradeus ('the man in rags'), founder of the Jacobite Church in the sixth century.

241 JACQUARD

Joseph Marie Jacquard (1752–1834) was a Frenchman who invented a device for assisting pattern weaving on a loom, named after him as a *jacquard*. Jacquard's apparatus (or the Jacquard-loom, as it came to be called), controlled the movement of the warp threads with perforated cards, and was the first loom to weave patterns successfully.

Jacquard's use of perforated cards could be said to have anticipated the punch-card of the modern computer and his name is often referred to in accounts of the development of the computer. Other inventions of Jacquard included a machine for weaving nets.

242 JACUZZI

Candido Jacuzzi (1902–86) invented and gave his name to one of the most successful inventions of recent times, the *Jacuzzi*, a bath with a device giving the effect of a whirlpool. It was originally intended to provide hydro-massage for one of Jacuzzi's sons who was suffering from rheumatoid arthritis, but it has since become widely used as a pleasurable style of bathing and something of a status symbol.

Jacuzzi was born in Italy, the youngest in a family of seven sons who emigrated to the USA in the early years of this century. The brothers formed an engineering business and specialized in making propellers which they supplied to the United States Air Force during the First World War. After the war, they turned to manufacturing their own aircraft; a fatal accident, however, in which one of the Jacuzzi brothers died, brought an end to the enterprise. The manufacturing of water-pumps became the Jacuzzi's next venture and resulted in the invention of an original type of jet-pump, which in turn led to Candido Jacuzzi's 'whirlpool' bath.

The Jacuzzi was manufactured and distributed in a number of countries, including the Jacuzzi's native Italy. Candido did indeed return to Italy for some years where he became a successful viniculturist, as well as designing a scanty swimsuit known as a 'monokini'.

243 JAMESONITE
Robert Jameson (1772 – 1854) was the Scottish geologist who identified and gave his name to the mineral compound of lead, antimony and sulphur, *Jamesonite*.

Born in Leith, he studied at Edinburgh (where he was later appointed Professor of Natural History) and at Freiburg. It was there that he became influenced by the theories of Werner (q.v.), though he was later persuaded towards those of his fellow-countryman, James Hutton (q.v.).

244 JANSENISM   JANSENIST
Cornelius Jansen, Bishop of Ypres in Flanders (1585 – 1638), was the Dutch theologian who founded and gave his name to the *Jansenists*, a sect within the Catholic Church, opposed to the Jesuits. The doctrine of the Jesuits in this controversy was typified by the Spanish theologian Luis Molina (q.v.), though the two men were not strictly contemporary.

The Jesuits were eventually suppressed, and the Jansenists ceased to exist as an organized force by the middle of the eighteenth century; but the long term effects of *Jansenism* extended beyond the Church and were arguably a significant factor in the events which led to the French Revolution.

245 JEHU
Jehu was King of Israel (*circa* 843 – 816 BC) and a great warrior, who was also renowned for driving his chariot at high speed ('and the driving is like the driving of Jehu, the son of Nimshi; for he driveth furiously.' II Kings 9:20). Any fast, reckless driver may be referred to as a *Jehu*.

246 JEREMIAH   JEREMIAD

Jeremiah (or Jeremias) was the reputed author of the *Lamentations of Jeremiah* in the Old Testament. From his name we have the word *jeremiad* – a tale of woe or a lamentation – and a *jeremiah* is someone who prophesies grief ('... he is gone forth from his place to make thy land desolate: and thy cities shall be laid waste without an inhabitant' Jeremiah 4:7).

The story of the English composer, *Jeremiah* Clarke (1670? – 1707), is certainly a 'tale of woe'. He became involved in a hopeless love affair and committed suicide by shooting himself. But it seems that fate was still against poor Jeremiah, long after his death. He had written a piece of music for the harpsichord, entitled *The Prince of Denmark's march* (presumably dedicated to Queen Anne's consort, George of Denmark), which was subsequently arranged for the organ and mistakenly attributed to the better known Henry Purcell. The famous arrangement of this piece by Sir Henry Wood became known as 'Purcell's Trumpet Voluntary'; and it is only recently that Jeremiah Clarke has been credited as the rightful composer.

247 JEROBOAM

Jeroboam I was King of Israel (*circa* 912 BC) and 'a mighty man of valour' who 'did sin and made Israel to sin' (I Kings 11:28 and 14:16). The *jeroboam* – a large bottle or bowl, roughly equivalent to four standard bottles – is named after him. Two jeroboams are equal to one *rehoboam* (q.v.).

248 JEZEBEL   PAINTED JEZEBEL

Jezebel (or Jezabel) was a Phoenician princess and a daughter of Ethbaal, King of Tyre and Sidon. She became the wife of Ahab, King of Israel, bringing him to worship Baal, the god of the Phoenicians, while she persecuted the prophets of the Hebrew god, Jehovah.

Jezebel met her end at the hand of Jehu (q.v.), who had earlier killed her son, Jehoram. And, characteristically, one of her last acts was to put on some make-up ('Jezebel ... painted her face' II Kings 9:30), which has given rise to the expression *a painted Jezebel*. Any woman of loose morals used to be referred to as a *Jezebel* ('... the whoredoms of ... Jezebel and her witchcrafts' II Kings 9:22), especially one who flaunted herself shamelessly.

249 JOB   JOBING   JOB'S NEWS   JOB'S COMFORTERS

Job, the central figure in the Old Testament *Book of Job*, has given his name to a number of words and phrases in the English language. These are mostly to do with Job's great patience and fortitude in adversity ('Behold, we count them happy which endure. Ye have heard of the patience of Job' James 5:11) and the reproof of his friends, who mistakenly attribute his misfortune to some wrong-doing, *Job's comforters* ('. . . miserable comforters are ye all.' Job 16:2). The name of Job is applied to anyone displaying great patience, and we speak of *jobing*, or *jobation*, after the sanctimonious manner of Job's comforters. *Job's news* is bad news, while someone who brings such news is *Job's post*.

250 JOE MILLER   JOE MILLERISM

Joseph (or Josias) Miller, known as Joe Miller (1684–1738), was a popular English comic actor whose name was used for the title of a book of old jokes, *Joe Miller's Jest-book or The Wit's Vade-mecum*, published in the year after his death. Subsequently, a *Joe Miller* came to mean a rather stale or hackneyed joke, or what nowadays might be described as a 'chestnut'. Any such collection of jokes is also known as a *Joe Miller*, while *Joe Millerism* refers to the all too familiar practice of repeating old jokes ad nauseam.

Ironically, the much maligned Joe Miller had little to do with the notorious *Jest-book* which bears his name. The book was compiled by one John Mottley, a somewhat second-rate playwright of the time, who it appears had not even obtained Miller's permission to use his name in the title. Miller, furthermore, was virtually illiterate.

251 JOEY

Joseph Hume (1777–1855) was an English politician with the nickname of 'Adversity Hume', from his frequent predictions of impending national disaster. Eponymously, however, he is remembered for the fourpenny-piece, the *joey* (also known as the *Britannia groat*), a small silver coin introduced through his advocacy, in 1836.

The old silver threepenny-piece was also called a joey; and the word is sometimes used as a synonym for a clown, after the celebrated pantomimist, Joseph Grimaldi (1779–1837), whose memoirs were edited by Charles Dickens (q.v.).

252 JOHN INNES

John Innes (1829–1904) was a Scottish horticulturalist who inherited an estate in the county of Surrey, in England, and set apart the larger part of his land for the cultivation of trees. On his death, he bequeathed his property 'for the study of the growth of trees and for the improvement of horticulture by experiment and research'. The John Innes Institute was established in 1909; and some 30 years later, a director of the Institute, Daniel Hall, developed a formula for a soil-based compost which he named in honour of John Innes. This was a standardized and sterilized potting and seed compost which has since come to be so widely used that it is now known simply as *John Innes*, or 'J.I.'.

253 JONAH

Jonah (or Jonas) was the Hebrew prophet in the Old Testament story whose presence on the ship going to Tarshish was identified as the cause of stormy weather ('So they took up Jonah, and cast him forth into the sea; and the sea ceased from her raging.' Jonah 1:15).

From this part of the story the name of *Jonah* has come to be given to anyone who brings bad luck along with him or her – though of course not all Jonahs are dealt with as drastically as the man who gave his name to the word.

254 JOSEPH

Joseph, the eleventh son of Jacob (q.v.), and the first by his wife Rachel, gives his name to anyone who resists temptation. This comes from Joseph's rejection of the overtures of Potiphar's wife. ('And it came to pass ... that his master's wife cast her eyes upon Joseph; and she said, Lie with me. But he refused, and said ... because thou art his wife; how then can I do this great wickedness, and sin against God?' Genesis 39:7–9).

A *Joseph*, or a *Joseph coat*, is a woman's overcoat with a cape, dating from the eighteenth century. This is no doubt in allusion to Joseph's 'coat of many colours'. ('Now Israel loved Joseph more than all his children, because he was the son of his old age: and he made him a coat of many colours.' Genesis 37:3).

255 JOULE

James Prescott Joule (1818–89), the English scientist, is remembered in the main for his determination of the mechanical equivalent of heat and his discoveries concerning the conservation of energy. The unit of energy, work and heat, the *joule*, is named after him. He was a pupil of John Dalton (q.v.).

Joule is usually pronounced as 'jool', but it seems that J. P. Joule took the pronunciation of 'jowl', which was to give rise to the clerihew (q.v.):

> James Prescott JOULE
> Let out a great HOWL,
> 'Listen, you fool!
> I gave my name to the jowl, not the jool.'

256 JUDAS   JUDAS KISS   JUDAS TREE   JUDAS HOLE

Judas Iscariot (meaning *man of Kerioth in Judaea*) is remembered as the apostle who betrayed Jesus Christ (q.v.) through a number of words and phrases in the English language. His very name has become a synonym for a traitor, or a betrayer; while a *Judas-kiss* refers to some treacherous act which is made even worse by an accompanying false show of affection ('Now he that betrayed him gave them a sign, saying, Whomsoever I shall kiss, that same is he: hold him fast. And forthwith he came to Jesus, and said, Hail, Master; and kissed him.' Matthew 26:48–9).

Judas is supposed to have been a red-head, and from this we get *Judas-coloured hair*. And since he apparently hanged himself on an elder-tree, this tree and others of the same family (the *Cercis siliquastrum* and the American *Cercis canadensis*, or redbud) are sometimes known as *Judas-trees*. Also named from Judas is the *Judas-hole*, or *Judas-slit* (sometimes referred to as simply a *judas*) which is a peep-hole, or spy-hole, especially the kind in a cell door for the purpose of observing a prisoner.

257 JUVENALIAN

Decimus Junius Juvenalis (*circa* AD 60 – *circa* 140), the celebrated Roman lawyer and poet, was renowned for his brutally frank satires of the Romans under the Empire. His main targets for criticism were unnatural vices, the extravagant lifestyle of the ruling classes in contrast to the poverty of others, and his contempt of sycophancy. Unlike the writing of most other great satirists, however, his work contains virtually no humour; and this gives us *Juvenalian* as a description of a style of writing (with a particular reference to satire) which is predominantly bitter, rather than humorous.

Juvenal (as he is also known) served as a tribune in the Roman army and spent some time in Britain. He is also known to have been a misogynist and an anti-Semite.

K

258 KAFKAESQUE

Franz Kafka (1883–1924) wrote three novels, all of which were published after his death (from tuberculosis) at the age of 40. The first of these to be translated into English from the original German was *The castle*, which appeared in 1930; and as Kafka's works became increasingly well known, the word *Kafkaesque* edged its way into the English language, but as something more than just a description of the author's style, so that we now use the word in allusion to any dream-like or nightmarish situation where a seemingly real world is confused with a world of strange and disturbing dreams.

Kafka was of Austrian nationality, but born in Prague of Jewish parents. Almost unknown as a writer in his lifetime, he might well have become completely forgotten had his manuscripts been destroyed at his death, in accordance with his wish. In addition to the other novels (*The trial* and *America*), he produced a number of short stories and some verse. His influence on other writers has been considerable: George Orwell's *1984* is decidedly Kafkaesque, for example, while the surrealistic effects in many of the novels and plays of Samuel Beckett would seem to owe much to Kafka.

259 KALASHNIKOV

Mikhail Timoteyevich Kalashnikov (1919–   ) is the inventor of one of the most widely used firearms of modern times, an assault rifle named after him as the *Kalashnikov*, or the AKM. It is a modification of an earlier Kalashnikov rifle, the AK-47, which is still in use. Both weapons are 7.62mm gas-operated automatics, capable of being used as single-shot rifles.

Kalashnikov was a tank commander in the Red Army, and his interest in the invention of guns began when he was recovering from being severely wounded, in 1941. He produced a submachine-gun and a carbine before his AK-47 was adopted by the army as a replacement for the Simonov rifle of the Second World War. The AKM appeared in 1959, and Kalashnikov was subsequently honoured as a Hero of Socialist Labour.

The Kalashnikov has come to be the standard weapon of the Russian rifleman and of most other armies within the Soviet bloc, as well as being made available to a number of countries in the

Middle East and parts of Africa. Kalashnikov has produced other firearms, but his name is generally used to indicate the AK-47 and the AKM assault rifles.

260 KELVIN   KELVIN SCALE
Sir William Thomson, first Baron Kelvin of Largs (1824–1907), gave his name to the *kelvin*, symbol K, the unit of thermodynamic temperature on the *Kelvin scale*. The Kelvin scale is an 'absolute' scale, and a development of the Celsius (q.v.) scale, with absolute zero for zero and centigrade degrees. (Absolute zero is only obtainable in theory.)

Lord Kelvin made a number of important scientific discoveries, and was a prolific inventor. His theory of electric oscillations formed the basis of wireless telegraphy, and he was responsible for laying the first Atlantic telegraph cables.

261 KENNELLY-HEAVISIDE LAYER
Arthur Edwin Kennelly (1861–1939) was the American electrical engineer who identified and jointly gave his name to the *Kennelly-Heaviside layer*, a region in the ionosphere some 60 miles up, which reflects certain radio waves. Kennelly's discovery coincided with a similar identification by the British mathematician and physicist, Oliver Heaviside (q.v.), though the two men were working independently and had never met.

The Kennelly-Heaviside layer is also known as just the Heaviside layer or the E region in the ionosphere. It lies between the lower D region and the F region, the Appleton layer (q.v.).

262 KEPLER'S LAWS
Johann Kepler (1571–1630) formulated three laws of planetary motion, which are named after him as *Kepler's laws*. His discoveries marked the beginning of modern astronomy and can be said to have formed the link between the work of Copernicus and Newton (qq.v.).

Kepler was born in Württemberg (now in West Germany) and worked briefly as an assistant to the eminent Danish astronomer, Tycho Brahe, before succeeding him as court astronomer to the Holy Roman Emperor, Rudolf II. His *laws* state that (1) planets move around the sun in ellipses, with the sun as one focus or central body; (2) the line drawn from the focus to a planet in any position of its orbit describes equal areas in equal time; and (3) the square of a planet's revolution round the sun is proportional to the cube of its mean distance from the sun.

263 KEYNESIAN
John Maynard Keynes, first Baron Keynes (1883 – 1946), was one of the most influential economists of his day. His theory of full employment was largely contained in his *Treatise on money* and *The general theory of employment, interest and money*, and *Keynesian* economics were to revolutionize economic thinking universally. He advocated a planned economy with a degree of public control, but within the capitalist system.

Keynes was born in Cambridge, where his father was a lecturer at the university; and it was at Cambridge University that he was to become associated with the Bloomsbury Group. This gathering of intellectuals included the writers Virginia Woolf, E. M. Forster and Lytton Strachey, and took its name from its meetings at the houses of Virginia Woolf and her brother, in the Bloomsbury district of London. Keynes's interests, in fact, were far from being confined to economics and politics, and it was his particular love of the ballet which led to his marriage with the Russian-born ballerina and actress, Lydia Lopokova.

It is perhaps worth noting (at least for astrologers and the like), that Keynes was born on the same day of the year – 5 June – as another famous economist, Adam Smith, the author of the first work of importance on political economy, *An enquiry into the nature and causes of the wealth of nations*.

264 KING CHARLES SPANIEL
CAVALIER KING CHARLES SPANIEL
Charles II (1630 – 85), King of England, Scotland and Ireland from the Restoration in 1660 to 1685, was known as the 'Merry Monarch'. He was also known, among other things, for his fondness for women (there were at least 13 mistresses known by name) and a breed of toy spaniels, the *King Charles Spaniel*.

The King Charles is distinguished by its long pendulous ears and long-haired silky coat. It has specific markings in various colours, stands some 11 – 12 in. high and is an active and intelligent dog. The *Cavalier King Charles Spaniel* is a slightly larger and taller breed of spaniel.

Charles II was of course one of the best known cavaliers during the English Civil War. And it is in the sense of the cavalier or free-and-easy character associated with King Charles that he is also remembered in the English language for his response to the mock epitaph of his favourite courtier, John Wilmot, Earl of Rochester:

> Here lies our sovereign lord the king
> Whose promise none relies on;
> He never said a foolish thing,
> Nor ever did a wise one.

Charles remarked, 'This is very true: for my words are my own, and my actions are my ministers.'

265 KING CHARLES'S HEAD

Charles I (1600 – 49), King of England, Scotland and Ireland from 1625 until his execution in 1649, gives his name to the English language through a character in the novel by Charles Dickens (q.v.), *David Copperfield*. The eponymous hero of the novel (generally believed to be a thinly veiled younger Dickens), encounters an amiable lunatic, a certain Mr Dick, who is obsessed with a Memorial which he 'had been for upwards of ten years endeavouring to keep King Charles the First out of ... but he had been constantly getting into it, and was there now'. This has given us the expression *King Charles's head* as a synonym for a particular kind of obsession or fixed idea which keeps returning.

Charles I is also remembered eponymously (albeit indirectly), through Vandyke (q.v.), who painted a number of portraits of the king, and the hangman Richard Brandon (q.v. under *Gregorian tree*), his executioner.

266 KLIEG LIGHT

John H. Kliegl (1869 – 1959) and his brother Anton T. Kliegl (1872 – 1927) were pioneers in the development of lighting effects for the stage and film studios. *Klieg light* (also spelt as *Kleig light*) is a kind of incandescent floodlighting, or an arc-light making use of ultraviolet rays which have a strong effect on a photographic plate. And *Klieg eyes* is a description given to a strain on the eyes from floodlighting, especially in film production.

The Kliegl brothers were born in Germany and emigrated to the USA before the turn of the century.

267 KÖCHEL NUMERATION

Ludwig Ritter von Köchel (1800–77) holds a unique place in the world of music from his classification of the compositions of Wolfgang Amadeus Mozart. Originally a botanist and mineralogist by profession, he used his knowledge of scientific classification to catalogue the previously unnumbered works of the composer whose music he held in special reverence. The *Köchel numeration*, usually abbreviated to 'K' or 'KV' (the 'V' meaning *verzeichnis* or list), subsequently became universally accepted as the correct chronological classification of Mozart's musical compositions.

Köchel, like Mozart, was Austrian-born and lived some 13 years in Salzburg, Mozart's birthplace, while engaged in compiling his great catalogue. He died in Vienna where Mozart had died in 1791.

268 KOCH'S BACILLUS

Robert Koch (1843–1910) is best remembered for his discovery, in 1882, of the tubercle bacillus, *Mycobacterium tuberculosis* or *Koch's bacillus*, which represented the first real step towards the effective treatment of tuberculosis. Six years earlier, however, he had already attracted the attention of the medical world with a remarkable paper on the anthrax bacillus (also known as Koch's bacillus), stating that infectious diseases are frequently caused by definite micro-organisms.

Koch was born near Hanover, the son of a mining engineer, and made his first important discoveries while earning his living as a general practitioner. His subsequent researches took him to many countries, including India, where he discovered the cause of cholera and the source of the bubonic plague. He was awarded the Nobel prize (q.v.) for physiology and medicine in 1905.

L

269 LABANOTATION

Rudolf von Laban (1879–1958) was the German choreographer who invented a system of notation for movements in ballet, named after him as *labanotation*.

Of all the arts, ballet is unique in combining the arts of music, drama, and painting with that of dancing to produce (ideally) a balanced and blended presentation of all four. The dancers may command the immediate attention at a performance of the ballet, but the person responsible for the success of the ballet as a whole is more than likely to be the choreographer, the 'backroom boy of ballet'. And his task is no easier for the surprising absence of a standard notation of dance movements. Over the years, there have been a number of attempts to produce an acceptable notation, but Laban's system which he introduced in the 1930s, has probably been the most successful. At least Laban has been honoured in the dictionary for his efforts.

270 LAMARCKISM

Jean Baptiste Pierre Antoine de Monet, Chevalier de Lamarck (1744–1829), originated and gave his name to a theory of evolution which in many respects anticipated the celebrated Darwin (q.v.) theory. Yet *Lamarckism* (or *Lamarckianism*), in its turn, was largely developed from an even earlier theory of evolution suggested by Charles Darwin's grandfather, Erasmus Darwin.

Lamarck studied medicine and botany in Paris, and became the royal botanist and a custodian of the *Jardin du Roi*, which after the Revolution was renamed (at the suggestion of Lamarck) the *Jardin des Plantes*. Of Lamarck's numerous books on natural history, his major work is *Histoire naturelle des animaux sans vertèbres*.

Lamarckism differs from Darwinism in that it gives greater importance to the part played by the environment in the development of species; but this is less acceptable to scientists for lack of experimental proof, whereas Darwin's theory is supported by a mass of first-hand evidence.

271 LAWRENCIUM

Ernest Orlando Lawrence (1901–58) gives his name to the element of atomic number 103, *lawrencium*, an artificially produced element.

Lawrence was a professor of physics and director of the radiation laboratory at the University of California, at Berkeley, California, where *lawrencium* was originally produced. He invented the cyclotron, a device for accelerating charged particles, and by means of this he produced artificial radioactivity. In 1939, he was awarded the Nobel prize (q.v.) for physics.

Berkelium, the element of atomic number 97, is named from Berkeley where it was produced.

272 LECLANCHÉ CELL

Georges Leclanché (1839–82) was a French chemist who invented and gave his name to an original type of dry cell battery, the *Leclanché cell*. In contrast to earlier types of battery, such as the Daniell cell (q.v.), Leclanché's invention had no free flowing liquid and worked by the action of ammonium chloride on electrodes (the positive and negative points of the cell) of zinc and carbon.

The modern dry battery, of the kind used in torches etc., is a direct development of Leclanché's invention and is still the most common battery in use after more than a century.

273 LENINISM

Nikolai Lenin, originally Vladimir Ilyich Ulyanov (1870–1924), the Russian revolutionary leader, was the first man to attempt to put into practice the socialist theories of Karl Marx (q.v.). But Lenin was aware of the need to adapt principles to given circumstances ('We can and must begin to build up Socialism, not with the fantastic human material especially created by our imagination, but with the material bequeathed us by Capitalism'). Therefore, *Leninism* can be seen as a development of Marxism.

Lenin was born in the Russian city of Simbirsk, which has since been renamed Ulyanovsk, from his original surname. He became actively involved in the socialist movement, following the execution of an older brother who had been party to a plot against the life of Czar Alexander III. Lenin lived in exile for a number of years before finally returning to Russia to lead the revolution in 1917 and to become premier.

Lenin died in January 1924, and on 22 April of that year, the 54th anniversary of his birth was marked by the renaming of

Petrograd (formerly St Petersburg) as Leningrad. But Leninism in Russia was already giving way to the virtual dictatorship of Lenin's successor, Joseph Stalin (q.v.).

274 LEOTARD

Jules Léotard (1842 – 70) was a French trapeze artist who wore a type of skin-tight garment during his act. Garments similar to his, with variations in the length of the sleeves and the legs, have come to be named after him as *leotards*; though it is doubtful whether half the men and women who wear leotards for gymnastics, dancing, or keep-fit classes, have ever heard of the Frenchman who gave his name to this garment.

In his day, however, Léotard was very well-known and highly successful. He appeared in a number of countries, including Britain, and his breathtaking act (he would fly literally over the heads of the audience from one trapeze to another) earned him the name of 'That Daring Young Man on the Flying Trapeze', from a popular song of the time – and a considerable amount of money.

But Léotard did not live long to enjoy the fruits of his success. He died of smallpox, at the age of 28.

275 LEWIS GUN

Isaac Newton Lewis (1858 – 1931) was an American army officer and an inventor. He gives his name to the best known of his inventions, the *Lewis gun*. This was a machine-gun of exceptionally light weight (some 26lbs.), compared with other machine-guns of its time. Invented shortly before the First World War, it was used extensively by the British army during the war and was manufactured in England. And it was a Lewis gun which was used in the first attack by one aeroplane against another in the first month of the war.

Colonel Lewis also invented a position finder for artillery, an artillery control system and a gas-propelled torpedo, among other things.

276 LIEBIG   LIEBIG CONDENSER

Baron Justus von Liebig (1803 – 73) was one of the most eminent chemists of his time. He discovered chloroform and aldehyde, invented the apparatus for converting vapour into liquid (named after him as the *Liebig condenser*) and prepared a beef extract without albumen, fat or gelatine, *Liebig*, or *Liebig's extract*.

Born in Darmstadt, in Germany, Liebig studied at Bonn and Erlangen and in Paris under Gay-Lussac. He eventually became professor of chemistry at Munich and is regarded as the founder of agricultural chemistry.

277 LINNAEAN CLASSIFICATION

Carolus Linnaeus, also known as Carl von Linné (1707–78), devised and gave his name to a system of classification for living things, and is regarded as the founder of modern botany.

Linnaeus was born in Sweden and studied at Uppsala, where he was a contemporary of Celsius (q.v.). He travelled to a number of countries, including England, before returning to Uppsala as professor of botany. Ten years after his death, the Linnean Society was founded, in London, by Sir James Edward Smith, who had bought the collections of Linnaeus.

278 LISTERISM   LISTERIA

Joseph Lister, first Baron Lister of Lyme Regis (1827–1912), is remembered as the surgeon who founded the antiseptic treatment of surgical wounds, known after him as *Listerism*. His method, using carbolic acid to prevent septic infection, was to revolutionize modern surgery.

Lister was the second son of the eminent microscopist Joseph Jackson Lister and was a house surgeon to James Syme (q.v. under mackintosh), whose daughter became his wife. His work was greatly indebted to the discoveries of Pasteur (q.v.).

Listeria, a genus of bacteria, was named in honour of Joseph Lister by the bacteriologist J. H. Pirie in 1929. This word has come into popular notice in recent times in relation to the contamination of pre-cooked food.

279 LOGANBERRY

James Harvey Logan (1841–1928) was a judge in the superior court of Santa Cruz County, California, 1880–92. He is mainly remembered, however, as a horticulturist and especially for the *loganberry*, which he produced in his garden. The fruit has a shape similar to the blackberry, with the colour of the raspberry; and, while its rather sharp taste is not to everybody's liking, it does have the advantage of being left alone by most birds.

280 LONSDALE BELT

Hugh Cecil Lowther, fifth Earl of Lonsdale (1857–1944), originated and gave his name to the *Lonsdale Belt* for boxing, which is awarded to a boxer gaining the same British title three times in succession.

Lord Lonsdale was much more than a patron of 'the noble art', and his ability in the boxing-ring was confirmed by no less than John L. Sullivan, the American world heavyweight champion, who used him as a sparring partner. His other main sporting interest was with horses and horse racing, and again he was an active participant and continued to ride to hounds almost to the end of his long life. Lord Lonsdale died at the age of 87, and attributed his good health in old age to sport and 'good-living'. (He always drank white burgundy at breakfast, it is said.)

Henry Cooper, who held the British heavyweight title longer than anyone else, was the first boxer to win three Lonsdale belts.

281 LOUIS   LOUIS-QUATORZE

Louis XIV (1638–1715), King of France from 1643 (at the age of four) until his death in 1715, reigned longer than any other European monarch. During this period there was a great flowering of the arts and literature in France and it has since become known as the Augustan Age (q.v.), with *Louis*, or *Louis-Quatorze*, being used to describe the architecture and furniture of the period.

Louis was a flamboyant character, devoted to amateur theatricals and known as the Sun King from the role of the Sun which he performed in a ballet. As a ruler he exercised the powers of pure despotism and led France into a long succession of wars which brought his country to the point of ruination. His attitude to government is perhaps summed up in his attributed utterance, 'L'état c'est moi.' (I am the state.)

282 LUCULLAN   LUCULLIAN   LUCULLIC

Lucius Licinius Lucullus (*circa* 110–*circa* 57 BC) was a Roman general who was particularly celebrated for his defeat of Mithridates (q.v.). He is remembered in the English language, however, for the life he led in retirement, when he became famous for his luxurious style of living and his sumptuous banquets. From this then, we have the adjectives *Lucullan*, *Lucullian*, etc., describing the *epicurism* (q.v.) of Lucullus.

There is also the expression 'Lucullus sups (or dines) with

Lucullus'. This is said to have come from an occasion when, on sitting down to an exquisite meal, Lucullus was asked who were his fellow diners: the reply was that Lucullus was dining with Lucullus. And a latter day equivalent of this quotation might well be attributed to the noted epicure Nubar Gulbenkian who said that the ideal number for dinner was three: the chef, the head waiter and himself.

283 LUDDITES   LUDDITE RIOTS
Ned Lud (or Ludd) was apparently the name of a half-witted Leicestershire labourer who, in 1799 or thereabouts, attracted a certain amount of attention to himself by going berserk and smashing two knitting-machines belonging to a local stocking-maker. Little more is known of him, but in 1811, a group of Nottinghamshire textile workers set about destroying new labour-saving machines, recently acquired by their employers, and took the name of *Luddites*.

These men saw the new machines as the cause of unemployment and its subsequent hardships, and the *Luddite riots* (as they became known) soon spread to other parts of the north of England and the midlands. The riots continued to break out for the next five years, and inevitably men were killed and property was destroyed, while many Luddites were put on trial and executed. Charlotte Brontë took the Luddite riots in her native Yorkshire as the basis for her novel *Shirley*.

It could be argued that there is a *Luddite* instinct in most of us, striving to preserve and protect those things we know and understand against innovation and change. And many of today's latest technological advances are undoubtedly regarded by many workers with the same kind of distrust as the Luddites regarded the new machines of the early nineteenth century. The spirit of Ned Ludd lives on, it would seem.

284 LUTHERAN
Martin Luther (1483–1546), the great German Protestant reformer, was also a musician of considerable talents. He wrote a number of hymns which are still sung (*Away in a manger* being one of the best known), as well as introducing the *Lutheran chorale*, or the *Lutheran hymn*, into the reformation church service. Lutheran congregations were encouraged to join in the singing of hymns, and Luther liked his church music to be tuneful, insisting that 'the devil should not have all the best tunes'. This

famous saying has been variously attributed to the Reverend Rowland Hill, General William Booth of the Salvation Army and John Wesley (q.v.).

285 LYSENKOISM

Trofim Denisovich Lysenko (1898 – 1977) was the Russian scientist who originated and gave his name to the theory of genetics known as *Lysenkoism*. Lysenko's theories were much in accord with those of another Soviet scientist, I. V. Michurin (1855 – 1935), who had been a leading opponent of principles of heredity propounded by the Austrian botanist Mendel (q.v.), in the nineteenth century.

Lysenko was also in accord with Lamarck (q.v.) in claiming that acquired characteristics could be inherited, and his theories found much favour with the Soviet authorities. But Lysenkoism had its detractors inside as well as outside the USSR. And from around the time of the death of Stalin (q.v.), in 1953, Lysenko's influence began to wane within the Soviet scientific establishment, until today the main claims of Lysenkoism are largely discounted.

M

286 MACADAMIZE   TAR-MACADAM   TARMAC
John Loudon McAdam (1756–1836) invented and gave his name to a method of surfacing roads known as *macadamizing*. The method utilized the weight of normal road traffic to crush layers of small broken stones of fairly uniform size into the road surface.

McAdam was born in Ayr but, like so many of his countrymen, he found it necessary to travel south of the border to further his career. And it was as the surveyor-general of roads in Bristol and later in the metropolitan area that he was eventually able to put his ideas on road-making into practice and 'macadamization' soon became a standard method of surfacing roads.

A development of McAdam's method was *tar-macadam*, which added tar to the crushed stones. And in 1903, 'Tarmac' was registered as a proprietary name in the USA. We use the word *tarmac*, of course, for the runways of an aerodrome, though John Loudon McAdam would surely have been surprised to know that he would give his name (or at least part of his name) to such things. After all, he died more than 60 years before the Wright brothers made their famous flights at Kittyhawk, in 1903.

287 McBURNEY'S POINT
Charles McBurney (1845–1913) was a distinguished American surgeon and one of the pioneers of antiseptic surgery. He was also a leading authority on appendicectomy; and it is in this respect he gave his name to *McBurney's point*, a pressure point discovered by him which marks the base of the appendix. This is of great importance in diagnosis.

Another surgical expression named after Professor McBurney is *McBurney's incision*, from a method he developed for operating in appendicectomy.

288 McCARTHYISM
Joseph (Raymond) McCarthy (1909–57) was the US senator who gave his name to a particular kind of political witch-hunting – *McCarthyism* – which flourished in America in the early 1950s. At that time, the involvement of America in the war in Korea, and the recent revelations of communist infiltration which had come to light through a number of treason trials, were very much

116

in the mind of the average American. McCarthy and his followers deliberately set out to exploit the situation and to create an atmosphere of fear and distrust; and the extent to which this scaremongering succeeded was largely due to the obsessiveness and determination of McCarthy himself.

McCarthy was elected to the senate as a Republican in 1946, and by 1950 had become chairman of the very powerful Permanent Subcommittee on investigations. He then declared that he had evidence that some 200 communists were employed by the State Department itself, and the ensuing investigations marked the start of a witch-hunt which left few sections of the community untouched. The film industry in particular became a prime target for the investigators. McCarthy was rarely able to produce real proof to back up his allegations, but evidence of 'guilt by association' was usually damning enough, and any number of innocent men and women were deprived of their usual means of earning a living as a result of McCarthyism.

The investigations were given maximum publicity, with the added dramatic effect of television coverage. Yet, ironically, it was television which played a considerable part in McCarthy's eventual downfall. There were others more skilled in TV presentation, notably the popular journalist and broadcaster, Ed Murrow, who fearlessly exposed McCarthy in a man-to-man confrontation, watched by millions of viewers. But there was growing opposition to McCarthyism from other quarters, too. Some of the generals had reacted strongly to accusations of 'commy-coddling' in the US army; and when McCarthy attacked President Eisenhower himself, he lost the support of the majority of his own party. In 1954, the senate took the unusual step of formally censuring McCarthy for his conduct, and this virtually ended his 'reign'.

The word *McCarthyism*, however, became a new word in the English language, together with a new phrase – 'Reds under the bed' – which effectively sums up the scaremongering aspect of McCarthyism.

289 MACH NUMBER

Ernst Mach (1838–1916) was the Austrian scientist and philosopher who defined speeds of objects in relation to the speed of sound, named after him by the expression *Mach number*.

The first officially recognized supersonic flight – i.e. a flight at a speed exceeding *Mach 1* – was made in 1948. And 28 years later, Anglo-French *Concordes* began the first scheduled flights by supersonic aircraft, capable of reaching speeds of *Mach 2*. In fact, travel at supersonic speeds is now a comparatively common experience for thousands of regular air passengers; whereas when Ernst Mach died, in 1916, the fastest aircraft could barely exceed 100 mph (or approximately a Mach number of 0.13).

290 MACHIAVELLIAN   MACHIAVELLIANISM
Niccolo Machiavelli, or Machiavel (1469–1527), the Florentine statesman and political philosopher, recommended that, 'Injuries should be done together in order that men may taste their bitterness but a short time' and that, 'Benefits ought to be conferred a little at a time, that their flavour may be tasted better'. This typically *Machiavellian* observation was one of many contained in his book *Il Principe* (The Prince), dedicated to Lorenzo de' Medici, the Florentine ruler, also known as 'Lorenzo the Magnificent'. And much of what Machiavelli wrote, more than 450 years ago, is still highly relevant to any number of people in power – or those aspiring to positions of power – in this day and age.

The term *Machiavellian,* however, has become somewhat misused over the years, for while Machiavelli condoned the most unscrupulous methods as a means to a political end, he was also a realist and a dispassionate observer of human nature. Another philsopher, the great Francis Bacon, wrote of him: 'We are much beholden to Machiavel and others, that write what men do, and not what they ought to do.'

Machiavelli's theories – unlike many political theories – were at least based on his own considerable personal experience of government and the precariousness of the 'power game'; moreover, despite his dismissal from office on suspicion of plotting against the Medici (he was also imprisoned for a while), he was returned to favour and died in retirement. It might well be said that no politician should be without his copy of *The Prince*.

291 MACKINTOSH
Charles Macintosh (1766–1843) invented and gave his name to a waterproof cloth known as *mackintosh*. The raincoat named the *mackintosh* or *mack* was not however his exclusive invention; and long before mackintosh was patented in 1823, there had been a number of attempts to produce a practical waterproof coat.

Macintosh (there is no 'k' in his name), was born in Glasgow and earned his living as an industrial chemist; and it was while he was working on the problem of utilizing a certain industrial by-product that – almost by accident – he discovered his original process for waterproofing cloth with indiarubber. Yet much of the credit for the eventual production of mackintosh as a practical material for making into clothes must go to another Scotsman, James Syme, who was later to become eminent as a surgeon. (An amputation of the ankle joint is named after him as 'Syme's operation'.)

After securing his patent, Macintosh founded Charles Macintosh & Company to produce and sell his waterproof cloth; but the first ready-to-wear 'mackintoshes' were not manufactured until 1830, when his firm amalgamated with another in – appropriately perhaps – Manchester, since, rightly or wrongly, Manchester is invariably associated with the rain in most people's minds.

In the 150 years or more since Macintosh patented his invention, the manufacture of rainclothes has, of course, undergone many changes and mackintosh has been largely superseded by other materials; the bulkiness of the early raincoats has in particular been overcome, too, with the introduction of the modern plastic product, which can be easily folded to fit in a trouser pocket or a small handbag. Nonetheless, we still tend to refer to any kind of waterproof, or semi-waterproof coat as a 'mack'.

292 MACMILLANITE
John Macmillan (1670 – 1753) founded and gave his name to a religious sect in Scotland which came from the Reformed Presbyterians, or the Cameronians (q.v.). The *Macmillanites* seceded from the original sect in a wish for a stricter adherence to the principles of the Reformation in Scotland and were also known as the 'Reformed Presbytery'.

293 McNAGHTEN RULES
Daniel McNaghten (also spelt M'Naghten, McNaughton, etc.) was a would-be assassin of British Prime Minister, Sir Robert Peel (q.v.). On 20 January 1843, near Charing Cross, McNaghten mistakenly shot Peel's private secretary, Edward Drummond, who bore a strong resemblance to the prime minister. Drummond died shortly afterwards and at the subsequent trial, McNaghten's acquittal on grounds of insanity gave rise to what became known as the *McNaghten rules*, defining criminal responsibility in such cases.

The McNaghten rules were based on the answers of the judges

to questions put to them by the House of Lords, and under these rules, it was accepted that a criminal pleading insanity through being unaware of doing wrong, or by not knowing that what he was doing was wrong, could be relieved of responsibility for his crime. McNaghten's motives for attempting to assassinate Sir Robert Peel were apparently vague and confused. He was a Scotsman of illegitimate birth and had been employed as a mechanic, among other things. And the various spellings of his name stem from the fact that he was illiterate.

The McNaghten rules were superseded in 1957, in English law, but they had long since been adopted by a number of states in the USA and we still refer to the McNaghten rules in a general sense as a definition of insanity in criminal cases.

294 MAE WEST

Mae West (1892–1980), the American actress, gave her name to a pneumatic life-jacket for airmen, which when inflated resembled a well-developed bust. Miss West's comment on this was: 'I've been in *Who's who* and I know what's what, but it's the first time I ever made the dictionary.'

Mae West was indeed as famous for her witticisms as for her vital statistics; and most of the lines she spoke on the stage or in films were her own. She wrote a number of plays, including the highly successful *Diamond Lil*, and was usually her own director. *Diamond Lil* was filmed in 1933 as *She done him wrong*, with Mae playing her original stage part as 'Lil'.

It was only in the previous year that Mae West had made her debut in films, at the unusually advanced age (for an actress of her kind) of 39. The film was *Night after night*, and she took a line from that film as the title of her autobiography, *Goodness had nothing to do with it*. (These words were her reply to the remark: 'My goodness, those diamonds are lovely!')

But the best-known of all Mae West's sayings must be the ultra-suggestive, 'Come up and see me sometime'. This catchphrase has become almost as much a part of the English language as the *Mae West* itself. Oddly enough, those actual words were never spoken by Mae West in any of her films.

295 MAGINOT LINE   MAGINOT-MINDED

André Maginot (1877–1932) was minister of war in numerous French governments from 1922 to 1931. He advocated and gave his name to a system of fortifications along the eastern frontier of France, extending some 200 miles from Switzerland to Belgium. This was constructed between 1928 and 1934. In the event, the German army invaded France by way of Belgium and the elaborate defences of the *Maginot Line* were rendered impotent.

From this we have the expressions *Maginot-minded* and the *Maginot mentality*, implying a preoccupation with the defensive or an unwillingness to consider alternatives. But the dictionary is possibly unfair to Maginot, who had fought in the First World War and observed the unexpectedly important part played by the old system of forts in the defence of Verdun. Had the Maginot Line been extended in full strength along the Belgian frontier, the events of 1940 might well have taken a different turn.

296 MAGNOLIA
Pierre Magnol (1638–1715) was a French physician and botanist who gave his name to the genus of flowering trees and shrubs, *Magnolia*. Chiefly native to North America and Asia, they are particularly notable for their striking dark-green foliage and large, solitary and fragrant flowers.

Magnol was a professor of botany at Montpellier; and it was the Swedish botanist Linnaeus (q.v.) who honoured his name. The system of classification of living things originated by Linnaeus was, in fact, in some degree anticipated by Magnol with his classifying of plants by families.

297 MALPIGHIAN   MALPIGHIAN LAYER
MALPIGHIAN TUFTS
Marcello Malpighi (1628–94), the Italian physician and anatomist, is regarded as the founder of microscopic anatomy through his use of the microscope in biological studies. His discoveries of the minute structures of the body and his descriptions of the organs and tissues were numerous and *Malpighian* is still applied to several of the body's structures, including the deeper part of the outer layer of the skin, the *Malpighian layer*, and the loops of capillaries in the kidney, the *Malpighian tufts*. He also discovered the corpuscles of the kidney and the spleen.

Malpighi was born near Bologna where he first studied medicine and became a professor, as well as holding professorships at Pisa and Messina. From 1691 he was the chief physician to Pope Innocent XII. His work was in many respects a continuation of that of the English physician, William Harvey, the discoverer of the circulation of the blood.

298 MALTHUSIAN   MALTHUSIANISM

Thomas Robert Malthus (1766–1834) was an English clergyman and economist whose anonymously published *Essay on the principle of population* (in 1798) caused a great deal of controversy among both the progressive and conservative thinkers at the time. The *Malthusian* doctrine argued that population increases faster than the means of subsistence and in turn advocated birth control, as well as anticipating aspects of Darwinism (q.v.) in regard to 'the survival of the fittest'.

Malthusianism, however, was often wrongly misrepresented; and Malthus himself was at great pains to dismiss any ideas that his theories were revolutionary or even original. In private life he was happily married and absorbed in his work as a political economist.

299 MANICHEAN   MANICHEANISM

Manes, or Manichaeus (*circa* AD 216–276) founded and gave his name to a religious sect compounded of Zoroastrianism and Christianity (qq.v.). Manes, a Persian, claimed that he had been sent into the world as God's prophet to banish 'darkness' and restore 'light'. His popularity eventually brought him into conflict with the Zoroastrian priests and he was imprisoned and put to death by crucifixion.

St Augustine, bishop of Hippo, was a *Manichean* before his conversion to Christianity; and the influence of *Manicheanism* continued into the thirteenth century.

300 MANSARD   MANSARD ROOF

Nicolas François Mansard, or Mansart (1598–1666), was a French architect who gave his name to a kind of roof in two sections, with a very steep slope on the lower half, a *mansard* or a *mansard-roof*. The mansard, however, was not the exclusive invention of Francois Mansard (as he is usually known). Some 50 years before he was born, the device had been employed by another French architect, Pierre Lescot, at the Louvre.

Mansard's work is represented in a number of French churches and châteaux, and the Hôtel de la Banque de France, in Paris. His grand-nephew, Jules Hardouin-Mansard, was one of the architects of the Palace of Versailles.

There are variations of the mansard-roof in different parts of the world. In America, for example, the mansard usually slopes up from all four sides of a building.

301 MAOISM

Mao Tse-tung (1893–1976) pioneered and gave his name to the Chinese form of Communism, known as *Maoism*. Maoism has much in common with Leninism (q.v.), in its application of Marxist (q.v.) theories to the special needs of China, while at the same time striving to retain an identity with the original aims of the revolution.

Mao Tse-tung dominated events in China from the outbreak of the revolution until his death in 1976, at the age of 82, though he was never a dictator in the way of Stalin (q.v.). He is particularly remembered for his wise sayings, or 'thoughts', which were deeply revered in China. 'Engage in no battle you are not sure of winning' is a typical example of the Maoist philosophy. And Mao invariably won his battles.

302 MARCONI   MARCONIGRAM
MARCONIGRAPH

Marchese Guglielmo Marconi (1874–1937), the Italian electrical engineer and inventor, is better known for his contributions to wireless telegraphy than those he made to the English language. Nonetheless, we do have the verb *marconi*, 'to communicate by wireless telegraphy', and the noun *marconigram*, 'a message so transmitted', as well as another verb in this connection, *marconigraph*.

Marconi was born of an Italian father and an Irish mother at Bologna, where he made his first successful experiments with wireless telegraphy in 1895. In the following year he went to England to further his experiments, and in 1899 conducted the first international transmission, sending a message from France to England. Then in 1901, Marconi received the first transatlantic radio signals, transmitted from Polhu, in Cornwall, to St John's, in Newfoundland, proving that radio waves could 'bend' around the earth.

Marconi was the first Italian to be awarded the Nobel prize (q.v.) for physics when he shared the 1909 prize with the German physicist Karl Braun.

303 MARIVAUDAGE

Pierre Carlet de Chamblain de Marivaux (1688–1763) was a French playwright and novelist whose subtle though over-affected style of writing has given us the word *Marivaudage* from his name. As well as describing this style, the term is also used as a synonym for a kind of precociousness in a writer.

Marivaux studied law before turning to the theatre with his first play, *L'Amour et la vérité*, in 1720. The writing of his outstanding novel, *La vie de Marianne*, occupied him for some ten years.

304 MARTENOT

Maurice Martenot (1898 – 1980) invented and gave his name to an electronic keyboard instrument, the *martenot*, also known as the *ondes musicales* (musical waves). There had been other electronic musical instruments before the martinot made its appearance (in 1928), but it was one of the first to attract the interest of serious musicians. Martenot, who was himself a musician of considerable repute in his native France, played the solo part in the first public demonstration of his invention, when a *Poème symphonique pour solo d'ondes musicales et orchestre* was performed at a concert in Paris; and two years later he was again the soloist in a performance of the same work played by the Philadelphia Orchestra under Leopold Stokowski.

A number of leading composers wrote music especially for the martenot, including Arthur Honegger, Olivier Messiaen and Darius Milhaud; and the eminent pianist Alfred Cortot wrote the preface to a text book on the instrument, *Méthode d'ondes musicales*, the first instructional publication for an electronic musical instrument.

Although the martenot has lost much of its original impact through recent developments in the field of electronics, it was unique in its day for its wide range of tonal effects and its ability to produce quarter-tones and eighth-tones, not usually obtainable on keyboard instruments. Unlike most keyboard instruments, however, the martenot was unable to produce more than one note at a time.

305 MARTINET

Marquis de Martinet (died 1672) was a French army officer and a commander of Louis XIV's (q.v.) personal regiment. He gave his name to a system of drilling young officers, which he devised and carried out with considerable success. In the broader sense, we use the word *martinet* (with its anglicized pronunciation) for any strict disciplinarian and not necessarily a military person.

Martinet was killed at the siege of Duisburg during the Anglo-French war against the Dutch.

306 MARTINI-HENRY

Frédéric de Martini (1832 – 97), a Hungarian-born Swiss engineer, invented a breech-action for a rifle which, combined with a barrel invented by the American gunsmith B. T. Henry (q.v. under Winchester), was known as the *Martini-Henry*. This rifle was adopted by the British army in 1871.

Martini served in the Austrian army in the war against Italy in 1859 before establishing his factory at Frauenfeld in Switzerland where his rifles were manufactured.

307 MARXISM   MARXIST

Karl Marx (1818 – 1883) could be said to have had a greater influence on social change in the twentieth century than any other one man. His theory of socialism was largely contained in his great work *Das Kapital* completed after his death by his friend and compatriot Friedrich Engels, who had earlier collaborated with Marx in writing *The communist manifesto*. *Marxism* was based on the principle 'from each according to his abilities, to each according to his needs' and the manifesto ended with the now well-known slogan, 'Workers of the world, unite!'

Marx was born in Prussia and educated at the universities of Bonn and Berlin. He became editor of a newspaper in Cologne, *Rheinische Zeitung*, but his radical views led to its suppression by the authorities and Marx was forced to leave the country. He was subsequently expelled from Paris and again from Prussia for his revolutionary and communistic views, before settling in London, where he began writing *Das Kapital* and founded the International Working Men's Association, the first International. Marx died in London and was buried at Highgate cemetery.

It was more than 30 years after the death of Karl Marx that *Marxist* theories were first put to the test – and then not in one of the more advanced countries, as he had predicted, but in 'backward' Russia.

308 MASOCHISM

Leopold von Sacher-Masoch (1836 – 95) gave his name to a form of sexual perversion known as *masochism*. The word was invented by the German neurologist, Baron Richard von Kraft-Ebing, who had studied the short stories and novels of Sacher-Masoch and noted the author's obsession with self-inflicted pain, linked with sexual gratification and domination by the opposite sex.

Sado-masochism refers to a form of masochism connected with the sexual perversion which takes its name from the French novelist and playwright, the Marquis de Sade (q.v.).

309 MASON AND DIXON LINE
Charles Mason (1730–87) and Jeremiah Dixon were English surveyors who were engaged by the proprietors of Maryland and Pennsylvania to survey their respective boundaries in order to settle a dispute of some 80 years. They began their work in 1763, but returned to England after four years with the survey uncompleted because of the activities of American Indians. The boundary, however, came to be known as the *Mason and Dixon Line* (or the *Mason-Dixon Line*) after the two Englishmen; and during the four decades or more up to the Civil War it was referred to in a general way (though largely inaccurately) as the dividing line between the 'free' North and the Southern 'slave' states.

Mason was an astronomer at Greenwich Observatory and with Dixon had observed the transit of Venus at the Cape of Good Hope in 1761. Little more is known of Dixon, despite the familiarity of his name through the famous 'Line'.

310 MAUSER
Peter Paul Mauser (1838–1914) was the inventor of the *Mauser magazine rifle*, the first practical rifle capable of firing a number of shots without being reloaded.

Mauser and his elder brother, Wilhelm, had earlier produced a successful needle-gun (a gun in which the cartridge is exploded on being struck by a spike, or a needle) and a breech-loading gun which was adopted by the Prussian army in 1871, the *Mauser model 1871*. There are many other kinds of firearms bearing the name of Mauser, which has come to be one of the best known in the manufacture of guns.

311 MAUSOLEUM
Mausolus was a king of Caria, in Asia Minor, who died about 353 BC. His widow, Artemisia, who was also his sister, ordered a tomb of great splendour to be erected in his memory, at the city of Halicarnassus (now Bodrum in Turkey), and this was named after him as the *Mausoleum*. The word has subsequently come to be used for any such magnificent tomb.

The Mausoleum became one of the seven wonders of the ancient world, but Halicarnassus was destroyed by Alexander the Great in 334 BC. Some remains of the sepulchre of Mausolus have been acquired by the British Museum.

312 MAVERICK

Samuel Augustus Maverick (1803 – 70) was one of the leaders in the fight for Texan independence, and like his famous contemporary, James Bowie (q.v.), he is mostly remembered today through giving his name to a word in the English language. Maverick was the owner of a large cattle ranch, but he neglected to brand his cattle, which led to many of them being stolen. From this, the word *maverick* came into being, to describe a stray animal or anyone with no particular attachment to a place or a group of people. And *to maverick* is to acquire something illegally.

313 MAXIM-GUN

Sir Hiram Stevens Maxim (1840 – 1916) invented and gave his name to the first fully automatic machine-gun, the *Maxim-gun*. Unlike the earlier hand-cranked machine-guns, such as the Gatling (q.v.), the Maxim utilized the force of the gun's 'kick', or recoil, to keep it firing. In other words, all the while the trigger was depressed, the Maxim would continue to fire until its belt of ammunition was expended.

Hiram Maxim was born in America, but in 1881, he emigrated to England and became a naturalized British subject. He was persuaded to apply his engineering skills (he had been the chief engineer of the United States Electric Lighting Co.) to producing a fully automatic machine-gun; and in 1884, the first Maxim was successfully demonstrated. Not unnaturally, other automatic machine-guns soon made their appearance; Vickers (in Britain) and Krupps (in Germany) produced guns based on the Maxim, though most of the new inventions came from America – the Browning, the Lewis, the Hotchkiss, and much later (after the First World War) the Thompson submachine-gun (qq.v.).

It was not until the First World War, in fact, that all but the most bigoted of military men were finally convinced that a modern army without machine-guns was doomed to defeat. The value of the machine-gun in defending a small body of men against an attacking force, vastly superior in numbers, had already been clearly demonstrated in Africa, where on many occasions the unsophisticated weapons of the native population were proved to be no match against the rapid fire of the Gatlings and (later) the Maxim-guns of the colonialists. But the onesidedness of this kind of warfare was neatly summed up by the poet Hilaire Belloc:

> Whatever happens, we have got
> The Maxim Gun, and they have not.

In 1914, *both* sides had the Maxim or its equivalent. And over the next four years it became horribly clear that the machine-gun was not just another new weapon, but a weapon which made nonsense of the existing conception of warfare. Yet the lessons were learned slowly – and at an appalling cost in human life and suffering. In battle after battle, soldiers were sent 'over the top' in their thousands, almost inevitably to be mown down by the deadly automatic fire. It has been estimated that machine-guns accounted for more than two-thirds of the casualties of the First World War; and in one day alone – on 1 July 1916, the first day of the battle of the Somme – over 21,000 men were killed and thousands more wounded, mostly by fire from the now ruthlessly efficient machine-guns.

314 MAXWELL

James Clerk Maxwell (1831–79) gave his name to the *cgs* (centimetre-gramme-second) unit of magnetic flux, the *maxwell*.

Maxwell (his name is also given as Clerk-Maxwell) was born in Edinburgh and displayed a remarkable aptitude for science at an early age, and wrote his first scientific paper at 15. He was professor of physics at Aberdeen and then London; and in 1871, became the first professor of experimental physics at Cambridge, where the famous Cavendish laboratory (named after the scientist Henry Cavendish) was built under his supervision.

Maxwell's theory of electromagnetism formed the basis for the discoveries of Hertz (q.v.).

315 MAZARINADE   MAZARIN BIBLE
MAZARIN HOOD

Jules Mazarin (1602–61) is remembered in the history of France as the highly influential head of state during the first 18 years of the reign of Louis XIV (q.v.), at which time he was virtually the ruler of France. Born in Italy of Sicilian parents, Mazarin went to France with a papal legate and was papal nuncio there (1634–36) becoming a naturalized Frenchman in 1639 and a cardinal two years later. He had gained the favour of Richelieu (q.v. under éminence grise) and succeeded him as prime minister, as well as becoming a favourite of Anne of Austria, the queen-regent; and despite many set-backs he was still in power at the time of his death.

Eponymously, Mazarin is best remembered for giving his name to the *Mazarin Bible*, the first printed bible and one of the first books of importance to be printed with movable type. This was also known as the *Gutenberg Bible*, from the German printer Johann Gutenberg who invented the movable type and probably produced the Mazarin Bible. Mazarin, however, gives it his name since the first known copies of the book were discovered in his library in Paris, the famous *Bibliothèque Mazarine*, which Mazarin founded in 1642.

The *mazarinade* was a pamphlet produced in opposition to the various measures instigated by Mazarin which brought about the formation of the Fronde (meaning 'sling' – and the Paris mob did indeed sling stones at the Cardinal's residence); but this was by no means a class struggle and there was factional fighting among the French nobles seeking to overthrow Mazarin.

The *mazarin hood* is one said to have been worn by the Duchesse de Mazarin.

316 MEKHITARIST

Peter Mekhitar (1676–1749) was an Armenian monk and the founder of a Roman Catholic congregation at Constantinople in 1701. The members of his community were known as *Mekhitarists* (or *Mechitharists*); and as Uniates, acknowledged the supremacy of the pope while retaining their own rights in regard to languages and liturgy. Mekhitar sought change by introducing western culture to the Armenian people.

In 1702, Mekhitar became abbot of a monastery in Southern Greece which in 1717 was transferred to the island of San Lazzaro, near Venice. It was noted for its printing of an Armenian translation of the Bible and various Armenian classics.

317 MENDELEVIUM

Dmitri Ivanovich Mendeleev, or Mendeleyev (1834–1907), gives his name to the element of atomic number 101, *Mendelevium*.

Mendeleev was born in Siberia and educated at St Petersburg (now Leningrad) where he studied chemistry. He inaugurated a system of classification of chemical elements, and element 101 was produced and named after him in 1955.

318 MENDELISM   MENDEL'S LAW
Gregor Johann Mendel (1822–84) was an Austrian monk who originated a theory of heredity, named after him as *Mendel's law*, or the *Mendelian principles of heredity*.

Mendel entered the Augustinian monastery at Brno, in Czechoslovakia, in 1843, and eventually became the abbot. He devoted a great deal of his time to the study of inheritance, and his experiments with common peas in the monastery garden led to the discovery of a definite pattern of hereditary characteristics. Mendel's law was discovered and published in 1865, but *Mendelism* was not generally accepted until the turn of the century.

319 MENIERE'S DISEASE
Prosper Menière (1799 – 1862) described and gave his name to an affection of the inner ear, *Menière's disease* or *Menière's syndrome*. This is characterized by sudden attacks of deafness, or obliterating noises in the ear, causing the patient to lose his balance and possibly to vomit.

Menière was the director of the Paris Institution for Deaf-Mutes when he presented his paper to the medical world, but he was already a sick man and died within a few months from influenzal pneumonia. Apart from being one of the leading physicians of his day and a specialist in otology, he had been a brilliant scholar and enjoyed the company of literary men such as Honoré de Balzac and Victor Hugo.

320 MENIPPEAN
Menippus was a Greek philosopher and satirist of the third century BC whose cynical and often bitter commentaries on the foibles of his fellow-men (and not least other philosophers of his time) made his name synonymous with a particularly sarcastic form of satirical writing. Another Greek satirist, Lucian, described him as 'the greatest snarler and snapper of all the dogs'; and the Roman scholar Marcus Terentius Varro acknowledged his name in his medley of prose and verse, the *Saturae Menippeae*. It was in imitation of this work that a French political satire was published in 1594, *Satyre Ménippée*, directed against the Catholic League. *Menippean* is generally used today to describe a bitter satire in imitation or in the manner of Menippus.

321 MERCALLI SCALE

Giuseppe Mercalli (1850–1914) was an Italian priest whose study of geology led him to an investigation of seismology. This resulted in his devising a scale for measuring the intensity of earthquake shocks, named after him as the *Mercalli scale*. This scale graded the degree of the shocks from 1 (weak) to 12 (catastrophic) and could be said to have anticipated the more sophisticated Richter scale (q.v.).

322 MERCATOR'S PROJECTION

Gerhard Kremer (1512–94) was the Flemish geographer better known as Gerardus Mercator, the latinized form of his name (Kremer meaning shopkeeper or merchant). He was one of the pioneers of modern cartography and devised a map with the meridians of longitude at right angles to the parallels of latitude, known after him as *Mercator's projection*.

Navigation was much simplified by Mercator's device, which was first used by him on a map dated 1568.

323 MESMERISM   MESMERIZE

Friedrich Anton, or Franz, Mesmer (1734–1815) gave his name to a kind of hypnotism, *mesmerism*. The *mesmerist* was supposed to possess some special power (animal magnetism) which could be used to cure disease.

Mesmer was born in Austria and studied medicine at Vienna. He moved to Paris in 1778 and attracted considerable attention with his theory of animal magnetism and his claims of having effected miraculous cures by this means; but in spite of some success, he was eventually exposed as a charlatan. Nonetheless, Mesmer's experiments aroused continued interest among medical men; and in 1843, a Scottish surgeon, Dr James Braid (q.v.), came to coin the word *hypnotism* in attempting to explain Mesmer's power's as a mesmerist.

324 METHUSELAH

Methuselah is remembered for his exceptionally long life and is the oldest man named in the Bible ('And all the days of Methuselah were nine hundred sixty and nine years: and he died' Genesis 5:27). His name consequently is used to describe any very old person. A very large wine bottle of some six quarts is also called a *Methuselah*.

325 METONIC CYCLE

Meton, an Athenian astronomer of the fifth century BC, calculated and gave his name to a cycle of 19 solar years, the *Metonic cycle*. It was in 433 BC that Meton made his discovery that, after a period of 19 years, the moon's phases fall on exactly the same day of the year. Meton's calculations were used as the basis of the Greek calendar and still serve for the placing of movable feast days.

Meton's cycle was 'corrected' by another Greek astronomer a century later (q.v. under Callippic period).

326 MILLERITE

William Miller (1782–1849) was the leader of an American religious sect whose followers were known as *Millerites*. Miller earned his living as a farmer before devoting himself to writing and preaching on the second coming of Christ, which he predicted would occur in 1843 or 1844.

In 1860, the Millerites changed their name to the Seventh-Day Adventists and today the membership of the sect totals more than a million. The Adventists observe Saturday as the Sabbath and practise strict abstinence from alcohol and tobacco.

Another William Miller, the English mineralogist William Hallowes Miller (1801–80), gives his name to the nickel sulphide *millerite*.

327 MILLS BOMB

Sir William Mills (1856–1932) invented and gave his name to the *Mills hand-grenade*, also known as the *Mills bomb*. Mills' invention appeared in the first year of the First World War and was used by the Allied armies with great success throughout the war, several millions of Mills bombs being manufactured.

Mills was a prolific inventor and a pioneer in research on alloys. He was also a manufacturer and his aluminium foundry was the first in the UK, while his Mills Munitions Co. produced the hand-grenade and other war munitions. There had been grenades of sorts since the seventeenth century, but the Mills bomb marked a significant stage in the development of the weapon, both in design and reliability.

328 MINIÉ

Claude Étienne Minié (1814–79) was the inventor of a conical lead bullet, as well as a rifle which was uniquely adapted to accommodate the special nature of his bullet. Both bullet and rifle were known after their inventor as *Minié*. Minié's bullet expanded to take the rifling and was highly advanced in the field of firearms at the time.

Minié joined the French army as a private and eventually rose to the rank of colonel. He made improvements to a number of firearms as well as inventing the Minié.

329 MITHRIDATE

Mithridates VI Eupator, or Mithridates (*circa* 132–63 BC), was King of Pontus, in Asia Minor, and was known as Mithridates the Great from his successes in three wars against the Romans, the *Mithridatic Wars*. He is also remembered for his apparent habit of taking regular small doses of poison as antidotes, which has given us the word *mithridate*, an antidote to poison. More specifically, mithridate was a paste made from honey or syrup and mixed with numerous small amounts of poisons of various kinds.

In the third Mithridatic War, Mithridates was finally defeated by Pompey and forced into exile in the Crimea, where he committed suicide – but not by poisoning himself.

There are two kinds of field cress named from Mithridates, *mithridate mustard* and *mithridate pepperwort*.

330 MÖBIUS STRIP

August Ferdinand Möbius (1790–1868) was a German mathematician and astronomer. He was particularly noted for his work on analytical geometry and theoretical astronomy; but he is remembered eponymously for the *Möbius strip*, a one-sided surface formed by the joining of the two ends of a long rectangular strip, after giving a half-twist to one end.

331 MOHAMMEDANISM

Mohammed, or Mahomet (*circa* AD 570–632), founded and gave his name to *Mohammedism* (also spelt *Mohammedanism*), or Islam, the Moslem religion. The sacred book of Islam, the Koran, is probably the most influential book in the world, next to the Bible.

The story behind the well known saying, 'If the mountain will not come to Mahomet, Mahomet must go to the mountain', has been told and is interpreted in various ways. Here is Francis Bacon's version in his essay *Of boldnesse*: 'Mahomet made the People beleeve that he would call an hill to him; And from the

Top of it, offer up his Praiers, for the Observers of his Law. The People assembled; Mahomet cald the Hill to come to him, againe, and againe; And when the Hill stood still, he was never a whit abashed, but said: "If the Hill will not come to Mahomet, Mahomet will go to the hil'''.

332 MOHS' SCALE
Friedrich Mohs (1773–1839) was a German mineralogist who defined and gave his name to a scale of hardness, *Mohs' scale*. This lists the degree of resistance of a mineral to abrasion or scratching and begins with the softest: (i) talc; (ii) gypsum; (iii) calcite; (iv) fluorite; (v) apatite; (vi) orthoclase; (vii) quartz; (viii) topaz; (ix) sapphire (or corundum); and (x) diamond.

Mohs held professorships at Graz, Freiburg and Vienna and wrote a number of books on mineralogy, in particular his three volume *Treatise on mineralogy*. And 150 years after his death, Mohs' scale of hardness is still in common use.

333 MOLINISM   QUIETISM
Luis Molina (1535–1600) was a Spanish Jesuit and theologian whose teaching concerning predestination and free will (named after him as *Molinism*) was the cause of a great theological controversy, which was to continue long after his death. One of the leading opponents of Molinism was the Dutch theologian Cornelis Jansen (q.v.). Miguel de Molinos (1640?–1696?) was a Spanish priest and the originator of *quietism*, or passive contemplation, also known as *Molinism*. The Molinism which takes its name from the Spanish Jesuit Molina (q.v. above) is unconnected with the later Molinism (or quietism) of Miguel de Molinos, which caused its originator to be condemned by the Inquisition.

334 MOLOTOV COCKTAIL
Vyacheslav Mikhailovich Molotov (1890–1986) was, for more than 20 years, one of the most influential men in the USSR. As a young man, he took an active part in the Russian revolution and was a friend of Lenin (q.v.). More importantly, perhaps, he became a close associate of Lenin's successor, Joseph Stalin (q.v.), who in 1939, appointed him as commissar for foreign affairs. From that time, Molotov was virtually Stalin's right-hand man, figuring prominently in all the negotiations with the leading powers

throughout the Second World War and then in the 'cold war' period which followed. It was during the often bitter international debates of these post-war years that Mr Molotov came to be known as 'Mr Niet' ('Mr No'), from his constant and uncompromising use of the veto.

With the death of Stalin in 1953, Molotov's influence began to wane. And though he avoided the fate of Beria (the former head of the secret police was executed for treason in December, 1953), it was clear that his active life in politics was at an end when he was made ambassador to Outer Mongolia; and in 1964 he was expelled from the Communist Party.

Molotov's reputation was one of a hard, ruthless man ('Molotov', in fact, means 'the hammer'), and the Finns expressed their dislike of him by giving his name to the *Molotov cocktail*. The 'cocktail', of course, is a kind of home-made hand-grenade, consisting of a bottle of inflammable liquid with a slow-burning fuse. It was first used by the Finns against Russian tanks, in 1940.

Molotov's original surname was 'Scriabin' (many of the Russian revolutionaries changed their names before 1917 to avoid detection by the imperial police) and the composer Alexander Scriabin (1872–1915) was an uncle of his. It seems doubtful, however, that the 'Scriabin cocktail' could have retained its name in the same way as the Molotov cocktail.

335 MONROE DOCTRINE   MONROEISM

James Monroe (1758–1831) was the fifth President of the USA and held office from 1817 to 1825. He is particularly remembered for his message to the United States Congress on 2 December 1823, in which he warned the European powers against any interference in the affairs of the American continent. The *Monroe doctrine* (as it has come to be called) was based on this proclamation and also implied that the 'New World' would avoid involvement with the political disputes of the 'Old-World'.

In 1823, however, America was ill-equipped to enforce Monroe's doctrine; but as the US grew into an effective military power, *Monroeism* played an increasingly important part in its foreign policy. In the two World Wars, for example, it could be said that Monroeism delayed the participation of the United States.

James Monroe is also remembered (by collectors of curiosities) for the fact that he was the third US president to die on 4 July, American Independence Day; the other two being John Adams and Thomas Jefferson, the second and third US presidents, who *both* died on 4 July 1826.

The capital of Liberia, Monrovia, takes its name from James Monroe, who was US president when this first Black African State was founded (of liberated slaves) in 1821.

336 MONTESSORI METHOD
Maria Montessori (1870 – 1952) originated a method of education for children, with the emphasis on the pupils' freedom of choice, and named after her as the *Montessori method*.

She studied medicine and philosophy at the University of Rome, and became the first woman in Italy to receive the degree of Doctor of Medicine. The Montessori method was developed through her interest in the care and training of mentally deficient children, and, in 1907, the first Montessori school was opened in the slums of Rome. Dr Montessori's teaching method encouraged the individual child to react spontaneously to school activities, with the teacher playing the part of a leader as distinct from the traditional instructor. And, like the earlier Froebel system (q.v.), the Montessori method has had a considerable influence on present-day education of children.

337 MONTEZUMA'S REVENGE
Montezuma II (1466? – 1520) was the last Aztec ruler of Mexico. At the time of the Spanish conquest of Mexico, he was captured and held hostage by the Spanish *conquistador* Hernando Cortes; and when the Aztecs rose against the Spaniards, Montezuma was mortally wounded as he attempted to intervene.

The historian Macaulay insisted that: 'Every schoolboy knows who imprisoned Montezuma.' And while it is doubtful whether the average traveller to Mexico at the present time is certain to know what happened to the unfortunate chief of the Aztecs, the vast majority of tourists will almost certainly know about *Montezuma's revenge*. This is the proverbial name for the intestinal disorder causing diarrhoea and other unpleasantness, which afflicts most Europeans who visit Mexico.

Montezuma's revenge (or the *Aztec Two-step* as it is also known) is relatively short-lived, however, lasting little more than three days.

338 MOONIES
Sun Myung Moon (1920 –   ) is the founder of the so-called Unification Church, whose members have come to be known as

Moonies. The activities of the Moonies have attracted much adverse publicity in recent years, particularly regarding alleged brainwashing of recruits to the church, as well as Moon's methods of fund-raising. Young English-speaking students have been especially vulnerable as potential converts.

'The Reverend' Moon emigrated to America from his native Korea after the Korean War, becoming a successful businessman. His declared anti-communism derives from his experiences in the Korean War.

339 MORISONIAN
James Morison (1816–93) was a Scottish minister of the United Secession Church until his expulsion with three other ministers for their views opposing Calvinism (q.v.). They formed the Evangelical Union and their members were called *Morisonians*, while *Morisonianism* refers to the principles of the denomination, affirming man's freedom to accept or reject salvation from God.

Three years after Morison's death, the Evangelical Union was united with the Congregational Union of Scotland, though Morisonians observed a degree of independence.

340 MORRISON SHELTER
Herbert Stanley Morrison, Baron Morrison of Lambeth (1888–1965), is particularly remembered as the Home Secretary in Churchill's wartime government. It was at this time that he introduced and gave his name to an air-raid shelter. The *Morrison shelter* was an indoor air-raid shelter, designed to serve as a table during the 'all clear' periods, but it provided shelter for only two or three people, whereas the Anderson shelter (q.v.) could accommodate the average family.

Apart from the Morrison shelter, Herbert Morrison as Home Secretary added a number of morale-boosting slogans to the common language of the day, such as 'Go to it' and 'Up housewives and at 'em'. This last one was actually used as the title of a popular song of the time. But don't forget there was a war on, as they used to say.

341 MORSE CODE
Samuel Finley Breese Morse (1791–1872) would probably be remembered as a painter, had he not invented the famous dot-and-dash code named after him. Born in Charlestown, Mass-

achusetts, he came to London as a young man and exhibited at the Royal Academy; and returning to America he established himself as a quite successful portrait painter.

In 1826 he founded and became the first president of the National Academy of Design; but after a few years, his interest in the electric telegraph led him away from painting, and in 1838 the first message by 'Morse' telegraph was successfully transmitted. Morse was subsequently involved in a great deal of litigation, but was eventually successful in obtaining the rights to his invention.

During the Second World War, the *Morse code* sign for the letter V (... −) was adopted by the BBC as a motif signifying 'V for Victory', or the equivalent in sound of Winston Churchill's famous V-sign. This was also identified with the opening bars of the Fifth Symphony of Ludwig van Beethoven − who, of course, was a German, though an opponent of despotism.

342 MORTON'S FORK
John Morton (1420? − 1500) was Archbishop of Canterbury from 1486 and Henry VII's chancellor; and it was in that capacity that he was required to obtain benevolences, or to force contributions, from merchants or other seeming men of means. Morton's argument to those attempting to escape payment was two-pronged, hence *Morton's fork*: an obviously wealthy man could clearly afford to contribute; while someone living frugally was assumed to have made considerably rewarding economies.

Before becoming Archbishop of Canterbury, Morton's career was somewhat chequered. He was on the side of Henry VI for the greater part of the Wars of the Roses, but after the battle of Tewkesbury in 1471 he made his submission to Edward IV. Subsequently imprisoned by Edward's brother Richard III, he escaped and joined Henry VII. He became a cardinal in 1493.

343 MOSAIC LAW   MOSES BASKET   MOSES' ROD
Moses is believed to have lived probably in about the thirteenth century BC. He was anciently regarded as the author of the first five books of the Old Testament (the Pentateuch), containing the law of the Jews given by him at Mount Sinai and known as the *Mosaic Law*.

The *Moses basket* (an old name for the 'carry-cot') is derived from the story of Moses in the bulrushes ('And when she could not longer hide him, she took for him an ark of bulrushes, and daubed it with slime and with pitch, and put the child therein; and she laid it in the flags by the river's brink' Exodus 2:3). And *Moses' rod* is a divining rod ('. . . and thou shalt smite the rock, and there shall come water out of it, that the people may drink' Exodus 17:6) or a magic wand ('Take thy rod, and cast it before Pharoah, and it shall become a serpent' Exodus 7:9).

The *Moses boat*, however, has no direct connection with the prophet Moses. This takes its name from one Moses Lowell, a renowned eighteenth-century boat-builder of Salisbury, Massachusetts.

344 MOSSBAUER EFFECT

Rudolf Ludwig Mossbauer (1929–) is the German-born physicist who discovered a method of producing and measuring gamma rays, named after him as the *Mossbauer effect*. His researches verified Einstein's theory (q.v.) and have been used as a tool for studying various scientific phenomena such as the nature of magnetism and the Doppler effect (q.v.).

Mossbauer was the joint recipient of the Nobel prize (q.v.) for physics in 1961 for his discovery of the Mossbauer effect.

345 MUGGLETONIAN

Lodowicke Muggleton (1609–98), and his cousin, John Reeve (1608–58), were the founders of the English religious sect known as the *Muggletonians*. They saw themselves as the two witnesses of Revelation 11:3 ('And I will give power unto my two witnesses, and they shall prophesy a thousand two hundred and threescore days, clothed in sackcloth'), and believed that Muggleton represented Aaron and Reeve Moses (qq.v.).

Both men earned a living as journeymen tailors in and around London. The sect was founded about 1651; and 'the prophets' (as they were known by their followers) soon came into conflict with leaders of the established churches, who condemned their publications as blasphemous. They suffered imprisonment and Muggleton was pilloried; but the Muggletonians (or 'the believers in the third commission of the spirit', as they preferred to be called) continued to thrive for some 200 years.

346 MULREADY ENVELOPE

William Mulready (1786–1863), the Irish-born painter and illustrator, was a well-known portrayer of scenes of everyday life, but he is best remembered for his ornamental design of Sir Rowland Hill's penny postage envelope, issued in 1840 and named from the artist as the *Mulready envelope*. Mulready's design, depicting Britannia and other allegorical figures, was received with much hostility and sarcasm from his contemporaries, notably the *Punch* cartoonist John Leech whose reputation was largely established with his caricature of the *Mulready*.

From a collector's point of view, however, the envelopes are highly prized items, since they were withdrawn from circulation within a year and millions of unused copies were destroyed. The Mulready envelope was in fact the first prepaid envelope issued in Great Britain for public usage and coincided with the issue of the first Penny Black and Twopenny Blue adhesive postage stamps.

N

347 NANSEN PASSPORT

Fridtjof Nansen (1861 – 1930), was a Norwegian arctic explorer and zoologist who led a number of expeditions into the arctic regions, including the first east to west crossing of Greenland. He is remembered eponymously, however, for his work as a statesman and humanitarian; and it was in this connection that he was awarded the Nobel peace prize (q.v.) in 1922 for relief work for Russian, Armenian and Greek refugees.

Nansen was prominent in the negotations concerning the separation of Norway and Sweden. He was the first Norwegian ambassador to Great Britain, and as the League of Nations high commissioner for refugees after the First World War he gave his name to the passport issued to stateless people, the *Nansen passport*.

348 NAPIERIAN   NAPIER'S BONES

John Napier, or Neper (1550 – 1617), invented and gave his name to a mechanical calculating device. The oddly named *Napier's bones* are in fact square rods made from wood or bone (hence the name), with numerical tables on the four sides, which placed in parallel, will facilitate the tasks of multiplication and division. Napier's invention was in effect the first calculating machine.

Napier was the laird of Merchiston, near Edinburgh, and was one of the leading inventors and mathematicians of his day. His achievements covered a wide field and included the invention of a hydraulic screw for pumping out coal-mines, a design for a prototype of the modern tank (q.v. under 'Big Willie') and the invention of the modern notation of decimal fractions. The word *Napierian*, or *Naperian*, is used to describe his system of logarithms, which he devised in 1614, the year before the invention of his 'bones'.

349 NAPOLEON   NAP   NAPOLEONITE

Napoleon I, Napoleon Bonaparte, or Napoleone Buonaparte, also known as 'le Petit Caporal' (the Little Corporal), 'The Corsican', etc. (1769 – 1821), never managed to get to England as he had intended, but he certainly did get into the English language.

There are at least four words named after Napoleon, against

141

only two for the man who is credited with finally defeating him in battle, the Duke of Wellington (q.v.). Yet it is doubtful whether the average Englishman of today would be familiar with the 20 franc gold coin called a *napoleon*, or a rich iced cake of that name; let alone a kind of rock, *napoleonite*, found in Corsica, where Napoleon was born. The card game of *napoleon* – usually abbreviated to *nap* – is, however, still played in many English homes and pubs.

Nap is a modified version of the American game of Euchre. Each player is dealt five cards and plays for himself; and the word 'napoleon' is used for a bid against *nap*, which is a bid for the maximum five tricks.

350 NELSON'S BLOOD
Horatio Nelson, Viscount Nelson (1758 – 1805), was killed at the battle of Trafalgar at his moment of victory – as every schoolchild knows. It is perhaps less well known that Nelson's body was preserved in rum for its journey back to England and eventual burial in St Paul's Cathedral; and that rum has since come to be known as *Nelson's blood*.

Nelson's name is also remembered in connection with the number *one-hundred-and-eleven* (known as *Nelson*), which is variously interpreted as 'one pound, one shilling, one penny', or 'One eye, one arm, one arse', etc. It is considered an unlucky score in the game of cricket.

The wrestling holds, the nelson and the half-nelson, are not apparently named from Lord Nelson.

351 NEWTON
Sir Isaac Newton (1642 – 1727) gave his name to the unit of force, the *newton*. He is remembered by most people, of course, as the man who saw an apple fall in the garden and then proceeded to formulate his famous law of gravitation on the spot, so to speak. No less a person than the French philosopher and writer, Voltaire, is said to have authenticated the story; and, certainly, there is an apple named after Newton.

Isaac Newton was born in Lincolnshire and studied at Trinity College, Cambridge. He was acknowledged as one of the great men of science in a great scientific age, and became president of the Royal Society in 1703. He was buried in Westminster Abbey, and there is a statue of him in the chapel of his old college, which is especially celebrated for Wordsworth's reference to it in his poem *The prelude*:

The marble index of a mind for ever
Voyaging through strange seas of Thought alone.

Another poet, Coleridge, saw Newton in a different light. He believed that 'the souls of five hundred Sir Isaac Newtons would go to the making up of a Shakespeare or a Milton.' And, to himself, the humble Newton seemed to have been '... only a boy playing on the sea-shore, and diverting myself in now and then finding a smoother pebble or a prettier shell than ordinary, whilst the great ocean of truth lay all undiscovered before me'.

352 NICOTINE   NICOTIANA

Jean Nicot (1530? – 1600) could be said to have done for the French what Sir Walter Raleigh was to do for the English a few years afterwards. He introduced tobacco into France after sampling its effects in Portugal, where he was the French ambassador from 1559 – 1561. The newly discovered plant was subsequently named after him as *Nicotiana*, from which we have the word *nicotine*.

Raleigh, on the other hand, received small thanks for his efforts. And his fall from grace when James I (q.v.) became king, in 1603, was perhaps not entirely unconnected with his association with the 'weed'. James, of course, hated tobacco with such a pathological intensity that he was hardly on the throne before he felt compelled to put his feelings on paper with *A counterblast to tobacco*, in which he refers to smoking it as, 'A custom loathsome to the eye, hateful to the nose, harmful to the brain, dangerous to the lungs, and in the black, stinking fume thereof, nearest resembling the horrible Stygian smoke of the pit that is bottomless'. The first of the Stuarts, in fact, could have been the spiritual founder of ASH (Action on Smoking and Health).

Apart from having his name honoured as part of the language, the Frenchman Nicot also came to the end of his life in a more natural way than his unfortunate English counterpart. Nicot was born, incidentally, in Nîmes, in Southern France, the place that gave the name to 'denim' – the cloth 'de' (of) 'Nîmes'.

353 NIETZSCHEAN   NIETZSCHEANISM

Friedrich Wilhelm Nietzsche (1844 – 1900) was the German philosopher and poet who invented the *superman* or *overman* (*Übermensch*), the embodiment of perfection in humankind who dominates all lesser mortals with ruthless efficiency and shows no pity or weakness. Nietzsche's philosophy, or *Nietzscheanism*, undoubtedly influenced the thinking of the German National Socialists in the 1920s, and led to the rise of Hitler and the Nazis.

As a young man, Nietzsche was influenced by the German philosopher, Schopenhauer, and the composer Richard Wagner (q.v.), but he came to reject their views and made a bitter attack on Wagner, who had once been a close associate of Nietzsche. *Also sprach Zarathustra* (*Thus spake Zarathustra*) is probably Nietzsche's best known work and contains his gospel of the superman, though he wrote extensively on a number of subjects.

Nietzsche was virtually insane for the last 11 years of his life and was nursed by his mother and his sister, Elisabeth Forster-Nietzsche, who was to write a biography of her brother.

354 NIGHTINGALE

Florence Nightingale (1820–1910) is remembered as *the Lady with the Lamp*, from her pioneering work in nursing in the Crimean War. She is undoubtedly less well remembered for having given her name to a flannel scarf with sleeves, designed for the benefit of invalids sitting up in bed, known as a *nightingale*. The name of Nightingale, however, in inevitably linked with those of Cardigan and Raglan (qq.v.) in connection with the Crimean War, and remarkably all three names have been given to articles of clothing; while even the Balaclava helmet takes its name from the place of the famous battle of the Crimean War.

Florence Nightingale was given her first name from the Italian city of Florence, where she was born.

355 NIMROD

Nimrod was an early king of Assyria or Babylonia, a great-grandson of Noah and a son of Cush, and 'a mighty hunter before the Lord' (Genesis 10:9). His name has been used to describe any great hunter; and *Nimrod* was the pseudonym adopted by the British sporting writer Charles James Apperley (1777?–1843), who was also a devotee of hunting.

In the world of music, *Nimrod* is well known as one of the famous *Enigma variations* composed by Sir Edward Elgar. The name was used to conceal the identity of one of his friends, A. J. Jaeger, in one of 14 musical portraits. *Nimrod* was also the name given (in acknowledgment of the 'mighty hunter') to a marine patrol aircraft, which first came into service with the British Royal Air Force in 1969 as an anti-submarine 'hunter' of the Strike Command of the RAF.

356 NISSEN HUT

Peter Norman Nissen (1871–1930) invented and gave his name to the *Nissen*, or *Nissen hut*, a semi-cylindrical construction of corrugated iron on a foundation of cement. The Nissen was first used on the Western Front, in the First World War, as a temporary shelter for troops and equipment.

Nissen was a Canadian who joined the British army and served in the First World War. He rose to the rank of lieutenant-colonel in the Royal Engineers. The Second World War Anderson shelter (q.v.) incorporated certain features of the Nissen, with its use of corrugated metal and the curved roof.

357 NITHSDALE

Winifred Herbert, Countess of Nithsdale (*circa* 1679–1749), was a daughter of William Herbert, first Marquis of Powis, head of the Roman Catholic aristocracy in England and a leading Jacobite (q.v.) who went into exile with James II. Lady Winifred married William Maxwell in 1699, in the same year that he succeeded his father as the fifth Earl of Nithsdale. In 1715 Nithsdale joined the Jacobites and took part in the rising of that year, being taken prisoner and sentenced to death for treason. And it was on the night before the day fixed for her husband's execution (23 February 1716) that the countess became famous through effecting his escape from the Tower of London by exchanging clothes with him.

The Countess of Nithsdale is remembered eponymously from a particular item of her clothing: a riding-hood of a kind which was in vogue during the eighteenth century. She was presumably wearing such a hood, subsequently named after her as a *Nithsdale*, when she went to visit her husband for the 'last' time. In the event, they both escaped to Rome where they lived together until the death of the earl in 1744.

358 NOBELIUM   NOBEL PRIZE

Alfred Bernhard Nobel (1833–96) gives his name to the element of atomic number 102, named in his honour as *nobelium*, and the prestigious *Nobel prize*.

Nobel, a Swede, first achieved universal fame with his discovery of dynamite, in 1866; and the vast fortune he amassed from the manufacture of explosives and oil interests went towards the funding of the Nobel prizes. The first of these annual awards was made in 1901, with prizes for physics, chemistry, physiology and medicine, literature, and peace, the respective recipients being Röntgen (q.v.), van't Hoff, Behring, Sully Prudhomme, and (jointly) Dunant and Passy. In 1969, a further prize was introduced, for economics, with the award being made jointly to the Dutchman Tinbergen and Frisch, a Norwegian.

In accordance with Nobel's will, the prizes are adjudged by three Swedish learned societies and five members of the Norwegian Parliament. There has more than once been a great deal of controversy concerning the awards, especially when international politics have been involved. It is in fact the great prestige of receiving the Nobel prize, rather than its monetary value (considerable though this is), which has bestowed it with such eminence. The scientist Marie Curie (q.v.) was the first Nobel prizewinner to win two prizes, as well as being the first woman to be honoured. She is also one of many prizewinners to be honoured through the eponym, of course.

Nobelium was first produced in 1957 at the Nobel Institute, in Stockholm, the birthplace of Alfred Nobel.

359 NORBERTINE

Saint Norbert (1085? – 1134) founded an order of canons named after him as *Norbertines*, or the Premonstratensians. The site of the first habitation of the order, at Prémontré, in the diocese of Laon in France, is said to have been pointed out to St Norbert in a vision (*Pré montré* meaning 'the meadow pointed out') and the order was devoted to penitence and preaching.

There were some 35 monasteries of the Norbertine order in England before the dissolution of the monasteries by Henry VIII and its members were known as White Canons.

360 NOSTRADAMUS   NOSTRADAMIC

Michel de Notredame, or Nostredame, known as Nostradamus (1503 – 66), was an astrologer who achieved considerable fame in his day, through his prophecies, which he published in annual *Almanacks* and a book entitled *Les centuries*. He was patronized by the influential Catherine de Medici, Queen of Henri II of France, and eventually became physician to one of Catherine's sons, Charles IX. One of the best known predictions of Nostradamus was concerned with the death of Henri II, who met his end through a wound received in a tournament – just as Nostradamus had prophesied.

Today, however, Nostradamus is regarded as something of a

charlatan and we speak of a *Nostradamus* as someone who claims to foretell the future but tends to be vague and evasive, or *nostradamic*, in his predictions.

O

361 OCCAM'S RAZOR

William of Ockham or Occam (*circa* 1300 – *circa* 1349) was an English scholar and philosopher and one of the most original and influential thinkers of his day. Born in Ockham, in the county of Surrey, he joined the Franciscans and studied under Duns Scotus (q.v. Dunce), who was later to become his great rival in theological debate. His doctrines were later advocated by Hobbes and Berkeley (qq.v.).

We particularly remember William of Ockham (or, as he was also known, 'Doctor Invincibilis') from his philosophical maxim *Occam's razor*, so-called since it is said he dissected all arguments as with a razor. This states that 'Entities ought not to be unnecessarily multiplied', or the principle that if anything can be explained without introducing additional assumptions, then these assumptions are pointless. There is an anecdote concerning the Irish writer James Joyce which illustrates Occam's razor in a colloquial way. Joyce and another (at that time) impecunious writer encountered the father of William Butler Yeats in the street and enquired whether he could loan them a small amount of money. The old man said that, not only had he not got the money, but even if he had it to give to them they would probably spend it on drink. To which Joyce replied, 'Have you not heard of Occam's Razor? It doesn't matter a damn what we're intending to spend the money on if you haven't got it.'

362 OERSTED

Hans Christian Oersted (1777 – 1851), the Danish scientist, is known as the founder of the science of electromagnetism.

Oersted observed that a magnetic needle turned at right angles to a conductor when the conductor was carrying an electric current. He realised then the connection between electricity and magnetism. Appropriately, the unit of magnetic field strength has been named after him as the *oersted*.

Anders Sandoe Oersted (1778 – 1860), the younger brother of Hans, was Prime Minister of Denmark in 1853.

363 OHM OHM'S LAW

Georg Simon Ohm (1787–1854) gave his name to the unit of electrical resistance, the *ohm*, and the law of electric current, *Ohm's law*. Ohm, a German, linked his name with those of Ampère, the Frenchman, and Volta (qq.v.), the Italian, in formulating his famous law, which states that electric current is directly proportional to electromotive force and inversely to resistance; or expressed in the familiar equation: electromotive force (in volts) = current (in amperes) × resistance (in ohms).

Despite Ohm's great contribution to electrodynamics, you will rarely see his name on a piece of electrical equipment, along with Ampère, Volta and Watt (q.v.). The resistor (or resistance), a device used in electrical circuits, is marked in *ohms*, but by means of a colour code (black, brown, red, orange, yellow, green, blue, violet, grey and white, representing the numbers 0, 1, 2, 3, 4, 5, 6, 7, 8 and 9, respectively). You will, of course, find the word 'ohm' in the dictionary.

364 ONANISM

Onan was the second son of Judah and Shuah ('And she conceived again, and bare a son; and she called his name Onan' Genesis 38:4). His name is used as a synonym for coitus interruptus, or masturbation, from his refusal to obey his father's command to have sexual intercourse with his elder brother's wife, Tamar ('And Judah said unto Onan, Go in unto thy brother's wife, and marry her, and raise up seed to thy brother. And Onan knew that the seed should not be his; and it came to pass, when he went in unto his brother's wife, that he spilled it on the ground, lest that he should give seed to his brother' Genesis 38:8–9).

365 ORRERY

Charles Boyle, fourth Earl of Orrery (1676–1731), gave his titular name to a clockwork model of the solar system or a kind of planetarium, an *orrery*. The invention was in fact the work of one George Graham.

Boyle is also remembered for his part in the controversy concerning the *Epistles of Phalaris*, letters attributed to the sixth century Sicilian ruler, which were proved to be spurious. These letters were edited by the fourth earl. And as a soldier he fought at the battle of Malplaquet, but was later imprisoned in the Tower of London for his connections with the Jacobites (q.v.).

366 OSMANLI   OTTOMAN

Othman or Osman I, also known as al-Ghazi, i.e. the Conqueror (1259–1326) was the founder of the empire of the Ottoman Turks. He succeeded his father, Ertogrul, in 1288 and proceeded to conquer a great part of Asia Minor. He gives his name to the adjective *Osmanli*, referring to the Turkish empire or the western branch of the Turks and their language; and as a noun, an Osmanli is an Ottoman Turk or an *Ottoman*.

An *ottoman* (usually without the capital letter) is a cushioned seat or sofa without a back or armrests, originally intended for several people sitting back to back; or a flat-topped chest with cushioning on the top.

367 OWENITE   OWENISM

Robert Owen (1771–1858) was one of the pioneers of the co-operative movement in industry and a great philanthropist. Born in Wales, he became successful as an owner of cotton mills in the north of England; but he was also dedicated to improving the lot of his employees and bringing about social reforms in industry through co-operation on a socialistic basis.

Owen's example undoubtedly played an important part in the passing of the Factory Act of 1819 and the eventual prohibition of children from industrial employment in Great Britain. His great aim, however, was to establish a whole society based on his ideals and he spent the greater part of his fortune in founding *Owenite* communities in Great Britain and America, though none of them was successful. In spite of the genuine beliefs of its founder, *Owenism* was found to be impracticable.

P

368 PAGET'S DISEASE

Sir James Paget (1814 – 99) gave his name to two diseases: *Paget's disease of bone*, or *osteitis deformans*, which can affect one or several bones; and *Paget's disease of the nipple*, a rare kind of breast cancer.

Paget was noted for his relentless industry in everything he undertook and in addition to his eminence as a surgeon and a pathologist, he was among other things a gifted orator, much admired by Gladstone (q.v.). He was created a baronet in 1871.

369 PALLADIAN

Andrea Palladio (1518 – 80) was the Italian architect who introduced a style of architecture based on the ancient Roman principles, which became known after him as *Palladian*.

To a great extent, Palladio modelled his style on the work of Marcus Vitruvius, the Roman architect and engineer of the first century BC, and military engineer to the Emperor Augustus (q.v.); though at the same time, he was able to reconcile contemporary requirements with the symmetrical planning and other features of the ancient Roman style. The Church of the Redeemer, at Venice, is probably the best example of his work.

Palladianism was introduced into England in the seventeenth century by Inigo Jones (who was known as 'the English Palladio'), and the Banqueting Hall, at Whitehall, represents his interpretation of the Palladian style of architecture.

370 PARKINSON'S DISEASE

James Parkinson (1775 – 1824) was an English surgeon who identified and gave his name to *Parkinson's disease* (also known as *paralysis agitans*, or *shaking palsy*), a disease marked by a stooping and shuffling way of walking, and shaking of the limbs. It was Parkinson too, who was the first to describe appendicitis and to attribute perforation of the appendix as a cause of death.

Parkinson was also interested in palaeontology (the study of fossils) and wrote a number of books on the subject. Yet on top of all these activities, he managed to involve himself in politics too, and at one time was suspected of being a participant in a proposed plot to assassinate George III (q.v.), known as 'the Popgun plot'.

371 PARKINSON'S LAW

Cyril Northcote Parkinson (1909–   ), the English historian and political economist, is best known for his book *Parkinson's law: the pursuit of progress*. In this, he set out to ridicule the self-perpetuating machinery of bureaucracy, and coined the phrase, 'Work expands so as to fill the time available for its completion', which has become famous as *Parkinson's law*.

The *law* can be applied to inefficient administration generally, or even adapted to suit a certain subject, such as road-planning, when it might well become, 'Vehicles increase in size and numbers so as to fill the road-space available to them'.

372 PARNELLISM   PARNELLITE

Charles Stewart Parnell (1846–91), the Irish nationalist politician known as 'the uncrowned king of Ireland', gave his name to the language through his advocacy of Home Rule for Ireland, *Parnellism*. Elected to Parliament in 1875, he united the opposing groups in the Home Rule campaign, employing obstructionist methods which brought about the defeat of both Conservative and Liberal governments before his eventual alliance with Gladstone (q.v.), who had earlier sent him to prison for obstructing the imposition of a new land act. His principles and policies were first given the name with the publication in *The Times* of 'Parnellism and Crime', accusing Parnell of connivance in politically motivated crimes in England and Ireland. A special commission of high court judges exonerated him of any complicity, but the *Parnellites* as a body were declared guilty of incitement and failure to denounce the crimes.

Parneil's political career came to an end in 1890 when he was cited as co-respondent in a divorce suit brought about by a former Parnellite, William Henry O'Shea. He died suddenly the following year, some five months after marrying Mrs O'Shea.

373 PASCAL   PASCAL'S LAW

Blaise Pascal (1623–62), the French scientist and philosopher, gave his name to a unit of pressure, the *pascal*. Pascal was a mathematical prodigy and invented one of the earliest calculating machines. He also gives his name to the *Pascal arithmetical triangle*, *Pascal's mystic hexagram*, and *Pascal's law of fluid pressures*.

As a young man, Pascal turned to religion and came under the influence of Jansenism (q.v.). He was strongly opposed to the 'pure reason' of the Cartesian philosophy (q.v.), maintaining that, 'The heart has its reasons which reason knows nothing of'.

374 PASTEURIZE   PASTEURISM

Louis Pasteur (1822 – 95) was surely one of the great benefactors of mankind ever in the field of science. His numerous discoveries ranged from an effective treatment for hydrophobia or rabies (named after him as *pasteurism*) to a method of preventing disease in silkworms, which virtually saved the silk industry in his native France.

Pasteur is in fact regarded as the founder of the science of bacteriology, and it was through his research that the English surgeon Joseph Lister (later to become Lord Lister, q.v.) was able to perfect the antiseptic treatment of surgical wounds.

But of all his achievements, the majority of people undoubtedly remember his name from the *pasteurized* milk products they consume. *Pasteurization* – the method of sterilization by heating which destroys bacteria in milk, etc. without affecting its food value – is, of course, named after Louis Pasteur.

375 PAUL JONES

John Paul Jones (1747 – 92) is remembered for his adventures during the American War of Independence, when he took part in a number of daring naval exploits against the British. He also gave his name to a popular dance, the *Paul Jones*.

Jones was born in Scotland and his original full name was John Paul. He went to sea as a boy and became involved in smuggling and slave trading among other things, before settling in Virginia and changing his surname to 'Jones'. At the outbreak of the war in 1775, Jones joined the American navy; and within a few years he was commanding a ship in action round the British Isles. His reputation as a dashing and courageous captain (he actually 'invaded' Britain on one occasion when he captured the fort at Whitehaven) earned him the command of the *Bonhomme Richard*, the flagship of a fleet of French and American ships which, in 1779, attacked the British and captured the *Serapis*. It was during this action that Jones, whose ship was virtually sinking (it did in fact sink two days after the battle), refused to surrender with the now famous words, 'I have not yet begun to fight'.

After the war, Jones served in both the Russian and French navies and ended his life in Paris. His remains were taken to America at the beginning of this century, and his name is now honoured in The Hall of Fame for Great Americans – along with another Scotsman whose name has become a part of the English language, Alexander Graham Bell (q.v. under decibel).

The *Paul Jones* – the dance in which the men and women change their partners throughout – is probably named after John Paul Jones from his relish in making fresh conquests.

376 PAVLOVIAN

Ivan Petrovich Pavlov (1849 – 1936) is remembered eponymously from his controversial theories concerning conditioned reflexes and his famous experiments with dogs in this connection. In effect, the *Pavlovian experiments* attempted to demonstrate that all animal behaviour, including that of man, could eventually be analysed and controlled.

Initially, Pavlov's theories made a considerable impression on the scientific world and in 1904 he became the first Russian to receive a Nobel prize (q.v.) when he was awarded the prize for physiology and medicine. But scientific opinion (especially outside Russia) was far from unanimous in accepting the implications of Pavlov's experiments; and today his theories are generally regarded as an over-simplification of the function of the brain. *Pavlovian* has consequently come to refer to any such theories and not just those of Pavlov.

377 PEACH MELBA

Dame Nellie Melba (1861 – 1931), the Australian operatic soprano, gave her name to the *peach Melba*. It is said that the famous singer – at the height of her career and her name a household word – paid a late and unexpected visit to a well known restaurant and demanded a certain dish. Unable to comply with the request, the resourceful restaurateur hastily improvised with peaches and ice-cream, and flatteringly informed his customer that his *peach Melba* had been specially created in honour of her. Melba was not only pleased with the substitute dish, but allowed her name to be used for it.

Melba's real name was Helen Porter Mitchell. She was born near Melbourne – her father was a Scotsman and her mother of Spanish descent – and took her professional name from that city (which in turn had taken its name from a British prime minister). Her married name was Armstrong.

Another famous Australian singer, the bass-baritone Peter Dawson, had a story about Melba and the great Caruso, which again was about food – but not exactly peaches and ice-cream. The two singers were performing Puccini's *La Boheme* and had come to the part of the first act where Rodolfo (played by Caruso) sings to Mimi (played by Melba), *Che gelida manina* (*Your tiny hand is frozen*). The scene is played in semi-darkness, with Rodolfo and Mimi groping for the lost key on the floor until their hands touch and Rodolfo sings. But on this occasion, Rodolfo added a little extra touch of his own, gently pressing a very hot sausage (which he had had specially heated in the wings) into Mimi's tiny, frozen hand . . .

378 PEPPER'S GHOST

John Henry Pepper (1821–1900) gave his name to a theatrical contrivance which was originally invented by one Henry Dircks. This was a device which gave the impression of a ghost-like figure moving on a stage and was produced by means of a sheet of glass reflecting the movements of an actor from a hidden lower stage. It became popularly known as *Pepper's ghost* from Pepper's demonstrations of the illusion, though he did also make some improvements to Dircks's invention.

Pepper was born in London and became an analytical chemist at the Royal Polytechnic and the author of a number of publications on science for the layman. He exhibited Pepper's Ghost in the USA and Australia, where he eventually settled in Brisbane in a scientific post.

379 PESTALOZZIAN METHOD

Johann Heinrich Pestalozzi (1746–1827) is remembered for his experiments in primary education, known after him as the *Pestalozzian method* of education.

Pestalozzi was born in Zurich of a wealthy family. As a young man, he was inspired by the educational theories of the French philosopher and writer, Jean Jacques Rousseau, and at his own expense, established a school for deprived children, under his personal charge. He dispensed with the traditional (and frequently brutal) methods of education and encouraged his pupils to observe and reason and to take a real interest in their lessons. Pestalozzi was too far ahead of his time, however, and the school failed. But the experiment in itself, and Pestalozzi's writing on the subject, continued to attract the attention of educationalists, until today the Pestalozzian methods have become accepted, by and large, as the basis of primary school education.

A follower of Pestalozzi is known as a *Pestalozzian* – and one of the best known is the German educationalist, Froebel (q.v.).

380 PETERSHAM

Charles, Viscount Petersham, later fourth earl of Harrington (1780 – 1851), designed and popularized a type of greatcoat with matching breeches, made from a heavy woollen cloth, with a round-napped surface. The coat was named from the fourth earl's courtesy title as a *petersham* and the cloth (usually of a dark blue) is also known by that name.

Before he succeeded his father, the third earl, in 1829, Petersham had been Lord of the Bedchamber to George III and George IV (qq.v.). In addition to his sartorial accomplishments, he was an inventor of various things, including an original mixture of snuff. His interest in snuff, in fact, became something of an obsession and his collection of snuffboxes was one of the finest in England.

Petersham is also a kind of heavy ribbon or belting.

381 PETRARCHAN SONNET

Francesco Petrarca, known as Petrarch (1304 – 74), the great Italian poet, is mainly remembered through his love-poems in praise of *Laura, Rime in vita e morte di Madonna Laura*. Laura, it is thought, was Laure de Noves, the wife of Count Hugues de Sade, of Avignon, where Petrarch had gone to live in 1313. The poems were largely written in the form of the sonnet, and it is through the sonnet that Petrarch gives his name to the English language. The *Petrarchan*, or *Petrarchian sonnet* has a rhyming scheme of *abbaabba cdcdcd*, with an additional rhyme in the last six lines in certain imitations.

Wordsworth's sonnets are basically Petrarchian in their form, and in one of these addressed to *The sonnet*, he makes a metaphorical reference to the great Italian sonneteer: '...the melody of this small lute gave ease to Petrarch's wound.'

Lord Byron, on the other hand, is more down-to-earth about Petrarch's poetry in his famous satire *Don Juan*:

> 'Think you, if Laura had been Petrarch's wife,
> He would have written sonnets all his life?'

382 PINCHBECK

Christopher Pinchbeck (1670? – 1732) was a London watchmaker and toymaker who invented an alloy of five parts of copper and one of zinc, which bore a resemblance to gold. It was used in the manufacture of cheap jewellery and named after him as *pinchbeck*.

The word pinchbeck is also used to describe anything sham, or cheap in quality.

383 PINDARIC ODE

Pindar (*circa* 522 – 443 BC), the celebrated Greek lyric poet of Thebes, gives his name to the English language through the *Pindarique odes* of the seventeenth-century English poet, Abraham Cowley (1618 – 67). Cowley's odes were written in English in supposed imitation of Pindar's verse and were characterized by irregularities of metre and rhyming patterns and an elevated style. The form of the *Pindaric ode*, as it came to be known (or the English ode), was subsequently copied by many other English poets, notably Dryden and Pope, and Dryden's *Alexander's feast* is one such example.

Little is known of Pindar's life, but there are various surviving fragments of his works, in addition to 44 complete odes written in celebration of victories in the great national games. The victors in these games could commission a suitable ode from the poet and together the odes are known as the *Epinicia*.

384 PINKERTON

Allan Pinkerton (1819 – 84) was a Scotsman who founded the first and most famous private detective agency in America. Consequently, any private detective has come to be called a *Pinkerton*.

Pinkerton was born in Glasgow and emigrated to America in 1842. He joined the Chicago police force and became its first detective officer before establishing his private detective agency in 1850. Pinkerton's reputation grew rapidly as his detectives solved a number of sensational crimes; and in 1861, an attempt to assassinate President Lincoln was thwarted by Pinkerton's men.

The American writer Dashiell Hammett had been a Pinkerton man before he began writing his best-selling detective stories. Furthermore, the 'private eye' of crime fiction is derived from an original trade mark of Pinkerton's, which depicted a wide-open eye with the slogan, 'We never sleep'.

385 PLATONIC

Plato (originally Aristocles), or 'the broad shouldered one' (*circa* 427 – 347 BC), was a pupil of Socrates (q.v.) and the teacher of

Aristotle. He gives his name to one of the most frequently misused expressions in the English language, *Platonic love*, or *Platonic friendship*. This is commonly used to describe a non-sexual relationship between a man and a woman, whereas Plato, in his *Symposium*, refers to the pure love shown by Socrates towards young men.

386 PLIMSOLL LINE   PLIMSOLLS

Samuel Plimsoll (1824 – 98) gave his name to the compulsory load-line for ships, the *Plimsoll line*, and the rubber-soled canvas shoes, *plimsolls*.

Plimsoll was born in Bristol and became a successful London coal merchant. His abiding interest and concern, however, was for the welfare of the British seaman; and in 1872 he made a scathing attack on the attitudes of the shipowners, with the publication of his book, *Our seamen*. At this time he was the Member of Parliament for Derby, and it was largely through his efforts that the Merchant Shipping Act of 1876 was passed. This was designed to prevent the overloading of ships. Plimsoll was known as 'the sailors' friend'.

387 POMPADOUR

Marquise de Pompadour, née Jeanne Antoinette Poisson (1721 – 64), was a mistress of the French king, Louis XV. From 1745 and until her death in 1764, she exercised the strongest influence on the king and the affairs of state and was largely responsible for taking France into the disastrous Seven Years' War, in 1756. (It was after the defeat of the French army at the battle of Rossbach that Mme de Pompadour is said to have uttered the frequently quoted, 'Après nous le déluge'.)

Mme de Pompadour is remembered eponymously, however, in connection with her influence on the fashions of the day; in particular, a style of hairdressing, a *pompadour*, which raised the hair by having it pulled back over a pad, and a colour, a purplish pink, also named after her.

388 POTT'S DISEASE   POTT'S FRACTURE

Percivall Pott (1714 – 88) might be said to have become eponymous through breaking his leg! At the time of his accident (he was thrown from his horse) Pott was already a surgeon of considerable repute at St Bartholomew's Hospital in London; and it was during his enforced convalescence that he began writing his original accounts of diseases and other ailments, including fractures. *Pott's fracture*, a severe fracture-dislocation of the ankle, causing the foot to twist outwards, was not however the injury which all but cost Pott his leg, amputation being the all too universal remedy of his day.

Pott's disease, a paralysis of the legs due to spinal tuberculosis, and another inflammatory condition, *Pott's puffy tumour*, were both described by Pott, who was also the first to identify cancer of the scrotum, or chimney sweep's cancer.

389 POUJADISM   POUJADIST

Pierre Poujade (1920 –   ) gives his name to the French *Poujadiste* *party*. But *Poujadism* in a more general sense has come to mean the protest of small men against the big political machine.

Poujade was born in Saint Cere, in Southern France, and after war service (two years of which he spent in the British Royal Air Force) he became a bookseller and publisher, and a member of his municipal council. In 1953 he organized a strike of local shopkeepers, aimed against the French tax department. This led to the founding, in the following year, of his *Union de Défense des Commercants et des Artisans* (*Union for defence of traders and artisans*). The *Poujadistes*, as they had now become known, went on to achieve considerable success in the 1956 elections to the National Assembly, polling over 2,000,000 votes in gaining some eight per cent of seats in the Assembly.

In subsequent elections the influence of Poujade's party has waned; but *Poujadism* in general, and in countries other than France, has come to be a force to be reckoned with. In Great Britain, for example, the National Association of Small Shopkeepers is just one of a number of pressure groups devoted to the interests of the small businessman.

Poujade himself has been content to remain a local councillor and has never sought election to the National Assembly.

390 PRE-RAPHAELITE

Raphael, in full, Raffaello Sanzio or Santi (1483 – 1520), was one of the three great masters of what has become known as the golden age of Italian art, or the High Renaissance (the other two being Leonardo da Vinci and Michelangelo). Yet ironically, it is in connection with a different period that Raphael's name gets into the English dictionary.

It was in 1848 that a group of British artists and writers decided to form the *Pre-Raphaelite Brotherhood* (or the PRB) with the aim of restoring art to its 'natural' state, or as they supposed it to be before the time of Raphael. The Brotherhood included the painters Holman Hunt and Millais, and the poet and painter Dante Gabriel Rossetti, and they published a periodical, *The germ: thoughts towards nature in poetry, literature and art*, which brought them a good deal of criticism, especially from Charles Dickens (q.v.). And though another famous writer, John Ruskin, championed their cause, the PRB was largely ineffective and *The germ* ceased to be published after only four numbers.

It remains a curious fact that painters (or for that matter composers too) have been notably unsuccessful in giving their names to words in the English language. Titian and Van Dyck (qq.v.) are the most obvious exceptions, but of the rest, Daguerre and Morse (qq.v.) are remembered as inventors, rather than painters; while 'divine' Raphael (or 'Rafael of the dear Madonnas', as the poet Robert Browning described him) is 'honoured' merely in a derogatory way.

391 PRINCE RUPERT'S DROPS
PRINCE RUPERT'S METAL

Prince Rupert, known as Rupert of the Rhine (1619–82), was a grandson of James I (q.v.) and a nephew of Charles I (q.v. under King Charles's head). As commander of the Royalist cavalry in the English Civil War and later as a naval commander, he became renowned for his fearlessness and flair in attack, while invariably finding himself on the losing side.

Eponymously, however, Prince Rupert is remembered as a man of science: *Prince Rupert's metal* or *Prince's metal*, a kind of brass alloy, was one of his inventions; and he also gives his name to *Prince Rupert's drops*, pear-shaped bulbs of glass, made by dropping molten glass into water, which explode into minute pieces when the tip of the tail is broken. Another of his unwarlike activities was his work on improving mezzotint processes.

Disraeli referred to Edward Stanley (later, as prime minister, the Earl of Derby) as 'the Rupert of parliamentary discussion . . . in his charge he is relentless, but when he returns from the pursuit he always finds his camp in the possession of the enemy'. Lord Lytton, too, made a similar allusion to Prince Rupert, but in verse:

> The brilliant chief, irregularly great,
> Frank, haughty, rash, – the Rupert of Debate.

392 PRISCIANIST   PRISCIAN'S HEAD

Priscian (also known as Priscianus Caesariensis) was one of the leading Latin grammarians of the sixth century. He was held in such esteem that his name was adopted as a synonym for a grammarian, *Priscianist*. Also in reverence to his scholarship, we have the expression *to break Priscian's head*, meaning a violation of the rules of grammar. The poet Samuel Butler, in his *Satire on the imperfection of human learning*, made reference to this: '...And counted *breaking Prisician's head* a thing / More capital than to behead a king.'

Priscian taught Latin at Constantinople and his highly revered *Institutionis grammaticae* was contained in 18 books.

393 PRZEWALSKI'S HORSE

Nikolai Mikhailovich Przewalski (1839–88) was a Russian army officer and explorer who discovered and gave his name to a wild horse, then believed to have become extinct, *Przewalski's horse*. The horse was observed in Mongolia in 1881; and it is estimated that a very small number, perhaps 30 or 40 still exist in the wild. There are many more, however, in zoos in various countries which are breeding successfully.

Przewalski's horse (also spelt Przhevalski) stands 12–14 hands high and is dun coloured with a lighter coloured belly and striped on its back, neck and legs. It is a common ancestor of most riding ponies and horses, but no one breed of horse can be said to have descended directly from the original wild animal.

Colonel Przewalski made many other discoveries in his wide-ranging travels, including a wild camel and numerous other animals and plants. He rediscovered Lake Lop Nor, in China, more than 500 years after Marco Polo's original discovery.

394 PULLMAN   PULLMAN CAR

George Mortimore Pullman (1831–97) gave his name to the luxury railway-car, the *Pullman*, or the *Pullman car*. The design of the original Pullman incorporated sleeping facilities, with a folding upper berth, and was jointly designed by Pullman and his colleague Ben Field.

Pullman was born in New York, where as a young man he learned the trade of cabinetmaker; but it was in Chicago that, with Field, he came to design the first Pullman, which in 1859 made its appearance on the Bloomington to Chicago line. The success of the Pullman cars led to the formation of the Pullman Palace

Car Company; and by 1874 Pullmans were in service in Great Britain, from London to Bradford. Nowadays, the name of Pullman is synonymous with luxury in rail travel internationally.

395 PURDONIUM
Purdon was the name of a nineteenth century English inventor who designed and gave his name to a kind of coal-scuttle with a hinged, sloping front and a shovel slotted into the back, a *purdonium*.

This was intended to reduce the dust caused by shovelling coal on to the fire. The purdonium also became a decorative item of furniture and upholstered designs were produced with models in the Chippendale (q.v.) style being very popular.

396 PUSEYITE   PUSEYISM
Edward Bouverie Pusey (1800–82) was one of the leaders of the Oxford Movement, a movement initiated by a group of Oxford clerics and aimed at reviving High Church practice in the Church of England. John Keble, John Henry Newman (later Cardinal Newman), and R. H. Froude were prominent in the group, and with Pusey and others became known as *Puseyites*. They were also called *Tractarians* from their *Tracts for the times*, which set out their views.

Pusey was regius professor of Hebrew at Oxford, and canon of Christ Church; but in 1843 he was suspended as a university preacher on account of his *Puseyism*. Pusey House at Oxford was founded in his memory.

397 PYRRHIC VICTORY
Pyrrhus (318?–272 BC) was king of Epirus, in Greece, whose victories over the Romans at Heraclea (280 BC) and Asculum (279 BC) marked him as a military genius. But Pyrrhus was only too well aware of the terrible cost of winning such battles in terms of the lives of his soldiers and is said to have declared, 'One more such victory and we are lost'. This has given rise to the phrase, a *Pyrrhic victory*, in the sense of a victory achieved at too high a price.

Pyrrhus was eventually defeated by the Romans and died in battle at Argos, in Greece. Another military genius, of a later period, the Duke of Wellington (q.v.), was perhaps echoing the words of Pyrrhus when after Waterloo he wrote, 'Nothing except a battle lost can be half so melancholy as a battle won'.

398 PYRRHONISM   PYRRHONIST   PYRRHONIAN

Pyrrho (*circa* 365 – *circa* 275 BC) was the Greek philosopher who founded and gave his name to the Sceptical or *Pyrrhonian* school of philosophy. *Pyrrhonism* is the ultimate form of scepticism and the true *Pyrrhonist* asserts that we have no certain knowledge of anything and that the acceptance of this is the key to real understanding and happiness.

The poet Tennyson might well have had Pyrrho in mind when he wrote: 'There lives more faith in honest doubt, ... than in half the creeds.' While one of Pyrrho's friends was somewhat less reverent about Pyrrhonism in a mock epitaph on the philosopher:

> 'And oh, dear Pyrrho!
> Pyrrho, are you dead?'
> 'Alas, I cannot tell,'
> Dear Pyrrho said.

Pyrrho was born in Peloponnese (or Peloponnesus), in Southern Greece, and fought in the army of Alexander the Great.

399 PYTHAGOREAN   PYTHAGOREAN LETTER PYTHAGOREAN THEOREM PYTHAGOREANISM

Pythagoras (*circa* 580 – 500 BC), the Greek philosopher and mathematician, left us nothing in writing, but he did give us a number of words and phrases from his name.

He was born in Samos (he is sometimes referred to as the *Samian Sage*), and after much travel, settled in Crotona, in Southern Italy, where he founded the *Pythagorean brotherhood*. The brotherhood advocated and practised moral and social disciplines, including vegetarianism, also called *Pythagoreanism*. Pythagoras taught a system of the universe, the *Pythagorean system*, which in some respects could be said to have anticipated the system of Copernicus (q.v.). He also taught the doctrine of metempsychosis, or the transmigration of souls. But Pythagoras is undoubtedly most remembered for his *Pythagorean theorem*, that the square on the hypotenuse of a right-angled triangle is equal to the sum of the squares on the other two sides.

The *Pythagorean letter* (or the *Samian letter*) is the 20th letter of the Greek alphabet, the letter upsilon or ypsilon (υ), which was seen by Pythagoras as a symbol of vice and virtue going their different ways.

Q

400 QUEEN ANNE STYLE
QUEEN ANNE'S BOUNTY

Anne (1665–1714), Queen of Great Britain and Ireland from 1702 and the last of the Stuart Sovereigns, was also the first sovereign of the United Kingdom through the union of Scotland with England in 1707. She was the second daughter of James II (q.v.) and his first wife Anne Hyde.

Queen Anne is especially remembered in the English language through the simplified rennaissance style of architecture, furnishing and handicrafts which flourished at around the time of her reign.

Queen Anne's Bounty was a fund established by Queen Anne in 1704 for the relief of the poorer clergy of the Church of England. It was provided for from revenues formerly paid to the Pope, but appropriated for the Crown by Henry VIII. The fund was increased by public grants and was eventually merged with the Ecclesiastical Commission in 1948 as the Church Commissioners.

Queen Anne's fan is the thumbing of the nose with extended fingers as an expression of contempt or defiance, or 'cocking a snook'. While the expression *'Queen Anne's dead'*, implying that something said is all too obviously well known or very out of date news, comes from a comedy by the dramatist George Colman the younger (1762–1836), *Heir-at-Law*, in which one of the characters declaims, 'Lord help you! Tell 'em Queen Anne's Dead'. Queen Anne, in fact, died on 1 August 1714 without issue, having given birth to 17 children, none of whom survived infancy.

401 QUEENSBERRY RULES

John Sholto Douglas, eighth Marquis of Queensberry (1844–1900), originated and gave his name to a set of regulations for boxing, known as the *Queensberry Rules*. The actual rules were first drawn up in 1867 by a noted athlete, John Graham Chambers, under Queensberry's supervision.

Among other things, Queensberry Rules specified the use of boxing gloves. At that time, bare-knuckle fighting was still very much the rule, although gloves had been in limited use for some time; but in 1885, the first world heavyweight boxing championship fought with gloves was staged at Cincinnati, when John L. Sullivan of the USA successfully defended his title against

Dominick McCaffery, also of the USA.

The Marquis of Queensberry is also remembered as the father of Lord Alfred Douglas, 'Bosie' (q.v.), the poet. It was, of course, Queensberry's intense disapproval of his son's friendship with Oscar Wilde which led to the sensational trials in 1895, and Wilde's eventual conviction and imprisonment. Ironically, Queensberry's behaviour in this affair, and the methods he used to attack Wilde, do not appear to have been in accordance with the spirit of 'fair play' laid down in the Queensberry Rules.

402 QUISLING

Vidkun Quisling (1887–1945) was a Norwegian politician who betrayed his country to the Germans and became 'puppet' Prime Minister of Norway during the Nazi occupation. His name has since been used to describe anyone who aids and collaborates with the enemy.

There were, of course, *Quislings* of lesser and greater importance in all countries occupied by Germany in the Second World War; and had the Nazis conquered Britain, there would have undoubtedly been a British *Quisling*.

Vidkun Quisling was executed by firing squad on 24 October 1945.

R

403 RABELAISIAN
François Rabelais (*circa* 1494 – 1553) was the author of two novels, *Pantagruel* and *Gargantua*, which have given rise to the word *Rabelaisian*, on account of their broad and outspoken humour, or (as some would say) their coarseness and indecency. *Rabelaisian*, however, does not accurately describe Rabelais himself.

He was born near Chinon, in central France, and became a monk of the Benedictine (q.v.) order; but he turned to the study of medicine and gave up his monastic dress. He travelled widely in his own country and in Italy, acquiring considerable fame as a physician and as a fearless critic of the establishment.

There is a statue of Rabelais in Chinon which is somewhat dwarfed by another of Joan of Arc on horseback. Saint Joan, though, was not born anywhere near Chinon – and neither is her name in the dictionary. It is doubtful, too, whether Rabelais would have acquired that distinction had he been better known by his pseudonym of 'Alcofribas Nasier', which is an anagram of 'Francois Rabelais'.

404 RACHMANISM
Peter Rachman (1920 – 62) was a Polish immigrant who became notorious (and subsequently eponymous) through his ruthless and unlawful exploitation of tenants in the slum area of Paddington, in London. Any activities of this nature have since come to be known as *Rachmanism*.

The 1957 Rent Act had lifted restrictions on the rent which could be lawfully charged for certain properties; and Rachman and his kind were quick to take advantage of the more vulnerable tenants, including a number of prostitutes. Exorbitant rents were demanded and the demands enforced by threats and other highly dubious methods of coercion, involving the use of 'strongarm men'. By 1963, however, the existence of Rachmanism had been widely exposed by the national press and eventually became the subject of parliamentary debate.

Rachman died of a heart attack in 1962; and in 1965 a new Rent Act introduced measures to counteract Rachmanism.

405 RAGLAN

Fitzroy James Henry Somerset, first Baron Raglan (1788 – 1855), the commander-in-chief of the British forces in the Crimean War, is probably remembered more for the part he played in the battle of Balaclava (when Lord Cardigan (q.v.) and the Light Brigade were mistakenly ordered to charge the Russian guns), than for his earlier military exploits. He had in fact been aide-de-camp to the Duke of Wellington (q.v.) in the Peninsular War; had fought at Waterloo, where he lost his right arm; and in the month before Balaclava, had won the battle of Alma.

Lord Raglan is also remembered in quite another way. He gave his name to the raglan, an overcoat (or other such garment) with each sleeve in one piece with each shoulder.

Raglan died of dysentery at Sebastapol, nine months before the Crimean War ended in 1856.

406 RAMAN EFFECT   RAMAN LINES

Sir Chandrasekhara Venkata Raman (1888 – 1970), was the Indian physicist who discovered and gave his name to a phenomenon of the diffusion of light, the *Raman effect*. This displayed the appearance of additional lines from the light of the original wavelength (*Raman lines*) when the spectrum of light was scattered or diffused. The Raman effect and its implications subsequently became important in the study of molecular science.

Raman was already distinguished in the world of science when he announced his discovery in 1928. He was knighted in 1929 and the following year became the first Indian scientist to be awarded the Nobel prize (q.v.) for physics.

407 RAMISM   RAMIST

Petrus Ramus, or Pierre de la Ramée (1515 – 72), was a French philosopher and mathematician who originated and gave his name to a system of logic, *Ramism*. He became a leading critic of scholasticism and in particular the philosophy of Aristotle, ultimately turning to Protestantism.

Ramus came of humble origins and as a servant at the College of Navarre he used the opportunity to study and eventually to become a graduate and a great scholar. He was one of the first to recognize the validity of the Copernican system (q.v.) and for some years after his death his theories were perpetuated by his followers, the *Ramists*. His death occurred on 24 August 1572,

167

when some 50,000 French Huguenots, including Ramus, were slaughtered in the Massacre of St Bartholomew at the instigation of Catherine de' Medici, mother of Charles IX, King of France.

408 RAPPIST   RAPPITE
George Rapp (1757–1847) was a German religious leader who broke away from the Lutheran (q.v.) church and emigrated to America with a group of his followers in 1803. The *Rappists*, or *Rappites*, as they were known, established a settlement in Pennsylvania which they named Harmony; and from this they took the alternative name of Harmonists and practised communal principles with rigid economy in order to amass wealth for the second coming of Christ.

In 1815, the community moved to Indiana and founded New Harmony; but eventually returned to Pennsylvania to build yet another township, Economy. The Rappists had by this time become extremely wealthy. Their strict rule of celibacy, however, finally led to their extinction.

409 RASTAFARIAN
Haile Selassie, formerly Ras Tafari (1891–1975), became Emperor of Ethiopia in 1930. His former name ('Ras' means 'Royal Prince') was soon afterwards adopted by adherents of the Jamaican Negro Marcus Garvey's 'Back to Africa' movement, who saw in the crowning of a black man as 'King of Kings' (one of the Emperor's various titles), an event of great significance and came to regard Haile Selassie as their patron.

At first, *Rastafarianism*, or *Rastaism*, was in the main confined to the poorer areas of Jamaica, but in recent years its influence has extended throughout the Caribbean, as well as to certain West Indian populated areas of Britain. *Rastafarians*, or *Rastamen*, are outwardly identified by their long plaited hair-styles (known as 'dreadlocks') and wispy beards (Haile Selassie wore such a beard), but the extreme members of the sect are also strict vegetarians and live apart from the rest of society in conditions of considerable frugality. The vast majority, however, have compromised their beliefs and there are clearly many young people who follow Rastafarianism just as they might become involved with any fashionable cult.

Haile Selassie was exiled in England during the occupation of Ethiopia by the Italians, 1936–41, and was eventually deposed by his armed forces in 1974 and died in custody the following year.

410 REAUMUR THERMOMETER   REAUMUR SCALE

René Antoine Ferchault de Réaumur (1683 – 1757) invented and gave his name to a thermometer with the freezing point of water at zero and the boiling point at 80 degrees. The *Réamur scale* was different from the Fahrenheit scale (q.v.) and the *Réaumur thermometer* used alcohol instead of mercury as its liquid.

Réaumur also invented and gave his name to Réaumur porcelain, an opaque white glass; and he was eminent in his day both as a naturalist and a metallurgist.

The Réaumur thermometer was known for some time as the *German thermometer*, though Réaumur was in fact a Frenchman.

411 REHOBOAM

Rehoboam was the son of King Solomon (q.v.) and became king of the two tribes comprising the Kingdom of Judah when the northern tribes revolted under Jeroboam (q.v.). He gave his name to a very large bottle or measure, equivalent to some eight standard wine bottles, a *rehoboam*.

A rehoboam is also a kind of broad-brimmed hat resembling a shovel, once worn by clergymen – according to Charlotte Brontë, in her novel *Shirley*.

412 RICARDIAN

David Ricardo (1772 – 1823) is remembered mainly for his influential work on political economics, *Principles of political economy and taxation*, in which he expounded what have since become known after him as the *Ricardian* theories concerning the causes determining the distribution of wealth. This contained his important theory of rent, profit and wages.

Born in London, the son of a Dutch Jew, he followed his father as a member of the stock exchange and made a large fortune as a broker. He then devoted himself to the study of political economy and is generally regarded as the founder of the 'classical' school of economics. As a young man, Ricardo had been greatly influenced by the writings of the Scottish economist Adam Smith (q.v. under Keynesian); and one of his contemporaries, Thomas Malthus (q.v.), wrote *An inquiry into the nature and progress of rent* some five years before Ricardo's magnum opus, anticipating much of its content.

413 RICHTER SCALE

Charles Francis Richter (1900 – 85) invented and gave his name to a scale for measuring the intensity of earthquakes, the *Richter Scale*.

Dr Richter, an American, was professor of seismology at the California Institute of Technology, Pasadena, and it was there that he worked with another seismologist, the German-born Dr Beno Gutenberg (1889 – 1960), in developing a method of calculating the magnitude of earthquakes. The *Richter Scale* is in fact also known as the *Gutenberg-Richter Scale*.

Earthquakes had been mentioned in some of the earliest records of civilization, but there was little or no attempt made to study the subject scientifically until the last century; and instruments were not used in a coordinated way on a world-wide basis until the 1920s. With Richter's method it is now possible to assess the intensity of an earthquake at any distance. Modern methods of detection and analysis cannot, of course, prevent earthquakes, though in some cases warnings can be given and measures accordingly taken to lessen their effect on people and property. Seismology has also told us a good deal about the structure of the earth.

414 RITZ   RITZY

César Ritz (1850 – 1918) was a Swiss-born hotelier who established and gave his name to a number of high-class hotels of international repute in New York, Paris and London. These hotels came to be identified with great wealth and luxury, which gave rise to a new word in the English language, *ritzy*, meaning expensive and luxurious, in the manner of the Ritz hotels.

But perhaps the ultimate acceptance of the word came with its inclusion in the title of a popular song by Irving Berlin – and sung by the immaculate Fred Astaire, complete with top-hat, white tie, and tails – *Putting on the Ritz*.

415 RONTGEN RAYS

Wilhelm Conrad von Roentgen, or Röntgen (1845 – 1923) discovered and gave his name to the electromagnetic rays of very short wavelength which can penetrate flesh and other matter, *Röntgen rays*, better known as *X-rays*.

Professor Röntgen's discovery has, of course, been of incalculable value to medical science and being 'X-rayed' is something which is now taken for granted in modern society. But the X-ray also has a wider scientific application, including its use in forensic science.

In 1901, Röntgen was awarded the Nobel prize (q.v.) for physics. He was the first man – and the first German – to receive the award.

416 RORSCHACH TEST
Hermann Rorschach (1884–1922) was a Swiss psychiatrist and neurologist who devised and gave his name to a technique for diagnosing mental disorders through a patient's interpretation of ink-blots, the *Rorschach test*. Rorschach claimed that the intelligence, character and mental state of his patient could be revealed from reactions to a certain series of standardized ink-blots, given a reasonable degree of cooperation from the subject.

417 ROXBURGHE
John Ker, third Duke of Roxburgh (1740–1804), is commemorated by a famous book club (the first of its kind) and a word in the dictionary. The third duke's remarkable collection of rare books was dispersed in 1812 and led to the founding of the Roxburghe Club, an association of leading bibliophiles and the first of the book printing societies.

Also in honour of Lord Roxburghe, a style of bookbinding, *Roxburghe*, was named after him. It is characterized by a leather back and a gilt top, the other edges being untrimmed, while the sides may be of cloth or paper.

418 RUBIK CUBE
Erno Rubik (1944–   ), a Hungarian sculptor, designer and architectural engineer, was until recently little known outside his own community. His invention of a toy-cum-puzzle in the form of a pocket-sized cube, the *Rubik cube*, has however made his name world famous; and the Museum of Modern Art, in New York, has honoured his invention with a place in its permanent design collection.

Originally named the Büvös Kocka Magic Cube, each side of the cube is made up of nine 'mini-cubes' that can be rotated in a number of directions to give numerous combinations of six colours. Professor Rubik originally designed his cube to give his students at Budapest's School for Commercial Artists a better understanding of three-dimensional problems, but solving the puzzles it presents now occupies the minds of millions of Rubik cube addicts, from young children to academics. Inevitably there have been books published on the solution to Rubik's cube, to say nothing of the manufacture of countless reproductions of the cube itself.

419 RUNYONYESE   RUNYONESQUE

Alfred Damon Runyon (1880 – 1946), the American writer whose highly colourful short stories depicting imaginary underworld characters in New York in the inter-war years, gives his name to the English language through his unique style of writing which invariably avoided the past tense. 'Last Tuesday, Harry the Horse is standing with me at the corner of Broadway and Forty-Second and I see that he is more than somewhat nervous . . . ' is a typical example of *Runyonese*.

His stories were successfully adapted as musical revues and films, with *The Lemon Drop Kid* and *Guys and Dolls* being the best known with their oddly-named *Runyonese* characters. And a number of the slang words that Damon Runyon (as he is usually known) put into the mouths of these characters have long since become accepted in popular usage, such as 'Hoorah Henry' and 'broad'.

420 RUSSELLITE

Charles Taze Russell (1852 – 1916) was the founder of the International Bible Students' Association, whose members took the name of *Russellites* and later (some years after Russell's death), Jehovah's Witnesses.

'Pastor Russell', as he was known, was born in Pittsburgh, Pennsylvania, where he established an independent church and preached a doctrine concerning the second coming of Christ (which it was maintained had already occurred). On his death, Russell was succeeded by the legal adviser to the Russellites, Joseph Franklin Rutherford, known as 'Judge Rutherford'; and when, in 1917, America declared war on Germany, Rutherford was imprisoned for his active opposition to military service, which was regarded as contrary to the beliefs of the Russellites, who recognized only the authority of 'Jehovah-God'.

The activities of the present-day Russellites, or 'Witnesses', are intensively organized and marked by a forceful door-to-door distribution of the official magazine, *The Watch Tower*. Their slogan (from the title of one of their pamphlets) is 'Millions now living will never die'.

421 RUTHERFORD

Ernest Rutherford, first Baron Rutherford of Nelson and Cambridge (1871–1937), is remembered as the first man to split the atom, and appropriately the unit of radioactive disintegration, the *rutherford*, is named after him.

Rutherford was born in Nelson, New Zealand, and came to England to continue his education at Cambridge. (He was later to acknowledge both places in his title.) His pioneer work in atomic research at Manchester and Cambridge brought him the Nobel prize (q.v.) for chemistry in 1908. And three years later, he announced his new atomic theory, which led to the splitting of the atom in 1919.

Ironically, Rutherford is on record as saying that, 'We cannot control atomic energy to an extent which would be of any value commercially, and . . . we are not likely ever to be able to do so'.

S

422 SADISM SADIST SADISTIC

Comte Donatien Alphonse François de Sade, known as Marquis de Sade (1740 – 1814), was the author of a number of novels and plays (*Justine, Philosophie dans le boudoir, Les crimes de l'amour*, etc.), which reveal a sexual perversion marked by a love of cruelty – or *sadism*, as it has come to be known.

De Sade spent much of his life in prison as the result of his malpractices, and more than once was lucky to escape the death sentence. He died in an asylum for the insane.

Sadism is often linked (or even confused) with masochism (q.v.).

423 ST ANTHONY'S FIRE ST ANTHONY'S NUT TANTONY PIG

Saint Anthony the Great (*circa* 250 – *circa* 350) is the patron saint of herdsmen and swineherds and his symbols include a pig and a bell. He is also associated with the cure of disease, especially the inflammatory disease erysipelas, named after him as *St Anthony's fire*.

St Anthony was born in Egypt and was the first Christian monk. He was known as 'the hermit of Egypt' and is regarded as the founder of Christian monasticism. His feast-day is 17 January.

St Anthony's nut is another name for the pig-nut or earth-nut (*Conopodium*) and a *tantony pig* is the smallest pig in a litter, reputed to cling to the heels of its owner wherever he goes. (The term has also come to be used to describe someone who fawns or follows blindly.) A *tantony bell* is any small bell and particularly one round the neck of an animal, such as the little pig frequently depicted at St Anthony's side.

424 ST BERNARD DOG GREAT ST BERNARD

Saint Bernard of Menthon (923 – 1008) was the founder of the famous hospices on what have been named from him as the Great St Bernard Pass and the Little St Bernard Pass, in the Alps. He also gives his name to *St Bernard dogs*, or *Great St Bernards*, which were kept at the hospices to rescue travellers who had become lost in the snow. And St Bernard of Menthon is, appropriately, the patron saint of Alpinists.

Great St Bernard Pass traverses the Alps from Aosta in Italy (St Bernard was Archdeacon of Aosta) to Martigny in Switzerland, and reaches a height of 8,120 feet. Napoleon's army crossed the Alps by Great St Bernard in 1800, on its way to capture Milan, while more than 2,000 years earlier, Hannibal had made his celebrated crossing via the Little St Bernard Pass. Modern communications have, of course, greatly reduced the difficulties of crossing the Alps, and by 1964 the Great St Bernard Pass road tunnel was completed.

425 ST HUBERT'S DISEASE

Saint Hubert (died *circa* 727) is the patron saint of hunters and his symbol is a stag. According to legend, he was out hunting when a stag appeared before him bearing a luminous cross between its horns. The experience brought about his conversion and eventually he became Bishop of Liège.

It was said that St Hubert's descendants were able to cure anyone bitten by a rabid dog and this has given us *St Hubert's disease* as an alternative name for rabies, or hydrophobia, since this disease is spread by the bite of an infected animal, such as a dog. Pasteurism (q.v.) can be effective in treating the disease in its early stages, but it is generally accepted that prevention, through the enforcement of strict quarantine rules, is the best cure.

426 ST LUKE'S SUMMER

Saint Luke the Evangelist is believed to have been a physician ('Luke, the beloved physician' Colossians 4:14) and a painter and the author of the third Gospel and the Acts of the Apostles in the New Testament. He is the patron saint of physicians and artists.

St Luke's feast-day is 18 October, from which we have the expression *St Luke's summer*, a short spell of mild weather in mid-October.

427 ST MARTIN'S EVIL   ST MARTIN'S SUMMER

Saint Martin of Tours (*circa* 315–399) has come to be regarded (albeit accidentally) as the patron saint of innkeepers and publicans, since St Martin's Day (or Martinmas, or Martlemas), 11 November, coincides with the date of a traditional feast of the Anglo-Saxons, when beasts were slaughtered to provide food for

175

the winter. From this we have the expression *St Martin's evil* as a synonym for drunkenness, as well as *Martin drunk* for extremely drunk.

St Martin became Bishop of Tours in 371 and is a patron saint of France and of soldiers. (It is said that he was a Roman soldier in France and was converted to Christianity (q.v.) after dividing his cloak in two to clothe a naked beggar.)

St Martin's summer is a spell of unexpectedly fine weather around the time of St Martin's Day, while in France *St Martin's bird* is another name for the hen-harrier (l'oiseau de Saint Martin), as it passes through the country in early November.

428   ST PATRICK'S CABBAGE
ST PATRICK'S PURGATORY

Saint Patrick (*circa* 389 – 461), the patron saint of Ireland, was the son of a Roman official and was born outside Ireland. Moreover, the plant to which he gives his name, *St Patrick's cabbage*, is not another name for the shamrock, the national emblem of Ireland. It is in fact the hardy perennial saxifrage better known as *London pride (Saxifraga umbrosa)* or *none-so-pretty.*

There are numerous legends concerning St Patrick and one of these tells of a cave on an island in County Donegal which was revealed to the saint as an entrance to purgatory. This became known as *St Patrick's Purgatory* and it was said that anyone visiting the cave in penitence might witness both the torments of Hell and the joys of Heaven. There were frequent pilgrimages to the cave until its entrance was sealed by order of Pope Alexander VI on 17 March (St Patrick's Day) 1497.

429   ST PETER'S FINGERS   ST PETER'S FISH
PETER'S PENCE

Saint Peter, also called Simeon or Simon, or Simon Peter, was a fisherman ('And Jesus, walking by the sea of Galilee, saw two brethren, Simon called Peter, and Andrew his brother, casting a net into the sea: for they were fishers' Matthew 4:18). He is the patron saint of fishermen and gives his name to a fish of the mackerel family, *St Peter's fish*, or the dory or John Dory. The fish is golden-yellow (golden in French being *doré*) except for a black spot on each side, which is said to represent the marks made by St Peter's hands after he had caught such a fish with a coin in its mouth.

176

The story of St Peter and his fish also gives us the expression *St Peter's fingers* for a thief's fingers, for a thief (according to an old saying) has fish-hooks on his fingers.

Peter's pence was originally a tax of a silver penny paid to the Pope (recognized by the Roman Catholic Church as the lawful successor to St Peter) by the people of England on the feast of St Peter, 29 June. It was abolished during the reign of Henry VIII and nowadays the term refers to voluntary contributions by Roman Catholics.

430 ST VITUS'S DANCE

Saint Vitus (died *circa* 303) was the son of a Sicilian nobleman and, it is said, little more than a child when he was martyred with his nurse, Crescentia, and his tutor, Modestus, at the time of the persecution of the Christians by the Roman Emperor Diocletian. He gives his name to the nervous disease *St Vitus's dance*, also known as Sydenham's chorea (q.v.).

There is no evidence that St Vitus suffered from chorea, though it is recorded that dancing in front of a statue of the saint on his feast-day was once believed to ensure good health for a year; and it is not inconceivable that such dancing was likened to certain symptoms of chorea and thence its association with the name of St Vitus.

The feast-day of St Vitus is 15 June and he is regarded as the patron saint of sufferers from various nervous diseases, and also of dancers.

431 SALK VACCINE

Jonas Edward Salk (1914–) gives his name to the first successful vaccine against poliomyelitis, *Salk vaccine*, which he developed and brought into use in 1954. In that year, well over a million children were immunized with the vaccine which contained a preparation of the dead virus and penicillin.

Salk was born in New York of Polish-Jewish parentage. He was a professor at the University of Pittsburgh when he developed his vaccine which he first tested on a member of his own family. The initial successes were soon marred, however, by the indiscriminate and unauthorized use of Salk's vaccine, resulting in a number of deaths.

The Salk Institute for Biological Studies, in San Diego, California, is named in honour of Dr Salk.

432 SALLY LUNN

Sally Lunn was the name of a young woman of the city of Bath, whose home-made tea cakes (which she sold on the streets of Bath in the last years of the eighteenth century) were so much in demand that they came to be named after her as *Sally Lunns*.

An astute local baker named Dalmer (who was also something of a musician) persuaded the young pastrycook to sell him her recipe for the *Sally Lunn* and then proceeded to write a song (or what would nowadays be called a 'commercial') in further praise of the celebrated buns. And some years later (in 1877), a more distinguished songwriter, one W. S. Gilbert (q.v.), confirmed the place of the Sally Lunn in the English language in the following lines from the Gilbert and Sullivan opera *The Sorcerer*:

> Now for the tea of our host,
> Now for the rollicking bun,
> Now for the muffin and toast,
> Now for the gay Sally Lunn!

433 SALMONELLA   SALMONELLOSIS

Daniel Elmer Salmon (1850 – 1914) was an American veterinary surgeon who identified and gave his name to a genus of bacteria, *Salmonella*. Infections caused by salmonella usually occur through meat or vegetables becoming contaminated with the bacteria and the patient experiences severe abdominal pain, with vomiting and diarrhoea. The disease (known as *salmonellosis*) can be fatal.

Salmon was employed by the US Department of Agriculture as an investigator and later became chief of the Bureau of Animal Industry. In this capacity he was responsible for the introduction of various safeguards against contagious diseases of cattle and a meat-inspection system.

Many recent instances of salmonella poisoning have been attributed to deep-frozen poultry which has not been completely defrosted before cooking.

434 SAM BROWNE

Sir Samuel James Browne (1824 – 1901) invented and gave his name to the *Sam Browne*. This is a sword or pistol belt for officers, with a strap supporting the left side and passing over the right shoulder. It has been adopted by armies all over the world; and while it has not been used for field service in the British Army since 1939, it is still worn with service dress.

Browne was born in India, where he spent his long and

distinguished army career. He gained an early reputation as a fearless fighter, and during the Indian Mutiny, he won the Victoria Cross (q.v.) for his part in a daring cavalry charge, in which he lost an arm. He continued to serve in the army, however, and retired as a general.

Sir Samuel Browne also has the distinction of being the only holder of the VC whose name has become part of the English language.

435 SANDEMANIAN

Robert Sandeman (1718–71) was a Scottish religious sectarian and a son-in-law of John Glas (q.v.). After service as an elder in Glassite churches in Scotland and England, he emigrated to America where he established the sect in New England. The congregations eventually became known from his name as *Sandemanians*.

436 SANDWICH

John Montague, fourth Earl of Sandwich (1718–92), is said to have invented the *sandwich* (which is certainly named after him) as the result of his passion for gambling. So reluctant was he to leave the gaming table – even for meals – that he ordered his waiter to bring him a cut of ham between two slices of bread, which he could eat without interruption of his play.

Lord Sandwich was nicknamed 'Jemmy Twitcher' (after a character in John Gay's *Beggar's opera*, who betrays Captain Macheath) – and not without good reason. He became notorious through the part he played in the prosecution of his former associate, the politician John Wilkes; and for the bribery and corruption at the Admiralty when he was the First Lord.

Sandwich was First Lord of the Admiralty when Captain Cook discovered a group of islands in the Pacific Ocean and named them in his honour as the 'Sandwich Islands'; but they were renamed the 'Hawaiian Islands', and in 1959 became the 50th state of the USA. The sandwich, however, is still named after the fourth Earl of Sandwich and is still much the same as the ones consumed by his lordship from 1762.

437 SANFORIZE   SANFORIZED

Sandford Lockwood Cluett (1874–1968) invented and gave his name to a process of 'pre-shrinking' cotton and other fabrics by mechanical compression of the fibres, *sanforizing*.

Sandford L. Cluett (as he was usually known) was one of an old established family firm of shirt and collar manufacturers of Troy, New York, George B. Cluett Brothers & Co., later incorporated as Cluett, Peabody & Co. Sandford L. Cluett became the firm's director of engineering and research in 1919.

438 SANTA CLAUS   ST NICHOLAS'S CLERK

Saint Nicholas, a bishop of Myra, in Asia Minor, during the first half of the fourth century, must surely be regarded as one of the most 'versatile' of saints. He is acknowledged variously as the patron saint of Russia, and of children, pawnbrokers, sailors, scholars, thieves, and virgins; not surprisingly, therefore, there are numerous legends concerning him and his works.

But St Nicholas is undoubtedly best known as the original of *Santa Claus* (a contraction of St Nicholas) and the idea of a cheery old man distributing gifts to young children at Christmastide stems from a similar custom when (especially in Germany) the feast-day of St Nicholas, on 6 December, was the occasion for various festivities.

The eponym *St Nicholas's clerk* – meaning thief or highwayman – is less easily explained. A very poor scholar was also a St Nicholas's clerk (a clerk in fact used to be another name for a scholar) and it could well be that more than one such fellow had been driven to stealing. Alternatively, the celebrations on St Nicholas's day might well have presented opportunities for any thief.

439 SAPPHISM   SAPPHICS

Sappho was a Greek poet of the seventh and sixth century BC, born on the Aegean island of Lesbos. She is alleged to have indulged in homosexuality and from this we have the words *Sapphism* (from her name) and *Lesbianism* (from her birthplace).

The *Sapphic stanza* was one of a number of metres employed by Sappho in her verse and is basically a quatrain comprising three lines of five feet followed by one of two feet. Variations of *Sapphics* (they are commonly referred to in the plural) have been used by poets of many kinds, from Horace to Sir Henry Newbolt, whose well-known poem *He fell among thieves* is one such example.

440 SAXOPHONE   SAXHORN

Antoine Joseph Sax, better known as Adolphe Sax (1814 – 94), invented and gave his name to the *saxhorn* and the *saxophone*. Born in Belgium, he followed the trade of his father, Charles Joseph Sax (1791 – 1865), who was a well-known maker of musical instruments. But it was Adolphe, with his invention of the saxophone in particular, who made the family name really famous; and he lived to see such composers as Berlioz, Bizet and Saint-Saëns writing music for the instrument, and military bands making use of it.

Nowadays, although most composers have accepted the saxophone as a regular instrument of the orchestra, there is comparatively little serious music written for it; and there are still musicians who regard it as a somewhat inferior instrument. In the field of jazz and popular music, however, it is a different story. From the beginnings of jazz in the early decades of the twentieth century, the sax (as it is usually called) has played a major part in the development of this form of music and its offshoots; and it is impossible to consider the history of jazz and modern dance music without reference to the saxophone and the influence of such men as Johnny Hodges, Charlie Parker and Paul Desmond (alto sax players), Coleman Hawkins, Bud Freeman and Lester Young (tenors), Harry Carney and Gerry Mulligan (baritones), and Sidney Bechet (who made the soprano sax virtually his own special instrument).

The larger jazz bands or dance orchestras (the 'big bands'), comprising some 14 or more musicians, came into being around the 1930s and usually had more saxes (four or five) than any other instruments. The sax 'section' – commonly made up of two altos, two tenors and a baritone (with one or more of the players alternating on the clarinet) – often gave a band its particular character: the famous 'Glenn Miller sound', for example, was largely achieved through a combination of four saxes and a clarinet. (Like the clarinet, the saxophone is a single reed instrument, but mostly of metal construction, whereas the clarinet is of the wood-wind family.)

441 SCAVENGER'S DAUGHTER
SKEVINGTON'S DAUGHTER

Sir Leonard Skevington (or Skeffington), was a notorious Lieutenant of the Tower of London during the reign of Henry VIII. He gives his name to an instrument of torture which he is believed to have invented, *Skevington's daughter*, or (from a perversion of his name) *the scavenger's daughter.*

This fiendish machine was designed to double up the victim's body until his head and feet came together and blood was forced from his nose and ears.

442 SEQUOIA

Sequoya, also spelt Sequoyah or Sequoiah (1770? – 1843), was a Cherokee Indian who made a study of the Cherokee language and became a famous teacher among his people. He helped thousands of them to read and write, and the *Sequoia*, a genus of giant conifers, was named in honour of his achievements.

Sequoya believed himself to be the son of a trader called George Guess, and he eventually adopted this name in preference to Sequoya, though it is as Sequoya that he is remembered.

The *Sequoia* tree is also known as *Wellingtonia*, after the Duke of Wellington (q.v.); and George Washington also gave his name to another genus of *Sequoia* – *Washingtonia.*

443 SHERATON

Thomas Sheraton (1751 – 1806) ranks with Thomas Chipppendale and George Hepplewhite (qq.v.) as one of the foremost in furniture making and designing in the eighteenth century. The *Sheraton* style was essentially one of strict adherence to classical designs, and Sheraton published a number of books on his subject, including *The cabinet-maker and upholsterer's drawing book* and *The cabinet dictionary.* He was also a teacher of drawing.

Like Chippendale and Hepplewhite, Sheraton came to work in London from the north of England. Strangely, however, and in spite of his success, he never acquired a shop of his own.

444 SHRAPNEL   SHRAPNEL SHELL

Henry Shrapnell (1761 – 1842) was a British army officer who invented and gave his name to the *shrapnel shell.* Shrapnel was a young lieutenant in the Royal Artillery when his invention was successfully tested in 1784; and 20 years later, *shrapnel* was first used in action, by British forces against the Dutch, at Surinam, in Dutch Guiana. The shrapnel shell was filled with explosive and ball-shot.

The effectiveness of this devastating new weapon of war was acknowledged by no less an authority than the Duke of Wellington (q.v.), and its use by the artillery at Waterloo was arguably a decisive factor in the outcome of that famous battle.

Shrapnel retired from the army as a general, but like so many inventors, he received little reward for his efforts or compensation for the money he had spent in developing his invention, and died a disappointed man.

445 SIDEBURNS   BURNSIDES

Ambrose Everett Burnside (1824–81) was one of the least distinguished generals of the American Civil War – on either side of the conflict. Yet, with the exception of the redoubtable 'Stonewall' Jackson (q.v.), he is the only one to have given his name to the English language.

Burnside was the commander of the Army of the Potomac in 1862, but his lack of success in the Fredericksburg campaign led to his dismissal the following year. Under General Grant, he again failed to prove his ability on the field of battle, and his conduct was later criticized by a court of enquiry. He resigned his commission in 1865 and went into politics.

General Burnside is in fact remembered for his distinguished side-whiskers – which he gave his name to as *burnsides*, or *sideburns* – rather than his somewhat undistinguished military career.

446 SILHOUETTE

Etienne de Silhouette (1709–67) gave his name to the *silhouette*, but the reason for this is disputed.

Silhouette was the French Minister of Finance for eight months, in 1759; and during his term of office, he introduced certain economies and reforms which particularly angered the nobility. In an attempt to ridicule the minister, the nobles (it is said) used his name to suggest someone without real substance, a mere 'outline' of a person. But another interpretation sees Silhouette's brief tenure of office as 'shadow-like', in being short-lived and fleeting.

It is possible, however, that Silhouette himself invented the *silhouette*. There is evidence that he collected a type of outline portrait (or portraits in silhouette) and that a number of these were displayed in his château.

447 SIMONY   SIMONIST   SIMONIAN

Simon Magus, the sorcerer of Samaria ('... a certain man called Simon ... used sorcery, and bewitched the people of Samaria' Acts 8:9), was converted by the apostle Philip. But he received a stern reproof when he tried to buy the power of performing miracles from the apostles Peter and John ('And when Simon saw that through laying on of the apostles' hands the Holy Ghost was given, he offered them money, Saying, Give me also this power, that on whomsoever I lay hands, he may receive the Holy Ghost. But Peter said unto him, Thy money perish with thee, because thou hast thought that the gift of God may be purchased with money' Acts 8:18–20).

From this we have the word *simony* for the bartering of holy things, or the buying or selling of a benefice. A *simonist* is someone who practises or believes in simony, while a *Simonian* was the name given to a disciple of Simon Magus.

448 SMITHSONIAN PARITY   SMITHSONITE

James Smithson (1765–1829) was the English chemist and mineralogist who discovered the zinc mineral calamine, named after him as *smithsonite*. He also gives his name to the Smithsonian Institution, the famous scientific and cultural institution in Washington, DC.

Smithson was born in France, the illegitimate son of Hugh Smithson Percy, the first Duke of Northumberland, and known in his early years as James Lewis (or Louis) Macie. (His mother's name was Elizabeth Keate Macie.) He became eminent in the world of science and also travelled widely, especially in the USA. In his will, some £100,000 was bequeathed for the founding of the Smithsonian Institution, whose buildings were designed by the architect James Renwick, Jr.

In 1971 an international conference at the Smithsonian Institution reached an agreement on a parity for the major currencies, which has become known as the *Smithsonian parity*.

449 SOCRATIC

Socrates (*circa* 470–399 BC) was the Greek philosopher who originated and developed the method of teaching by means of questions and answers and provoking discussion, named after him as the *Socratic method*. We also use the word *Socratic* in referring to his philosophy, or (as a noun) to describe a follower of Socrates.

Socrates was born in Athens, the son of a sculptor, and for a time he followed his father's calling. He then joined the army and fought with much bravery at the battle of Potidaea, and then at the battle of Delium, saving the life of a soldier named Alcibiades in the first battle and another named Xenophon in the second. Both men were to become the best known of his pupils, along with Plato (q.v.), and were to assist in the development of the Socratic method. But Socrates had his enemies and was eventually accused of impiety and the corruption of youth, for which he was sentenced to death by drinking hemlock. (His last moments were depicted in a famous painting by the French artist Jacques Louis David, *The death of Socrates*.)

Socrates left us nothing of his philosophy in writing, but his disciples (and Plato in particular) have preserved much of his teaching, including the Socratic method.

450 SOLOMON

Solomon, the son of David and Bath-sheba, was a king of Israel (*circa* 973 – *circa* 933 BC) who was especially noted for his wisdom ('And Solomon's wisdom excelled the wisdom of all the children of the east country and all the wisdom of Egypt. For he was wiser than all men' I Kings 4:30 – 31). We therefore use the name of *Solomon* to describe anyone of great wisdom.

Solomon's name is also associated with various other words and phrases of lesser or greater relevance to Solomon himself. Possibly the best known is *Solomon's-seal*, a genus of the lily family, or an alternative name for the six-pointed Star of David.

451 SOUSAPHONE

John Philip Sousa (1854 – 1932) was known as 'the March King' – and not without good reason. He became the bandmaster of the US Marine Band, in Washington, at the age of 25 and quickly established a reputation as both an inspiring leader of his musicians and a talented composer of march tunes. Many of his compositions – such as *The Washington Post* – became very popular with the American public; and in 1892 he formed his own band and toured the world with great success. Sousa was also the composer of a number of light operas, though it must be by his marches (*Liberty Bell, The Stars and Stripes forever, Hands across the sea*, etc.) and the *Sousaphone* – an instrument of the tuba family and named after him – that he is best remembered.

Sousa was of Portuguese descent from his father, but he was

born in Washington, DC – on 6 November 1854. This date is possibly of interest to astrologers and suchlike, since it is exactly 40 years after the birthday of Adolphe Sax (in 1814) – who gave *his* name to the saxophone (q.v.).

452 SPARTACIST
Spartacus (died 71 BC) was a Roman gladiator from Thrace, in South-East Europe (now partly in Greece), who in 73 BC led an uprising against his captors. This became known as the Third Slave War.

Spartacus and his followers, the *Spartacists*, achieved several remarkable victories over the Roman armies, but were eventually defeated by Marcus Licinius Crassus and Spartacus was killed in action. Crassus exacted a terrible revenge on the surviving Spartacists and lined the Appian Way with their crucified bodies.

In Germany, during the First World War, a group of extreme Socialists adopted the name of Spartacists; and although an attempted revolution in 1919 resulted in the murder of its leaders, Karl Liebknecht and Rosa Luxemburg, and the subsequent suppression of the movement, the spirit of the Spartacists led to the development of modern German Communism.

453 SPENCER
George John Spencer, the second Earl Spencer (1758–1834), gave his name to a very short outer coat, a *spencer*, which came into fashion in the early years of the nineteenth century. It is believed that the second earl conceived the idea of the coat after being thrown from his horse and tearing his long-tailed riding coat on a thorn bush. From this, however, various garments bearing the name of spencer have evolved, notably a close-fitting woman's bodice.

Other than eponymously, Earl Spencer is remembered as an effective First Lord of the Admiralty under Prime Minister William Pitt the younger, when he was instrumental in quelling the naval mutinies at Spithead and The Nore and giving Nelson (q.v.) command in the Mediterranean. He was also an ardent bibliophile and the first president of the famous Roxburghe Club (q.v.).

The youngest daughter of the eighth Earl Spencer, Lady Diana Spencer, was married to the Prince of Wales in July 1981, at St Paul's Cathedral in London.

454 SPENSERIAN STANZA

Edmund Spenser (1552? – 99), the English poet, devised and gave his name to a verse pattern of nine lines, known as the *Spenserian stanza*. The stanza was made up of eight iambic lines of 10 syllables and one of 12, with the rhyming scheme *ababbcbcc*. Spenser's major poem, *The Faerie Queen*, was written in such stanzas.

In 1580, Spenser went to Ireland as secretary to Lord Grey de Wilton, the Lord Deputy of Ireland, and acquired Kilcolman Castle, near Cork, and it was here that he wrote the greater part of *The Faerie Queen*. But in 1598, the castle was burnt down by insurrectionists and Spenser lost the youngest of his four children, as well as a number of his manuscripts. He died in London in the following year, in some poverty.

Spenser was known as the 'Poet's Poet' and a number of famous English poets have paid him the compliment of writing in Spenserian stanzas: notably, Byron (*Childe Harold's pilgrimage*), Keats (*The Eve of St Agnes*) and Shelley (*Adonais, an elegy on the death of John Keats*).

455 SPOONERISM

William Archibald Spooner (1844 – 1930) gave his name to the *Spoonerism* – the accidental transposition of sounds in a phrase or a sentence. One of the best known of Spooner's *Spoonerisms* was coined in New College Chapel when he announced the hymn, 'Conquering kings their titles take' as 'Kinquering congs their titles take'.

The Reverend Spooner was Dean of New College, Oxford, from 1876 to 1889, and warden from 1903 to 1924; and his Spoonerisms and other eccentricities became something of a cult. Yet many of the Spoonerisms attributed to Spooner were probably never spoken by him at all.

It is said that a little imbibing can assist the production of Spoonerisms; and no doubt old Spooner had already had a glass or two at a certain dinner in Oxford when, rising to propose the loyal toast, he said (or is supposed to have said), 'Let us drink to the queer old Dean'.

456 STAKHANOVITE   STAKHANOVISM

Alexei Grigorievich Stakhanov (1906 – 77) was a Russian coal-miner who, in 1935, became the central figure of a movement directed at increasing productivity through the efforts and efficiency of individual workers. This movement was named after him as *Stakhanovism*.

The achievements of Stakhanov and others received personal praise from Stalin (q.v.) and a great deal of publicity in the USSR. The word *stakhanovite* has since come to be used in a general sense to describe any worker whose extra productivity is officially recognized.

457 STALINISM   STALINIST

Joseph Stalin, originally Joseph Vissarionovich Djugashvili (1879 – 1953), took his name (Stalin meaning 'Man of Steel') from his pre-revolutionary activities, which included the organized stealing of money for the Bolshevik Party funds. During the Second World War, Stalin was known to the British and American public as 'Uncle Joe', with the popular image of an avuncular, pipe-smoking elder statesman and a staunch ally in the fight against Nazi Germany. At this time, with President Roosevelt of the USA and Winston Churchill, he was one of the 'big three' amongst the allies, yet his position as leader of his people was radically different from that of the other two men.

When Lenin (q.v.) died in 1924, Stalin had already established himself in a position of considerable power through his intimate knowledge of the party machine and his expertise in manipulating the bureaucracy to his own ends. Trotsky (q.v.), his principal rival for the leadership, was soon removed from the government and, eventually, from the Communist Party, and Stalin became the virtual dictator of the USSR, ruthlessly eliminating all opposition to his plans. At the end of the war, in 1945, *Stalinism* gradually extended to most of the new communist states where puppet leaders were installed who effectively took their orders from Moscow. Marshall Tito of Yugoslavia was one of the few successful opponents of Stalinism amongst the communist leaders at that time.

Stalin retained his power up to his death in 1953, when the new collective leadership of the USSR started to dispense with some of the more extreme measures of his rule, though certain aspects of Stalinism remained, in particular the Soviet domination of the countries in the communist bloc. Stalinism was satirized in the well-known book *Animal farm*, by George Orwell, in which the author introduced the much-quoted line, 'All animals are equal, but some animals are more equal than others'.

458 STETSON

John Batterson Stetson (1830–1906) was the best-known member of a family of hatters of New Jersey. He joined the family business as a boy and, in 1865, opened a hat-making factory of his own in Philadelphia. The family name eventually came to be used for a popular wide-brimmed felt hat, much favoured by American cattle-men.

The *stetson* became well-known outside the USA, largely through the popular novels and films about the highly glamorized 'Wild West' era, and was soon to be as familiar as the Colt (q.v.) to avid followers of the 'Westerns'.

The slouch-type hat associated with Australia and New Zealand is also referred to by some as a stetson.

459 STEVENGRAPH

Thomas Stevens (1828–88) was a master weaver of Coventry, the English cathedral city, who gave his name to the language with his invention (in 1879) of small silk pictures, produced on a loom and mounted on cardboard, and named after him as *Stevengraphs*.

The pictures were usually of famous scenes and events, or celebrated people, and were originally sold for two shillings and sixpence, framed, or unframed for one shilling. Nowadays, Stevengraphs are regarded as antiques and a picture in good condition could be worth many hundreds of pounds.

460 STONEWALL   STONEWALLING

Thomas Jonathan Jackson, known as Stonewall Jackson (1824–63), was one of the outstanding generals on the Confederate side in the American Civil War. He was nicknamed *Stonewall* at the first battle of Bull Run, in 1861, when a fellow officer was inspired by the sight of 'Jackson standing like a stone wall'.

From General Jackson's nickname then, we have the *stonewaller* – someone who obstructs or blocks anything opposing him with dogged, *wall-like* resistance. And *stone-walling* is particularly associated with the game of cricket, when a batsman concentrates on stubborn defence with the object of wearing down the opposition, and makes no attempt to attack the bowling by scoring runs.

On 2 May 1863, Stonewall Jackson was accidentally shot and wounded by his own soldiers at the battle of Chancellorsville, and died eight days later. On hearing of Jackson's death, General

Robert E. Lee, the commander-in-chief of the Confederate armies, is reported to have said, 'I have lost my right arm'.

461 SYDENHAM'S CHOREA

Thomas Sydenham (1624 – 89) has been described as 'the English Hippocrates' (q.v.) and not without good reason. He carried out important researches on various diseases and ailments, including gout, hysteria, malaria and smallpox; and he described and gave his name to *Sydenham's chorea*, a nervous disease affecting children and causing spasmodic twitching of the face and limbs, also known as St Vitus's dance (q.v.) or chorea minor.

As a young man, Sydenham served in the Civil War with Cromwell's parliamentary forces.

T

462 TAWDRY   TAWDRY-LACE

Saint Audrey, or Saint Etheldreda (630? – 679), was the daughter of Anna, King of East Anglia, and patron saint of Ely. She is said to have died of a tumour in her throat, which she believed was a punishment for having worn ostentatious jewelled necklaces as a young woman.

From this came the *tawdry-lace*, a woman's silk necktie sold at the annual St Audrey's Fair (on 17 October) in the Isle of Ely. Cheap and showy products of the article subsequently led to the current use of *tawdry* to describe anything gaudy and of little value.

463 TEDDY BEAR

Theodore Roosevelt, known as 'Teddy' Roosevelt (1858 – 1919), was the twenty-sixth President of the USA and a distant cousin of the thirty-second President, Franklin Delano Roosevelt. He gives his name to the English language by way of the perennially popular soft toy bear cub, the *teddy-bear*.

Roosevelt was well known as a soldier, as well as an explorer and a hunter, before he became president, following the assassination of President McKinley in 1901. He was elected for a full term of office in 1904, and two years later, became the first American Nobel (q.v.) prizewinner, when he was awarded the peace prize for 1906.

There are conflicting accounts of the teddy-bear's origin, but there can be little doubt that through his own accounts of his hunting exploits, Roosevelt's name was strongly associated with bears in the mind of the average American; and when the first *teddies* appeared, shortly after he came to the presidency, the familiar version of his Christian name soon became attached to the new cuddly toy. It was perhaps ironic that Roosevelt the hunter had killed so many of the real bears in the world, though he was apparently a dedicated naturalist and had written a number of books on animals. And Roosevelt had more than once been at the 'wrong end' of a gun himself, both as a soldier and a politician. During one election campaign, he was shot and wounded by a would-be assassin, but insisted on finishing his speech with the bullet still in him.

464 TESLA TESLA COIL

Nikola Tesla (1857–1943) gave his name to the unit of magnetic flux density, the *tesla*. He also invented and gave his name to the *tesla coil*, a transformer for producing high voltages at high frequencies.

Tesla was born in what is now Yugoslavia and emigrated to the USA in 1884. He became an American citizen and worked for a number of years with the great American inventor, Thomas Alva Edison, producing numerous electrical inventions.

The tesla has virtually succeeded the *gauss* (q.v.) as the unit of magnetic flux density.

465 THESPIAN

Thespis, a Greek poet of the sixth century BC, is generally acknowledged as the founder of the tragic drama, through his introduction of the individual actor and the monologue (and subsequently dialogue) into the traditional mixture of chorusing and dancing. Since Thespis is also believed to have spoken these monologues, he was in effect the first 'actor'; and consequently we use the word *thespian* for an actor (or more specifically a dramatic actor) and, as an adjective, to describe a relationship with the drama.

The innovations of Thespis mark the beginnings of the modern theatre, though like most new ideas, his were not enthusiastically received by certain sections of society; and for more than 2,000 years, the actor or strolling player was regarded as little more than a vagabond. It is said that Thespis travelled about in a cart which he also used as a 'stage' for his performances; and certainly as recently as the Second World War, the British ENSA (Entertaiments National Service Association) concert parties improvised in a similar manner with army lorries on numerous occasions.

466 THOMASITES

John Thomas (1805–71) founded and gave his name to an American religious sect, the *Thomasites*, also known as Christadelphians or Brethren of Christ. His followers believed in 'conditional immortality', or immortality only to believers in Christ, as well as Christ's return to reign on earth.

Thomas was born in England and trained as a physician. He went to Brooklyn in 1844 where he established the sect some five years later.

467 THOMISM   THOMIST

St Thomas Aquinas (*circa* 1225 – 74) was known as the 'Angelic Doctor' and the 'Prince of Scholastics'. He is also known (among other things) as the 'Father of Moral Philosophy', and his system of philosophy, named after him as *Thomism*, has played an important part in shaping the doctrines of the Roman Catholic Church.

Thomas Aquinas was born at Aquino, in Southern Italy (he is sometimes called Thomas of Aquino), and was educated by the Benedictines (q.v.) at Monte Cassino and at the University of Naples. Against the wishes of his father, the Count of Aquino, he became a Dominican friar and travelled widely on pilgrimages and in pursuance of knowledge. The philosophy of Aristotle exerted a strong influence on his thoughts and it was his belief in the need to reconcile faith and reason which was eventually to bring his followers, the *Thomists*, into conflict with the Dunses (q.v.).

The main work of Thomas Aquinas is his *Summa totius theologiae*, though it remained unfinished. He was canonized in 1323 and his feast-day was originally 7 March (the date of his death in 1274), but since 1970 has been 28 January. He is the patron saint of students and Catholic schools.

468 TICH

Harry Relph, known as 'Little Tich' (1868 – 1928), was one of the most celebrated music-hall comedians of his day. His professional name was derived from the central figure in the famous Tichborne impersonation case (of 1873 – 4), who, like the young Harry Relph, was of a rather podgy appearance. The false claimant to the Tichborne estate (whose real name was Arthur Orton) was eventually exposed and sentenced to prison, but 'Little Tich' retained his nickname as it became clear that the boy was not going to grow much taller. His natural talents as an entertainer, however, more than compensated for his lack of height (he was hardly four feet tall), and by the turn of the century his performances were acclaimed internationally.

Little Tich not only gave immense pleasure to his many admirers – he also gave a new word to the English language. For we now use *tich* or *tichy* (usually in an affectionate way) to describe any diminutive person or object.

469 TITIAN

Tiziano Vecelli, known as Titian (1487? – 1576), the great Venetian painter, was especially renowned for the rich colouring of his paintings; and appropriately, he gives his name to a colour, *titian*, a reddish-brown or reddish-yellow. The word is particularly used to describe a colour of hair, but with the emphasis on a shade of red or reddish-brown.

Of the numerous works of Titian still in existence, his *Bacchus and Ariadne* in the National Gallery is generally considered to be one of his best, and a good example of the *Titianesque* art.

470 TODD-AO

Mike Todd (1909 – 58), the American showman and film producer, sponsored and gave his name to *Todd-AO*, a wide-screen system of filming, using a single camera and giving the effect of 'Cinerama'.

Todd (his real name was Avrom Hirsch Goldenborgen) was born in Minneapolis, the son of a rabbi, and his flair for showmanship and making money was apparent at an early age. He was still in his teens when he first ventured into the film-making business – as a technical 'expert'; but his interests were not wholly confined to the cinema and over the years he made and lost large amounts of money in various spectacular projects. His greatest success, however, was his Academy Award-winning production of Jules Verne's *Around the world in eighty days*, in 1956. Filmed in *Todd-AO*, it featured David Niven in the leading role, as well as any number of other famous film stars in cameo appearances; and in spite of the enormous production costs, the film was a considerable money-spinner for Todd. Then, two years later, he was killed in an air crash.

In the year before his death, Todd married his third wife, the film actress, Elizabeth Taylor (he was her third husband).

471 TOMMY-GUN   THOMPSON SUBMACHINE-GUN

John Taliaferro Thompson (1860 – 1940) gave his name to the Thompson submachine-gun, popularly known as the *tommy-gun*.

Thompson was an American army officer who, on retiring from the army, devoted himself to the invention of firearms and other devices. He collaborated with other inventors (notably a Commander Blish of the US navy) and the invention of the tommy-gun in its final form cannot be credited to Thompson alone, though of course it takes its name from the familiar form of Thompson.

The tommy-gun made its appearance too late to be used in the First World War, and despite the efforts of Thompson and his salesmen, the US army showed little interest in adopting the gun for general use until the Second World War. Not everyone, however, was slow to realize its potential − notably the up-and-coming American gangster of the Prohibition Era. The tommy-gun had been designed particularly for close-range fighting, in trenches, etc., and was comparatively light yet highly effective; and within a few years, a number of the rival bootlegging gangs were using Thompson's gun − often against each other. The notorious 'Saint Valentine's Day Massacre' in 1929, when seven members of the Moran gang were gunned down in a Chicago garage, is believed to have been carried out by Al Capone's men (posing as policemen), using sawn-off shotguns and tommy-guns.

472 TOMPION

Thomas Tompion (1639−1713) has been called 'the father of English watchmakers' and watches of his making or of the kind made by him were known as *tompions*.

With the English inventor and mathematician Robert Hooke, Tompion was one of the first to use the balance spring in a watch; and his invention of the dead-beat escapement represented one of the most significant advances in the history of watchmaking.

Tompion was appointed clockmaker for the Royal Observatory in 1676 and also constructed barometers and sundials for William III.

473 TONTINE

Lorenzo Tonti was a seventeenth-century Neopolitan banker who devised and gave his name to a form of life insurance, a *tontine*, and introduced the system in Paris in 1653.

The tontine provides annuities from a fund raised by subscriptions and the annuities *inc*rease as the number of subscribers *dec*reases through the normal process of death, until the last survivor is receiving the whole income. Tonti's system was soon adopted in other countries, including England.

Robert Louis Stevenson collaborated with his American stepson, Lloyd Osbourne, in a story of a tontine, entitled *The wrong box*, in which two brothers become the last survivors.

474 TONY

Antoinette Perry (1888 – 1946) was an American actress whose name is perpetuated through an award named after her, a *Tony*. These awards are presented for outstanding performances in the American theatre.

Antoinette Perry made her theatrical debut in 1905, and following a successful career both as an actress and a producer of plays, she was appointed chairman of the American Theatre Council. She died on 28 June 1946, the day after her 58th birthday, and the Tony (named from the familiar form of her Christian name) was instituted in her honour.

The origin of the *Oscar*, Hollywood's equivalent of the Tony, is relatively unknown. It is said that a secretary at the American Academy of Motion Picture Arts and Sciences (the body which awards the Oscars), on first seeing one of the statuettes, remarked that it reminded her of her Uncle Oscar. But then it is also claimed that the award takes its name from the Irish playwright Oscar Wilde. Both the Oscar and the Tony, however, have become a part of the English language and can be used in a general sense to indicate any such awards.

475 TROTSKYISM   TROTSKYIST

Leon Trotsky, originally Lev (or Leib) Davidovich Bronstein (1879 – 1940), the Russian revolutionary leader, gave his name to a form of communism which advocated world-wide revolution, known as *Trotskyism*. Trotsky's theories conflicted with the plans of Stalin (q.v.) and this led to his eventual downfall.

Trotsky was the People's Commissar for Foreign Affairs in the first Soviet government, and later as Commissar for War, he founded the Red Army. But with the death of Lenin (q.v.) in 1924, and the emergence of Stalin, Trotsky's political career in the USSR was virtually at an end. In 1929 he was sent into exile, eventually finding a haven in Mexico, where he continued to pursue his political activities until, on 20 August 1940, he was assassinated by Stalin's agents.

In recent years, there has been a marked reaction throughout the communist world to the concentration of power and authority in the USSR and this has led to a revival of Trotskyism.

U

476 UNCLE SAM

Samuel Wilson, known as 'Uncle Sam' (1766–1854), is widely believed to have been the original *Uncle Sam*, the personification of the US government or its citizens. Unlike England's *John Bull*, a fictional character created by the physician and writer John Arbuthnot (a Scotsman, incidentally), the origin of *Uncle Sam* has been disputed, but Samuel Wilson's claims would seem to be as strong as any.

Wilson was a meat packer who was employed as a government inspector during the War of 1812. The initials of his nickname coincided with the initials of the United States which he had to stamp on barrels of meat; and on 7 September 1813 the *Troy Post* printed the first known reference to the US government as 'Uncle Sam'. Samuel Wilson was in fact a resident of Troy, a city in the state of New York.

477 URSULINE

Saint Ursula is said to have been a British princess of the fifth century who was put to death with some 11,000 virgins, after being captured by Huns near Cologne, on their return journey from a pilgrimage to Rome. (There is also a belief that she was saved from the massacre to become a bride to the king of the Huns, but on her refusal was transfixed by arrows, which is how St Ursula is often represented in art.)

St Ursula has become the patron saint of a number of educational institutes, in particular the teaching order of the *Ursulines*, an order of nuns founded by St Angela Merici of Brescia in 1535 and primarily concerned with the education of girls.

V

478 VALENTINE

Saint Valentine is the name of two martyrs, a Roman priest and a Bishop of Terni, who were put to death during the latter half of the third century within a few years of each other and on the same day of the year, 14 February. There is a rural tradition that birds choose their mates on this day; and the old custom of young people choosing a lover or a *valentine* on St Valentine's Day probably originates from this.

Over the years, the custom has become increasingly exploited by the manufacturers of greetings cards and nowadays the number of valentine cards anyone receives is taken as a measure of his or her eligibility or attractiveness to the opposite sex.

For students of naval history, St Valentine's Day is particularly remembered for the battle of Cape St Vincent, in 1797, when the Spanish fleet was defeated by the English under Admiral Jervis with Nelson (q.v.) in support. And in 1929, in Chicago, 14 February was chosen for the 'St Valentine's Day Massacre' (q.v. under Tommy-gun).

479 VAN ALLEN BELTS

James Alfred Van Allen (1914–) became famous for his discovery of two belts of radiation surrounding the earth at distances of some 1,000 and 15,000 miles, respectively. They are now named after him as the *Van Allen belts*, or the *Van Allen radiation belts*.

The discovery was sparked off by information received via Russian and American satellites during the International Geophysical Year, 1957–58. Van Allen was one of America's leading representatives concerned with this project and his original explanations of the satellite data were subsequently confirmed by space probe observations.

Van Allen was born in Iowa and during the Second World War served in the US Navy as a gunnery officer. After the war, he supervised experiments in space research with captured German V2 rockets, which led to the development of purpose-built space rockets. He is now a professor at the University of Iowa.

480 VANDYKE   VANDYKE BEARD

Sir Anthony (or Antoon) Van Dyck, or Vandyke (1599–1641), is one of the few great painters to have given his name to a word in the English language. In fact, there are several words derived from his name. A *vandyke* is a collar shaped in the deeply cut fashion of those painted by Vandyke; and *to vandyke* is to shape in this zig-zag fashion. *Vandyke* (usually without the capital letter) is also a deep brown colour favoured by the painter. And best-known of all, perhaps, is the short pointed *Vandyke beard*, particularly associated with the Vandyke portraits of Charles I (q.v. under King Charles's head).

Vandyke was born in Antwerp, where he became first a pupil and then chief assistant to the great Rubens. He first came to England in 1620 and found favour with James I (q.v.). And on his return, in 1632, he was appointed as court painter to James's son, Charles I, who honoured him with a knighthood.

Circumstances were largely responsible for restricting Vandyke to portrait painting in the main, but he was nonetheless regarded as among the finest in this form of art. Another famous portrait painter of a later period, Thomas Gainsborough, is said to have uttered the name of Vandyke on his death-bed ('We are all going to heaven, and Vandyke is of the company') – which was possibly an even greater honour to him than getting his name in the dictionary.

481 VARDON GRIP

Harry Vardon (1870–1937) is generally regarded as one of the outstanding golfers of all time. He won the British Open Championship a record six times (in 1896, 1898, 1899, 1903, 1911 and 1914), as well as the US Open (in 1900) and the German Open (in 1911).

Vardon, who was born on the Channel Island of Jersey, is also noted eponymously for the *Vardon grip*, an overlapping method of holding a golf-club which he popularized and which is still employed by many players. This grip prevents the player's hands slipping apart; and with the hands operating as virtually one unit, the weaker hand (i.e. the left hand of the right-handed player) is compensated.

482 VENN DIAGRAM

John Venn (1834–1923) was an English mathematician and the author of several books on logic. He devised and gave his name to a diagrammatic system, the *Venn diagram*, in which circles and other figures represent groups or sets (of various things) and their relationships.

Venn diagrams have become an accepted device in the teaching of logic.

483 VERNER'S LAW

Karl Adolph Verner (1846–96) was a Danish philologist, and a professor of Slavic philology at Copenhagen University. He formulated and gave his name to *Verner's law*, a revision of the philological law named after Jacob Grimm (q.v.). Verner's law is contained in his *Eine Ausnahme der ersten Lautverschiebung*.

484 VERY LIGHT   VERY PISTOL

Edward Wilson Very (1847–1910) was an American naval officer and the inventor of the illuminating flare signal, named after him as the *Very light* (or *Verey light*). Very served in the American navy from 1867 to 1885, and retired with the rank of admiral. He was a gunnery expert, and he designed his flares to be fired from a pistol, also named after him as the *Very pistol*. Very's invention was patented in 1878.

485 VICAR OF BRAY

Simon Aleyn is believed to have been the vicar of Bray, in Berkshire, from 1540 to 1588. These years spanned the reigns of Henry VIII, Edward VI, Mary I and Elizabeth I (qq.v.) and witnessed extremes of religious persecution as the balance of power vacillated from Papists to Protestants. It was remarkable, therefore, for a man of religion such as the vicar of Bray to retain his living during these troubled times; and when he was challenged as a time-server on this point, he is said to have rejoined, 'Not so, neither, for if I changed my religion, I am sure I kept true to my principle, which is to live and die the vicar of Bray'.

Consequently we have come to apply the term of *Vicar of Bray* to any turncoat, or someone who changes his position to suit a particular situation. And there is a well-known song, dating from the early eighteenth century, in which one vicar of Bray defends his changes of faith throughout the reign of Charles II, James II, (qq.v.), William III, Anne and George I. The best known version of this is of six verses and begins:

In good King Charles's golden days,
When loyalty no harm meant;
A furious High-Churchman I was,
And so I gain'd preferment.

and ends with the chorus:

And this is law, I will maintain,
Unto my dying day, Sir,
That whatsoever King shall reign,
I will be the Vicar of Bray, Sir!

486 VICTORIAN   VICTORIA CROSS

Victoria (1819–1901), Queen of Great Britain, gave her name to
Victoria Falls, Lake Victoria, Victoria Land, the state of Victoria,
the city of Victoria, numerous towns, a river, a railway station
– and, jointly with her consort Prince Albert (q.v.), a famous
museum. She also gave her name to (and you will find *these* in
an English dictionary) a giant water-lily, a four-wheeled carriage
with a folding hood, a plum, and a medal – the *Victoria Cross.*

The Victoria Cross, usually abbreviated to VC, is awarded to
members of the British and Commonwealth armed forces for
outstanding bravery 'on the field of battle'; and since it was
founded by Queen Victoria in 1856, 1,351 men have received the
award, including three soldiers who were twice awarded the VC.
The most recent VCs to have been won were posthumously
awarded to an officer and a sergeant of the Parachute Regiment
who fought in the Falkland Islands conflict in 1982. The medal,
in the shape of a Maltese cross, was originally made from the
metal of cannon captured from the Russians at Sevastopol (also
spelt Sebastopol), in the Crimean War (q.v. under Nightingale).

The word *Victorian* refers not only to the reign of Queen
Victoria, but the strictly moral attitude and conservative outlook
usually associated with the period. On the other hand, *Victorian*
is also used to describe someone from the state of Victoria in
Australia – who, of course, is not necessarily 'Victorian' in the
other sense.

Victoria's reign was the longest of any king or queen of Great
Britain, lasting more than 63 years, and was more than four years
longer than the longest reign of a king of Great Britain – which
was that of her grandfather, George III (q.v.).

487 VOLT   VOLTAIC PILE

Count Alessandro Volta (1745 – 1827) invented the first electrical battery, named after him as the *voltaic pile*. He also gave his name to the unit of electromotive force, the *volt*.

Volta, an Italian, had studied the researches of his fellow-countryman, Galvani (q.v.), but his own discoveries were to disprove much of what Galvani had concluded.

The title of 'Count' was bestowed upon Volta by Napoleon (q.v.), who at that time was self-assumed King of Italy. Yet a greater honour, perhaps, was to know that his name (or at least an abbreviation of it) had become part of our language.

W

488 WAGNERIAN   WAGNER TUBA

(Wilhelm) Richard Wagner (1813 – 83) is one of the few composers to have given his name to a word in the English language. Words such as 'Mozartian', 'Handelian', and many more, are accepted in musical circles but are unlikely to be found in a standard dictionary; whereas no one could have failed to notice the existence of words such as *Wagnerian, Wagnerite* and even *Wagnerianism* and *Wagnerist.*

There is too a range of musical instruments named after the composer, the *Wagner tubas,* which he devised to enrich the harmonies for his mammoth production, *The Ring of the Nibelung,* in 1876. These instruments could be described as a cross between the French horn and the saxhorn (q.v.), though Wagner tubas of today differ considerably from those of Wagner's day.

The name of Wagner can also be found in the dictionary under 'music-drama', for in originating this new form of art, Wagner revolutionized the opera as it then existed, writing his own libretti and giving detailed instructions on every aspect of the production, including costumes and scenery. This new conception of the role of music in its relation to the theatre was as enthusiastically received by some as it was roundly condemned by others; and there is surely no other major composer who has been so violently and consistently attacked by his detractors as Wagner has.

But much of the criticism of Wagner has been not so much concerned with his operas as such, as what they appeared to represent in the minds of some people. His association with the German philosopher and poet Nietzsche (q.v.) is often cited as proof of his sympathy with the more sinister aspects of German nationalism – though Nietzsche eventually became a scathing critic of everything associated with Wagner. Yet the performance of Wagner's music was, for many years after the Second World War, banned in a number of places, notably Israel, just as music by Mendelssohn and other Jewish composers had been suppressed in Nazi Germany.

Ironically, there are two pieces of music, by Wagner and Mendelssohn respectively, which have probably been played together more often than any other two pieces by any other two composers: *The bridal chorus* from *Lohengrin* and *The wedding march* from the incidental music to *A midsummer night's dream.*

489 WATT

James Watt (1736–1819), who gave his name to the unit of power, the *watt*, is invariably associated with steam engines – and electric light bulbs. He did not in fact invent the electric light bulb; but he certainly did invent steam engines (in particular, the first steam engine with a separate condenser, which eliminated much of the power-wasting of earlier engines) and many other things besides.

Watt was born in Greenock, in Scotland, the son of a mathematical instrument-maker, and at first he followed his father's trade. The full potential of his inventive genius was not realized, however, until in 1775, he entered into partnership with a businessman from Birmingham, Matthew Boulton; and it was at Boulton's engineering works that Watt's engines and other inventions were to be manufactured for the next 25 years. Boulton, an engineer and inventor in his own right, originated the term 'horsepower' with Watt.

Apart from his steam engines, Watt's inventions included a mechanized method of copying manuscripts, a screw-propeller, and an apparatus for reproducing sculpture. He was also greatly interested in chemistry and carried out original researches on the composition of water.

It was characteristic of the man that he approached all his many and varied activities with equal enthusiasm and attention to detail. He was devoted to music and drawing – and remarkably skilled at both.

490 WEBER

Wilhelm Eduard Weber (1804–91) was the German physicist who gave his name to the unit of magnetic flux, the *weber*. He was also the inventor of the electrodynamometer, an instrument for measuring electric currents.

Weber carried out a great deal of research with his fellow-countryman, Karl Friedrich Gauss (q.v.), and also worked with his elder brother, Ernst Heinrich Weber, the distinguished anatomist.

491 WEDGWOOD

Josiah Wedgwood (1730–95) gave his name to a superior kind of pottery known as *Wedgwood*, or 'Etruria ware' from its distinctive designs based on the ancient Etruscan ware.

Wedgwood was born at Burslem, one of the 'five towns' of Arnold Bennett's novels and now a part of Stoke-on-Trent. In

1769 he established his famous pottery works in Hanley (another of the 'five towns') and built a village there for his workmen, which he named *Etruria*, after the ancient Etruria in Italy, also famous for its pottery. Many of the designs on Wedgwood's newly patented pottery were executed by a young sculptor named John Flaxman, who was provided with financial assistance from Wedgwood to further his studies abroad. Flaxman was to become the first professor of sculpture at the Royal Academy of Art.

The poet S. T. Coleridge was another to benefit from the generosity of Wedgwood and, later, his son Thomas. Thomas Wedgwood is also remembered as the world's first photographer, while Josiah Wedgwood's eldest daughter was the mother of another famous man, Charles Darwin (q.v.).

492 WEIL'S DISEASE

Adolf Weil (1848–1916) was the German physician who identified leptospirosis, an infectious disease of animals which can be transmitted to humans, named after him as *Weil's disease*. This is caused by a spirochaete (a spirally coiled bacterium), a species of Leptospira.

The disease is most commonly associated with rats. Consequently, any person occupationally involved with rats (the sewage worker or the rodent operative, for obvious example) is at most risk from infection; but since the parasite is contained in the vermin's urine, there are many ways in which Weil's disease can be contacted. The rat seems to have developed an immunity to illness from the spirochaetes, though it can be fatal to humans.

493 WELLINGTONS   WELLINGTONIA

Arthur Wellesley, first Duke of Wellington, also known as 'the Iron Duke' (1769–1852), gave his name to a genus of Californian conifers, *Wellingtonia* – and, of course, to *wellingtons* (or 'wellies').

Both as a soldier and a statesman, Wellington was one of the best-known men in Britain (he was actually an Irishman) of his day and, not unnaturally, many things were named in his honour, from the capital city of New Zealand and a public school, to any number of public houses called *The Duke of Wellington*. And one of the most successful bomber-aircraft of the Second World War, the Vickers-Armstrong *Wellington*, was named after the Duke.

Yet for all this, the 'Great Duke . . . England's greatest son' (as the poet laureate, Tennyson, described him in his *Ode on the death of the Duke of Wellington*) is only in the dictionary by virtue of little more than a pair of 'wellies'. (*Wellingtonia*, after all, was originally named after the Cherokee Indian Sequoyah (q.v.)). As the Great Duke himself said, after the battle of Waterloo: 'It has been ... the nearest run thing you ever saw.'

494 WERNERIAN
Abraham Gottlob Werner (1750–1817) was a German geologist whose theories concerning the formation of the earth's crust through the agency of water were known as Neptunian (after the Roman sea-god Neptune) or, from the geologist's name, *Wernerian*. Werner was a pioneer in the systematical classifications of minerals and rocks; but his advocation of the theory that all geological phenomena can be attributed to deposition by water brought him into controversy with other geologists and mineralogists, notably the Scottish geologist James Hutton (q.v.), and is now regarded as obsolete.

Wernerite, or scapolite, a silicate of aluminium, calcium, sodium and chlorine, is also named after Werner.

495 WESLEYAN
John Wesley (1703–91), the English evangelist and the founder of Methodism and the *Wesleyan Methodists*, was acutely aware of the importance of music in his religious teaching though he was not a trained musician. His youngest brother, Charles, however, was an exceptionally gifted and prolific hymn-writer, and a great number of his hymns remain among the most popular. *Jesu, lover of my soul*, *Soldiers of Christ, arise*, and *Hark! the herald angels sing*, are just three out of an immense total of some 6,500 hymns accredited to Charles Wesley.

And while John Wesley is regarded (rightly) as the founder of Methodism, it was the regular and methodical life-style adopted by Charles as a student at Oxford that gave rise to the word *Methodist*.

496 WHEATSTONE'S BRIDGE
Sir Charles Wheatstone (1802–75) has been credited with numerous inventions and scientific discoveries, yet the only invention to bear his name, *Wheatstone's bridge*, is not believed to have been invented by him. *Wheatstone's bridge* is a device for measuring electrical resistance and Wheatstone certainly made

much use of it in his researches in electricity.

One of his best-known inventions was the concertina (most appropriately for one coming from a family of musical instrument makers) and he collaborated with the electrical engineer Sir William Fothergill Cooke in devising the first practical electric telegraph.

497 WINCHESTER

Oliver Fisher Winchester (1810–80) was an American industrialist who gave his name to the famous *Winchester repeating-rifle*. The Winchester came to be one of the best-known rifles of its day, as well as acquiring a glamorous association with the 'Wild West' period of American history (as portrayed in numerous popular novels and films) when the Winchester and the Colt (q.v.) were the most favoured firearms of the sharp-shooters on both sides of the law.

Oliver F. Winchester, however, came into the arms manufacturing business through the rather less glamorous business of manufacturing men's shirts. His particular ability was that of acquiring and successfully developing the inventions of other men, and the Winchester rifle was largely a development of the Henry repeating-rifle, which had been used with considerable effect in the Civil War. Its inventor, B. T. Henry, was employed by Winchester, who later acquired the patent of the successful Hotchkiss bolt-action repeating-rifle (q.v.).

The name of Winchester has now become a trade-name for various firearms produced by the Winchester Repeating Arms Company.

498 WINDSOR KNOT

Edward Albert Christian George Andrew Patrick David, Duke of Windsor (1894–1972), became Edward VIII, King of Great Britain and Ireland, with the death of his father, George V, on 20 January 1936. Then on 11 December of the same year, he made his historic adbication speech in a broadcast to the nation, in which he declared, 'I have found it impossible to carry the heavy burden of responsibility and to discharge my duties as King as I would wish to do, without the help and support of the woman I love'. He was subsequently created Duke of Windsor and married the American divorcée Mrs Wallis Simpson (who became the Duchess of Windsor) in 1937.

The Duke of Windsor is remembered eponymously, however,

for purely sartorial reasons. He had long been a leader of fashion and the *Windsor knot* – a neat triangular knot made by tying a necktie with extra loops – was appropriately named after him.

The name of Windsor was adopted by the British royal house in 1917, replacing the existing German titles which had become clearly embarrassing to the British people since the beginning of the war with Germany in 1914. Windsor-chairs, Windsor-soap, etc., are named from Windsor in Berkshire, the site of the royal residence of Windsor Castle; while 'the Widow at Windsor' was the sobriquet coined by Rudyard Kipling for Queen Victoria (q.v.).

499 WOOLTON PIE

Frederick James Marquis, first Baron Woolton of Liverpool (1883–1964), became well-known to the British people as the Minister of Food during the Second World War. It was in 1940 that he was given the vital and daunting task of feeding a nation at war, having already supervised the kitting-out of the newly increased armed forces as Director-General of Equipment and Stores at the Ministry of Supply.

Lord Woolton had come to political life from the world of commerce, but apart from his proven skill as an organizer, he possessed a natural ability to communicate with the public at large on a personal level. With typical thoroughness he applied himself to the art of broadcasting; and soon the homely and reassuring voice of 'Uncle Henry' (as he got to be nicknamed) was to become a familiar feature of wartime radio in Britain, especially to the housewives.

In conjunction with his broadcasts, Lord Woolton conducted an advertising campaign with a particular emphasis on the merits of the home-grown and relatively plentiful potato and the carrot, which were promoted as two cartoon characters, 'Potato Pete' and 'Dr Carrot'. These and other common vegetables – parsnips, swedes, etc. – were the main ingredients for *Woolton pie*, the recipe for which was given out by the minister in his broadcasts.

It is perhaps remarkable that no fewer than *six* members of Britain's wartime administration – the others being Anderson, Bevin, Eden, Hore-Belisha and Morrison (qq.v.) – gave their names to words in the language.

500 WYKEHAMIST

William of Wykeham, or Wickham (1324–1404), Bishop of Winchester and Lord Chancellor of England, was the founder of

New College, Oxford, and Winchester College, one of Britain's oldest public schools. Any pupil, or former pupil, of Winchester is known as a *Wykehamist*, after the school's founder.

One famous Wykehamist, Dr Thomas Arnold, became well-known as the headmaster of another public school, Rugby, and was memorably depicted in Thomas Hughes's novel, *Tom Brown's schooldays*. Some other notable Wykehamists were the Reverend Sydney Smith, Anthony Trollope, Field Marshal Lord Wavell, Sir Stafford Cripps, Professor Arnold Toynbee, Marshal of the Royal Air Force Lord Portal, and Hugh Gaitskell.

X

501 XANTIPPE

Xantippe, or Xanthippe, was the wife of Socrates (q.v.). She had the reputation of being a woman of a shrewish disposition who was constantly nagging and quarrelling with her husband; and consequently her name has come to signify any wife or woman who behaves in this manner. Shakespeare, in his play *The Taming of the Shrew*, makes a specific reference to her: '. . . as curst and shrewd / As Socrates' Xanthippe . . .'.

It is also said that Xantippe was the subject of a great deal of gossip in Athens, but Socrates apparently bore all this and his wife's scolding with the philosopher's composure.

502 XENOCRATIC

Xenocrates (396–314 BC) was a Greek philosopher renowned for his strict abstemiousness towards all earthly pleasures. From his name, therefore, we have the word *Xenocratic* to describe the doctrine of Xenocrates, or someone subscribing to his ideals.

Xenocrates was a disciple of Plato (q.v.) and succeeded his nephew, Speusippus, as principal of the Academy at Athens. He is also associated with Pythagoreanism (q.v.).

Y

503 YALE LOCK
Linus Yale (1821–68) was an American locksmith who invented various kinds of locks, including a small cylinder type, the *Yale lock*, which was named after him. The Yale lock was patented in 1851 and is now, of course, one of the most widely used locks in the world, especially on motor cars – which had hardly been invented when Linus Yale died in 1868.

Yale, the inventor, should not be confused with Elihu Yale (1649–1721), a benefactor of Yale University.

504 YAPP
William Yapp was a London bookseller of the nineteenth century who specialized in religious literature. He was in the habit of carrying a Bible about his person; and noting the wear and tear sustained by the edges of the pages, he conceived the idea of an overlapping soft cover with rounded corners to protect a book's edges, as well as the lining of a pocket holding it. This kind of binding subsequently became known as *yapp*.

In America, yapp binding (especially of Bibles and prayer books, etc.) is sometimes referred to as 'divinity circuit binding'.

505 YARBOROUGH
Charles Anderson Worsley, the second Earl of Yarborough (1809–62), was noted for his devotion to the card-table and in particular for a famous bet of 1,000 to one which he would lay against the occurrence of a hand containing no card above nine. Such a hand has consequently come to be named after him as a *Yarborough* and it is calculated that the odds against its occurrence are 1,827 to one.

Lord Yarborough is sometimes represented as a fanatical *bridge* player, but it is more likely that whist was his main game since bridge is generally believed to have been introduced into England some years after Yarborough's death.

Z

506 ZEPPELIN

Count Ferdinand von Zeppelin (1838–1917), the German soldier and airship designer and manufacturer, saw active service in the American Civil War (with the Union army), the Austro-Prussian War and the Franco-Prussian War, before retiring as a lieutenant-general at the age of 52. He then turned his attention to the manufacturing of airships. And by the turn of the century he had produced the first dirigible airship of rigid construction, which was named after him as the *Zeppelin*.

Zeppelins were used in a military role during the First World War. And the first casualties of an air-raid over Britain occurred when a Zeppelin dropped bombs on Great Yarmouth, in 1915. The airships proved vulnerable to attack by fighter aircraft, however, and in 1916 Captain Leefe Robinson was awarded the first Victoria Cross (q.v.) to be won in England, for shooting down the *Zeppelin L21*. Yet, though largely unsuccessful as war machines, the Zeppelins' effect on the morale of the civilian population of Britain at that time was considerable, by all accounts.

In 1929 the *Graf Zeppelin* flew round the world in 21 days (a record at the time); and despite a number of airship disasters, it remained in service until 1938. It is worth noting that before the 1914–18 War, Zeppelins were being used in Germany for an inter-city transport service – the first commercial airline in the world. It is also a fact that not one accident occurred to the 35,000 or more passengers who used this service up to the outbreak of war.

507 ZEUXIAN

Zeuxis was a Greek painter in the latter half of the fifth century BC. He is remembered for his great skill in the painting of still life pictures, which were so realistic that his name has come to be given to painting in such a manner, or employing the *Zeuxian* style.

It is said that he engaged in a competition with another painter of even greater skills, one Parrhasius. Zeuxis executed a picture of a bunch of grapes which even convinced the birds of their apparent reality as they attempted to eat them. But when he was invited by Parrhasius to draw aside a curtain to reveal his rival's own picture, he discovered that it was in fact the curtain that was the painting!

508 ZOILISM   ZOILIST
Zoilus, a Greek orator and grammarian of the fourth century BC, gave his name to the English language through his scathing criticism of the works of Homer, Plato (q.v.) and Isocrates. Consequently, we call any severe or carping critic a *Zoilist*, or one who resorts to *Zoilism*.

Zoilus was also known as 'Homeromastix', i.e. 'scourge of Homer'.

509 ZOLLNER'S LINES   ZOLLNER'S ILLUSION
Johann Karl Friedrich Zöllner (1834–82) was a noted German astrophysicist of his day. His scientific interests were widely spread, however, and he is particularly (and eponymously) remembered for his work on optical illusions, as a result of which he came to devise his *Zöllner's lines*, or *Zöllner's illusion*. This consists of parallel lines which give the optical illusion of not being parallel through the addition of oblique intersecting lines.

Among Zöllner's other work of note was his expansion of the electrodynamical theory of Wilhelm Weber (q.v.).

510 ZOROASTRIANISM
Zoroaster (or Zarathustra), was the Persian prophet who founded *Zoroastrianism*, the national religion of Persia from the sixth century BC to the seventh century AD.

Zoroaster probably lived in the sixth century BC and his followers held him to be the prophet Ormuzd, the spirit of light and good. According to the sacred book of Zoroastrianism, *Zend-Avesta*, the spirit of light and good will triumph over the spirit of evil and darkness, called Ahriman; and life after death or, alternatively, eternal punishment or death, will depend on man's earthly 'balance sheet'.

Zoroastrianism is now almost entirely confined to the Guebres and the Parsees (*People of Pars, or Persia*) in India, but once it was one of the great religions of the world.

511 ZWINGLIANISM
Ulrich (or Huldreich) Zwingli (1484–1531) was rector of Zurich

Cathedral and the most prominent leader of the Reformation in Switzerland. His radicalism eventually brought him into conflict with Luther (q.v.) on a number of points of doctrine, and gave rise to the word *Zwinglianism*, referring in particular to Zwingli's interpretation of the sacraments.

Civil war broke out in Switzerland as a result of the religious differences, and the influence of Zwinglianism was virtually brought to an end with the death of Zwingli at the battle of Kappel on 11 October 1531. The *Zwinglians* survive as the Swiss Evangelical Church, with their activities largely confined to Zurich.

Subject Index

References are to eponym numbers – not page numbers

217